Beyond the
Ultimate Question

Also available from ASQ Quality Press:

Measuring Customer Satisfaction and Loyalty: Survey Design, Use, and Statistical Analysis Methods, Third Edition
Bob E. Hayes

Managing the Customer Experience: A Measurement-Based Approach
Morris Wilburn

Customer Satisfaction Research Management
Derek Allen

Competing for Customers and Winning with Value: Breakthrough Strategies for Market Dominance
R. Eric Reidenbach and Reginald W. Goeke

Analysis of Customer Satisfaction Data
Derek Allen and Tanniru R. Rao

Six Sigma Marketing: From Cutting Costs to Growing Market Share
R. Eric Reidenbach

ANSI/ISO/ASQ Q10002-2004: Quality management—Customer satisfaction—Guidelines for complaints handling in organizations
ANSI/ISO/ASQ

The Certified Manager of Quality/Organizational Excellence Handbook, Third Edition
Russell T. Westcott, editor

The Quality Toolbox, Second Edition
Nancy R. Tague

Making Change Work: Practical Tools for Overcoming Human Resistance to Change
Brien Palmer

Innovation Generation: Creating an Innovation Process and an Innovative Culture
Peter Merrill

To request a complimentary catalog of ASQ Quality Press publications, call 800-248-1946, or visit our Web site at www.asq.org/quality-press.

Beyond the Ultimate Question

A Systematic Approach to Improve Customer Loyalty

Bob E. Hayes

ASQ Quality Press
Milwaukee, Wisconsin

American Society for Quality, Quality Press, Milwaukee 53203
© 2010 by Bob E. Hayes
All rights reserved. Published 2009
Printed in the United States of America
15 14 13 12 11 10 09   5 4 3 2 1

Library of Congress Cataloging-in-Publication Data

Hayes, Bob E., 1963–.
  Beyond the ultimate question : a systematic approach to improve customer
loyalty / Bob E. Hayes.
      p. cm.
  Includes bibliographical references and index.
  ISBN 978-0-87389-772-3 (alk. paper)
  1. Customer loyalty.   2. Consumer satisfaction.   3. Customer services.
I. Title.

  HF5415.525.H39 2009
  658.8'343—dc22

                                                                    2009023442

Publisher: William A. Tony
Acquisitions Editor: Matt Meinholz
Project Editor: Paul O'Mara
Production Administrator: Randall Benson

ASQ Mission: The American Society for Quality advances individual, organizational, and community excellence worldwide through learning, quality improvement, and knowledge exchange.

Attention Bookstores, Wholesalers, Schools, and Corporations: ASQ Quality
Press books, videotapes, audiotapes, and software are available at quantity
discounts with bulk purchases for business, educational, or instructional use. For
information, please contact ASQ Quality Press at 800-248-1946, or write to ASQ
Quality Press, P.O. Box 3005, Milwaukee, WI 53201-3005.

To place orders or to request a free copy of the ASQ Quality Press Publications
Catalog, including ASQ membership information, call 800-248-1946. Visit our
Web site at www.asq.org or http://www.asq.org/quality-press.

∞ Printed on acid-free paper

Quality Press
600 N. Plankinton Avenue
Milwaukee, Wisconsin 53203
Call toll free 800-248-1946
Fax 414-272-1734
www.asq.org
http://www.asq.org/quality-press
http://standardsgroup.asq.org
E-mail: authors@asq.org

*As always, this book is dedicated
to my daughter, Marissa.*

*You have grown into a great person with decent values
and a sense of fun that is matched only by your sense
of responsibility. You bring me joy beyond what words
can express. You will probably never know how much
your loving, supportive words mean to me, but I hope
you know that I will always be here for you.*

Contents

List of Figures and Tables

Preface

I have had a desire to write a book on the best practices of customer feedback programs (CFPs) for a few years. My interest in writing this book is directly the result of my professional experience in the field of customer satisfaction and loyalty. Over the past several years, I have built up experience as a consultant to large Fortune 500 companies and as an employee of major corporations. During this time, I have acquired much practical insight into the workings of CFPs. In these various roles, I have seen differences in how companies organize their CFPs. Some companies have top executive support for their programs while others do not. Some companies integrate their customer feedback data into their daily business processes while others keep them separate. Some companies use customer feedback results as part of their employee incentive programs while other companies rely on more traditional incentive programs. Still some companies conduct in-depth customer research using their feedback data while others rely on basic reporting of their customer feedback data for their customer insight. These examples are only some of the many differences in how companies structure their CFPs.

Because of the diverse business practices companies can employ with respect to their CFPs, there are hundreds of ways a company can structure its particular program. Are there critical elements of a CFP that are necessary for its success?

Can a company exclude some elements from its CFP without adversely impacting its effectiveness? How important are certain components in increasing customer loyalty? There is a lack of knowledge regarding what works and what does not. Consequently, it is difficult for companies to know what elements are necessary to create a successful CFP. Practitioners and consultants try to provide guidance in this area and have, in fact, advocated their own laundry lists of best practices based on their experiences. While personal experience is a good start into understanding the elements that are needed for a successful CFP, a more systematic and scientific approach is needed.

Toward that end, I formally collected information from many CFP professionals regarding the programs that they manage in their respective companies. I developed a survey with a set of standardized questions that allowed these professionals to indicate how they structure their CFPs. As of this writing (January 2009), I do not know of any other scientific studies that have tried to identify the best practices of CFPs. While my attempt is the first published study of its kind, it is by no means the final answer to the question, What are the best practices of customer feedback programs? It is my hope that other researchers and practitioners will extend the knowledge gained in this study and pursue additional scientific studies on this topic. There are many more questions that should be addressed. Future studies can examine the differences in best practices across industries (service vs. manufacturing), organizational size (small vs. medium vs. large), and organizational type (business-to-business [B2B] vs. business-to-customer [B2C]), to name a few.

Chapter 1 discusses the central role of the customer in understanding the growth of business. In fact, popular business models include the customer as a key variable in understanding a business's growth. These business models also help companies understand how they should look at their customer feedback data in order to make sense of it. This chapter includes a critical review of the Net Promoter Score (NPS), a popular measure of customer loyalty that is widely used today. Also, this chapter introduces new research that supports the notion that customer loyalty is made up of three distinct types of loyalty.

Chapter 2 introduces the basic structure of a CFP. While there are many moving parts to a CFP, the elements of these programs can be grouped into six major areas: strategy, governance, business process integration, survey methods, reporting, and applied research. Strategy involves the executive-level actions that set the overarching guidelines around the company's mission and vision regarding the company's objectives. Governance deals with the organization's policies surrounding the CFP. Business process integration deals with the extent to which the CFP is integrated into the daily business processes. The area of survey methods deals with the way in which customer feedback data are collected. Reporting looks at how customer feedback data are summarized and disseminated throughout the company. Finally, applied research focuses on the extent to which companies gain additional customer insight through systematic research using their customer feedback data. While there is overlap among these six areas with respect to the elements in each (the element of "use feedback to resolve customer issues" could reflect both business process integration and reporting), this configuration provides a useful way of examining the major areas of CFPs.

Chapter 3 presents a recently completed study designed to identify best practices of CFPs. The results show that companies with high loyalty rankings (Loyalty Leaders) adopted a wide variety of business practices in their respective CFPs that their counterparts (Loyalty Laggers) did not. This study helped quantify the impact that specific business practices had on a company's customer loyalty rankings as well as how satisfied the companies were with their customer feedback in helping them manage their customer relationships. Study results suggest that some business practices of CFPs play a role in improving a company's loyalty scores or its customer relationship management (CRM) practice or both.

As we will see, while not all elements are considered best practices, it is important to present the many elements that are typically included in a CFP so that the reader understands the potential complexity involved in creating one.

Rather than rely on the survey results as the sole source of information for the book, CFP professionals were interviewed to help illustrate how these programs are implemented in a company. Chapters 4–8 present best practices of the CFPs (as determined by the study) and provide real-life examples of how these best practices are implemented in existing companies. I draw from my professional experience and include generally accepted standards as part of the best practices in CFPs. Chapters 4 and 5 focus on the management process surrounding CFPs. Specifically, Chapter 4 presents the results regarding elements of strategy and governance and illustrates how companies can accomplish the task of building CFPs with these elements. This chapter answers such questions as, Is executive support of a CFP necessary for its success? How can a company create a customer-centric culture? and How should companies use customer feedback data as part of their incentive program? Chapter 5 focuses on elements related to business process integration and demonstrates the importance of integrating the CFP into the company's business processes. Specifically, this chapter presents best practices that show how the goals and processes of the company's CFP can be effectively communicated throughout the company, how the resolution of customer issues that are identified with the customer feedback data can be integrated into the company's CRM strategy, and how to ensure customer feedback is used at the executive level in making business decisions.

Chapters 6–8 deal with operational processes of the CFP. Chapter 6 focuses on the process and method of collecting customer feedback data. There are different methods of collecting customer feedback data (for example, Web-based, telephone, interviews). This chapter illustrates how companies use different methods of data collection and how the use of Web-based surveys has helped companies improve the process of collecting customer feedback. After customer feedback data are collected, they need to be analyzed, organized, and disseminated throughout the company. Toward that end, Chapter 7 presents best practices around the reporting of customer feedback data. To help analyze customer feedback data, a data model is used to help guide in the analysis and organization of customer feedback data. Additionally, to whom the results of the analysis should be reported will be presented to maximize their usefulness. Finally, Chapter 8 presents information regarding the impact that applied research has on the effectiveness of a company's CFP. The existence of applied research in a company has been shown to have a bigger impact on improving customer loyalty than any other area of a CFP. Applied research can take a variety of forms and address different topics. This chapter presents general types of applied research projects that span across organizational roles. Furthermore, research programs and specific projects are presented to demonstrate how companies address specific questions around how to improve the customer experience and maximize customer loyalty.

Customer feedback professionals were asked to list the major roadblocks that prevent them from improving customer loyalty. Chapter 9 summarizes this list to help the reader understand problems commonly experienced by companies in their attempts to improve customer loyalty.

The last two chapters include stories of two companies that have developed CFPs. Chapter 10 looks at Oracle Corporation, and Chapter 11 focuses on Akamai Technologies. We will see that, while each company has a unique way of implementing its CFP, there is an underlying common theme that is supported by the specific practices they employ in their programs. These examples are by no means a template for how you should structure your program. They merely show what is possible.

The appendices provide additional information for the interested reader. While they provide substantial details beyond the content of the main chapters, they are not required reading to get a complete understanding of the central theme of the book. The appendices simply provide more detail regarding methods used in the main body of the book. Appendix A includes a discussion on methods of determining customer requirements—those elements of your business that are important to your customers. Appendix B includes a complete discussion on how to write survey questions. Appendices C–L include brief discussions on particular statistical analysis methods that can help you understand how customer feedback data are analyzed.

The key to improve your CFP's success rests on the design of your program. Toward that end, I have developed a free self-assessment tool to help you evaluate the design of your CFP. This tool is intended to help you understand the extent to which your company adopts best practices with respect to its CFP. Complete this short questionnaire to learn how you can create a world-class CFP. This free survey is available at http://www.businessoverbroadway.com.

Several people helped in the writing of this book. First, I would like to thank the customer feedback professionals, who were generous with their time during the early stages of the research for the book. The information on their CFPs brought the study findings to life, allowing the reader, I hope, to get a glimpse of how companies organize and structure their CFPs. The customer feedback professionals include the following:

- Doug Doyle, Microsoft
- Daniel Penney, Microsoft
- Jeremy Whyte, Oracle
- Kristal Ray, Oracle
- Stephanie Ekins-Parnell, Harris Stratex Networks
- Craig Adams, Akamai
- Steve Braje, American Express Business Travel

Two companies provided the resources that helped me pursue my research over the past two years: MSI International (http://www.msimsi.com) and GMI (http://www.gmi-mr.com). They facilitated my research efforts on both the NPS and CFPs best practices through the use of their panels and online data collection tools.

Special thanks to Jeremy Whyte for his assistance throughout this project. Jeremy has taught me much about the strategic and operational aspects of CFPs and played a key role in the genesis of this book. We have known each other for close to a decade and have worked together in the past. Our conversations are always educational, interesting, and fun and have led to specific outcomes, some of which are covered in this book.

My friends have always supported my work and play in many different forms. They give me words of encouragement, the occasional free coffee, and best of all, hugs. I try to repay them through my baked goods, but my simple scones and chocolate chip cookies do not even come close to conveying how much I love them. I will always be there for them just as they have always been there for me. These wonderful people are Michele Boyer, Tim Carter, Laura DiMarco, Traci Eggleston,

Eric Kong, Wade Gibson, Amita Gupta, Stephanie Kincaide, Stephen King, Roger Lloyd, Jennifer Meyers, Renah Seay, Optimus Rhyme, Erica Seddig, Craig Silva, Brandie Smith, Benjamin Verdoes, Josh Waterman, and Brenda Zeimet.

I would also like to thank my family. Throughout the writing of this book, they have been a great source of support through their words and actions. My family includes my sister, Lamona, and her husband, Bob, and their three children, Stephen, Jonathan, and Lauren. Even though my brother, Tom, lives three hours away, we talk every single day. I thank him, his wife, Sherry, and their three kids, Amanda, Chris, and Josh. My mom, in her own special way, keeps my siblings and me together. Thanks, Mom.

Finally, I would like to thank the staff at Kinetic Publishing Services, LLC. Their work on the book was excellent and far exceeded my expectations. In loyalty terms, I would be an advocate for their work, I would likely purchase additional publishing services from them, and I would likely remain a customer.

I try to keep my interests varied yet focused on matters of importance to the progress of society and science. Toward that end, I have a couple of interests that keep me busy and happy. I am pursuing bringing the science of customer loyalty management to the masses, specifically small to midsize companies that do not have the resources to employ large-scale survey vendors. I am currently chasing technological experts who can help me fulfill this dream. I hope to have something to offer the public later this year under the moniker of Loyalty Widget (http://www.loyaltywidget.com). In addition, I provide my market research skills in an advisory role for Mob4Hire (http://www.mob4hire.com), a leader in crowd testing and research for mobile applications. Our goal is to connect mobile application developers with a global community of eager, tech-savvy testers and professional testing houses for functional testing, usability testing, and product/market research. To satisfy my social conscience, I raise money through a Web site aimed at spreading the word about global warming. You can find out more about that effort at Without The Planet (http://www.withouttheplanet.com).

PART I

Introduction to Customer Feedback Programs

1

Beyond the Ultimate Question, and Measurement and Meaning of Customer Loyalty

Improving the customer relationship is seen as the key to improving business performance. Popular business strategies have emerged that are shining the spotlight on the importance of understanding customers' attitudes, expectations, and preferences (Ang and Buttle 2006; Reinartz, Krafft, and Hoyer 2004). Specifically, customer-centric business strategies, such as CRM (customer relationship management) and CEM (customer experience management), focus on managing customers' attitudes about their experience.

Additionally, formal business models espoused by both researchers and practitioners incorporate customers as an essential variable in explaining and predicting business performance and growth (Gupta et al. 2006; Heskett, Sasser, and Schlesinger 1997). A business model incorporating common customer-related elements appears in Figure 1.1.

The premise of these customer-centric business models is that the financial success of the business rests on the effective management of customers. The effective management of customers is a process by which the company understands the needs of the customers and is able to deliver products and

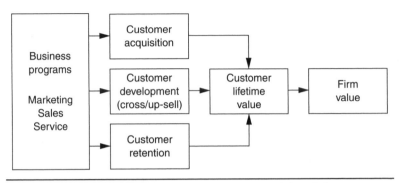

Figure 1.1 Marketing/sales/service business model and the relationship among key organizational variables.
Adapted from Gupta et al. 2006.

services that the customers value. The successful delivery of these products and services leads to increases in customer satisfaction and loyalty, and consequently, increases in financial performance. To improve business performance as measured by financial metrics, executives have looked to variables such as customer satisfaction and customer loyalty to help improve their company's performance. This deeper customer-centric understanding helps businesses identify ways to increase customer satisfaction and loyalty, therefore improving business performance.

The customer-centric business models and, consequently, the need of executives to better understand their customers' needs and expectations have fueled the proliferation of customer feedback programs (CFPs) and customer feedback vendors. CFPs are designed to help companies understand their customers' attitudes and experiences. I use the term "customer feedback program" to be inclusive of different types of customer programs where formal customer data are collected on customers' perceptions and attitudes about their customer experience. These programs are also commonly referred to as customer satisfaction programs, customer advocacy programs, and customer loyalty programs.

A discussion of CFPs needs to include a thorough review of a popular measure of customer loyalty, the Net Promoter Score (NPS). I will present the results of some recent research on the NPS that calls into question the merits of using this single question as the only measure of customer loyalty. The conclusions will be surprising to those who believe measuring loyalty is as simple as asking a single question. Following will be a discussion on the measurement and meaning of customer loyalty that will present research illustrating that customer loyalty can be conceptualized as reflecting three components.

THE MYTH ABOUT THE NPS AS THE ULTIMATE QUESTION

Many of today's top businesses use the NPS to monitor and manage customer relationships. Fred Reichheld and his code-velopers of the NPS say that a single survey question is the only loyalty metric companies need to grow their business. They refer to this single survey question as "the ultimate question." The use of this question has seen widespread adoption by such companies as General Electric, Intuit, T-Mobile, Charles Schwab, and Enterprise.

NPS Methodology

The NPS is calculated from a single loyalty question, "How likely are you to recommend us to your friends/colleagues?" On the basis of their rating of this question using a 0–10 likelihood scale, where 0 means "not at all likely" and 10 means "extremely likely," customers are segmented into three groups: (1) Detractors (ratings of 0–6), (2) Passives (ratings of 7 and 8), and (3) Promoters (ratings of 9 and 10). A company can calculate its NPS by simply subtracting the proportion of Detractors from the proportion of Promoters.

$$NPS = \text{prop(Promoters)} - \text{prop(Detractors)}$$

NPS Claims

Fred Reichheld, codeveloper of the NPS (along with Satmetrix and Bain & Company), has made very strong claims about the advantage of the NPS over other loyalty metrics. Specifically, Reichheld and the other codevelopers have said the following:

1. The NPS is "the one number you need to grow" (Reichheld 2003, 54)

2. The NPS is "the single most reliable indicator of a company's ability to grow" (Netpromoter.com 2007)

3. "Satisfaction lacks a consistently demonstrable connection to . . . growth" (Reichheld 2003, 49)

Recent Scientific Challenges to NPS Claims

Researchers, pointing out that the NPS claims are supported only by Reichheld and his codevelopers, have conducted rigorous scientific research on the NPS with startling results. For example, Keiningham et al. (2007), using the same technique employed by Reichheld to show the relationship between the NPS and growth, used survey results from the American Customer Satisfaction Index (ACSI) to create scatter plots to show the relationship between satisfaction and growth. Looking at the personal computer industry, they found that satisfaction is just as good as the NPS at predicting growth (see Figure 1.2). Keiningham et al. (2007) found the same pattern of results in other industries (for example, insurance, airlines, and Internet service providers). In all cases, satisfaction and the NPS were comparable in predicting growth.

Still, other researchers (Morgan and Rego 2006) have shown that other conventional loyalty measures (for example, overall satisfaction, likelihood to repurchase) are *comparable to* the NPS in predicting business performance measures like market share and cash flow.

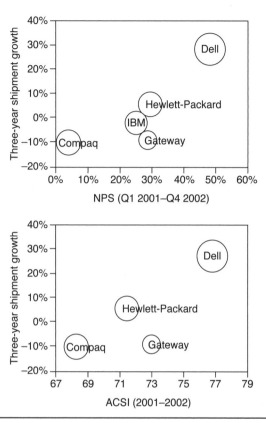

Figure 1.2 Predicting shipment growth using the NPS and satisfaction (ACSI).

Contrary to Reichhheld, other researchers, in fact, have found that customer satisfaction is consistently correlated with growth (Anderson, Fornell, and Mazvancheryl 2004; Fornell et al. 2006; Gruca and Rego 2005).

POTENTIAL LOSS OF REVENUE WHEN USING THE NPS: AN EXAMPLE

A company relying solely on the NPS as the ultimate metric may overlook disloyal customers defined in other ways. In the wireless service provider study, I found that 31% of nondetractors (those scoring 7 or above) were still likely to switch to a different wireless service provider. To manage customer relationships in order to minimize customer defections, the NPS falls short.

Relying solely on the NPS to manage customers would result in missed opportunities to save a large number of at-risk customers from defecting. This mismanagement of customer relationships in the wireless industry, where defection rate is a key business metric, can be detrimental to revenue growth. Using Q3 2008 data for T-Mobile USA (see Figure 1.3), it is estimated that, of nondetractors, over 900,000 T-Mobile USA customers are still likely to switch to another provider, with a potential annual revenue loss of over $30 million![1]

Problems with NPS Research

The recent scientific, peer-reviewed studies cast a shadow on the claims put forth by Reichheld and his cohorts. In fact, as of this writing, I know of no published empirical studies supporting the superiority of the NPS over other conventional loyalty metrics.

Keiningham et al. (2007) aptly pointed out that there may be research bias by the NPS developers. There seems to be a lack of full disclosure from the Net Promoter camp with regard to their research. The Net Promoter developers, like any research scientists, need to present their analysis to back up their claims and refute the current scientific research that brings their methodological rigor into question. To date, they have not done so. Instead, the Net Promoter camp only points to the simplicity of this single metric that allows companies to become more customer-centric. That is not a scientific rebuttal. That is marketing.

In their latest book, *Answering the Ultimate Question* (2008), Satmetrix authors Owens and Brooks never mention

---

[1] Based on only 5% of 984,583 customers who actually defected, and T-Mobile's average revenue per user of $52.

		Percentage of T-Mobile customers	Number of T-Mobile customers	Percentage highly likely to switch to another provider*	Number of T-Mobile customers highly likely to switch*
Recommend (NPS)	0	2	573,214	70	401,250
	1	2	573,214	29	163,776
	2	3	859,821	20	171,964
	3	3	859,821	8	71,652
	4	3	859,821	11	90,508
	5	9	2,866,071	8	218,071
	6	4	1,146,429	3	38,862
	7	12	3,725,893	6	216,622
	8	14	4,585,714	6	269,748
	9	19	6,018,750	7	440,396
	10	31	10,031,250	1	57,817
		100	32,100,000	6	1,958,437

Note: Calculations based on T-Mobile figures from Q3 2008.

*How likely are you to switch to a different wireless service provider within the next 12 months? "Highly likely" reflects ratings of 9 or 10 on a 0–10 scale, where 0 is "not at all likely" and 10 is "extremely likely."

Figure 1.3   T-Mobile USA example using NPS methodology.

the critique of the NPS claims or present evidence to rebut these critics' research regarding this metric. Instead, they repackage the NPS into the "Net Promoter operating model," incorporating other aspects of CFPs as part of a complete NPS solution. Their attempt at directing attention away from the downside of the NPS metric by introducing a methodology under the fashionable NPS moniker only magnifies the inherent problems with the premise of their NPS metric. The scientific evidence shows: The NPS is not the best predictor of business growth.

Why do commonly used loyalty questions show a similar pattern of relationship to revenue growth? The measurement process behind the loyalty questions plays a key role in understanding the meaning of customer loyalty. Let us examine how customer loyalty is measured.

OBJECTIVE MEASURES OF CUSTOMER LOYALTY AND FINANCIAL GROWTH

There are several objective measures of customer loyalty:

- Number of referrals: word of mouth/word of mouse

- Purchase again

- Purchase different products

- Increase purchase size

- Customer retention/defection rates

We can see how customer loyalty can lead to financial growth. Through the referral process, companies can grow through the acquisition of new customers. The idea is that the customer acquisition process relies on existing customers to promote/recommend the company to their friends, who, in turn, become customers. Another way of strengthening the financial growth of a company is through increased purchasing behavior (for example, increase amount of purchases, purchase different products/services) of existing customers. Finally, financial growth is dependent on the company's ability to not lose existing customers at a rate faster than it acquires them. Customer defection rate is an important metric in the wireless service industry, where processes such as number transfers and contract terminations make customer defections straightforward and routine.

CUSTOMER LOYALTY SURVEYS

Customer surveys remain a frequently used method for assessing customer loyalty despite the existence of objective measures of customer loyalty (for example, defection rate, number of referrals). There are a few reasons for their popularity. First, customer surveys allow companies to quickly and easily gauge levels of customer loyalty. Companies may not have easy access to objective customer loyalty data or may simply not even gather such data. Also, surveys allow companies to assess customer perceptions and prioritize initiatives to increase customer loyalty. Second, results from customer surveys can be used to more easily change organizational business processes.

Customer surveys commonly include questions about customer loyalty as well as the customer experience (for example, product, service, support). These questions can be used jointly (for example, driver analysis, segmentation analysis) to identify reasons why customers are loyal or disloyal. Finally, objective measures of customer loyalty provide a backward look into customer loyalty levels (for example, defection rates, repurchase rates). Customer surveys, however, allow companies to examine customer loyalty in real time. Surveys solicit questions regarding expected levels of loyalty-related behavior and provide opportunities for companies to "look into the future" regarding customer loyalty.

MEASUREMENT OF CUSTOMER LOYALTY

Customer loyalty, when measured through surveys, is assessed through the use of questions or items, mirroring the objective measures listed earlier. Typically, for each item, customers are asked to rate their level of likelihood of engaging in a specific behavior. Commonly used customer loyalty survey questions include the following items:

- Overall satisfaction

- Likelihood to choose again

- Likelihood to recommend

- Likelihood to continue purchasing same products/services

- Likelihood to purchase different products/services

- Likelihood to increase frequency of purchasing

- Likelihood to switch to a different provider

Most of the questions allow respondents to indicate their likelihood of behaving in different ways toward the company (for example, on a scale of 0–10, where 0 is "not at all likely" and 10 is "extremely likely"). The satisfaction question is sometimes used in customer loyalty measurement and is rated on a scale of 0–10 (0 = extremely dissatisfied, 10 = extremely satisfied). For all questions, higher ratings reflect higher levels of customer loyalty. It should be noted that different scale values (for example, 1–5, 1–10) can be used.

OBJECTIVE VS. SUBJECTIVE MEASURES OF LOYALTY AND MEASUREMENT ERROR

It is important that we distinguish between objective measures of loyalty and subjective measures of loyalty. Objective measures of customer loyalty have minimal measurement error associated with them. Because these measures are not subject to interpretation, they have unambiguous meaning. The number of recommendations a customer makes is clearly distinct from the number of repeat purchases that customer makes. This is not to say that these measures of customer loyalty are unrelated, but that they are measurably different entities (similar to the fact that height and weight are different constructs but are related to each other—taller people tend to weigh more than shorter people).

Measuring customer loyalty via questions on surveys is an entirely different process; customers' ratings of each loyalty question become the measure of customer loyalty. Even though we can calculate separate loyalty scores, one for each question, the distinction among the loyalty questions is not warranted. Because of the way customers interpret survey questions and the inherent error associated with measuring psychological constructs, ratings need to be critically evaluated to ensure we understand the meaning behind the ratings (American Educational Research Association, American Psychological Association, and National Council on Measurement in Education 1985). When using questionnaires to measure constructs, we need to be mindful of how customers interpret and respond to the questions.

In psychological measurement terms, the loyalty questions are simply observable indicators of a single underlying construct (see Figure 1.4). Specifically, customers' rating of each question (loyalty items) is simply a function of an underlying construct (loyalty). That is, customers respond consistently across all loyalty questions. A customer who is loyal will rate each loyalty question high, and a customer who is disloyal will tend to rate each loyalty question low.

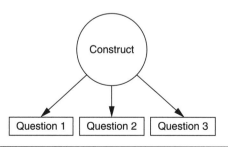

Figure 1.4 Relationship between a construct and its questions.

WHAT LOYALTY QUESTIONS ARE MEASURING: A FACTOR ANALYTIC VIEW

I set out to compare the differences, if any, among the following four commonly used loyalty questions:

1. Overall, how satisfied are you with Company ABC?

2. How likely are you to recommend Company ABC to friends/colleagues?

3. How likely are you to continue purchasing the *same* product and/or service from Company ABC?

4. If you were selecting a (company within the industry) for the *first time*, how likely is it that you would choose Company ABC?

An 11-point rating scale was used for each question. Question 1 was rated on a scale of 0 (extremely dissatisfied) to 10 (extremely satisfied). The remaining questions were rated on a scale of 0 (not at all likely) to 10 (extremely likely). With the help of GMI (Global Market Insite, http://www.gmi-mr.com), which provided online data collection and consumer panels, I surveyed about 1000 respondents (general consumers in the United States ages 18 and older) who were asked to identify and then rate their wireless service providers on the four questions.

I applied standard statistical analyses that are commonly used to evaluate survey questions. First, the average correlation among the four loyalty questions was very high ($r = .87$). This finding revealed that each customer responded to the four questions in a consistent manner. That is, customers who were highly likely to recommend the company were also highly likely to be satisfied with the company; conversely, customers who were not likely to recommend the company were also not likely to be satisfied with the company. The same pattern was seen across all pairings of the loyalty questions. Second, a factor analysis of the four questions showed a clear one-factor solution. Factor loadings, essentially representing the correlation between each question and the underlying factor, were all .90 or higher. This pattern of results clearly showed that all four questions, including the "likelihood to recommend" question, measure *one* underlying construct, customer loyalty.[2]

NPS VS. SATISFACTION VS. PURCHASE SAME

Of particular interest are three specific loyalty items: (1) satisfaction, (2) recommend, and (3) purchase same. The current factor-analytic findings cast additional doubt on the conclusions by the NPS camp. The "recommend" question appears to measure the same underlying construct as the other two loyalty questions. There is no scientific evidence that the "recommend" question (NPS) is, or should be, a better predictor of business growth compared to other loyalty questions.

SINGLE-ITEM MEASURES OR AGGREGATED METRICS

The NPS developers support the use of a single question to understand customer loyalty. This premise has two problems. First, this single-item approach is not supported with the present study findings; the four loyalty questions were shown to measure the same underlying construct. There was nothing unique about the "recommend" question. Second, single-item measures are less reliable (contain more measurement error) than multiple-item measures. Measuring loyalty with a single question is akin to measuring math skills with a single-item test. An answer to the single-item test is a less reliable reflection of math skills than the combined answers to a 50-item math test. Think back to when you took the SAT or a similar test. Would you have wanted your score to be determined by a single question on the

---

[2] A more detailed factor analysis of loyalty questions is presented later in the chapter.

test or the entire set of questions on the test? Using the loyalty indices (aggregating all items into a single metric) in customer loyalty management is statistically better than using any single question, because the indices provide a more precise measure of loyalty than any of the items used alone.

CUSTOMER LOYALTY 2.0 AND BEYOND THE ULTIMATE QUESTION

The field of customer loyalty has received much technological innovation over the past decade. Improvements are clearly seen in data collection (Web-based loyalty surveys), data analyses (reporting portals with automated reports), employees' accessibility to customer survey results (24/7 online reporting portals), and integration of attitudinal loyalty data with behavioral loyalty data in CRM and business intelligence/analytics applications.

While there has been much improvement in the quality of managing customer loyalty survey data, the quality of the measurement and meaning of customer loyalty has not kept pace. Our latest research on customer loyalty, however, tries to narrow this gap. Customer Loyalty 2.0 represents this advancement in the measurement and meaning of customer loyalty. The purpose of the discussion is to provide an overview of measures of customer loyalty and highlight our latest research findings on attitudinal measures of customer loyalty. Understanding the complexities of customer loyalty requires a look at the broader field of customer loyalty management and customer lifetime value.

CUSTOMER LOYALTY MANAGEMENT

While there has been a change in business nomenclature around the application of CFPs from "customer relationship management" to "customer experience management," the ultimate goal of a company, no matter what business nomenclature is used, is to maximize customer satisfaction and customer loyalty. You might think of customer loyalty as the most important criterion in customer relationship/experience management. While different companies' specific CFP practices differ (for example, program objectives, analytic techniques, and reporting results), they likely share the common goal to improve the customer experience and customer loyalty.

Customer Lifetime Value and Customer Loyalty Management

Companies are not static entities; they make business decisions in hopes of increasing customer loyalty and growing their business. The key to business growth is to make decisions that will improve customer loyalty. *Customer loyalty management* is the process by which companies identify what decisions need to be made in order to increase customer loyalty. To understand how improvements in customer loyalty will improve business growth, we need to first understand the value of customers to the organization.

Customer lifetime value (CLV) reflects the present total value of a customer to the company over his or her lifetime. The concept of CLV implies that each customer (or customer segment) differs with respect to his or her value to the company. Some customers, because they spend more and/or cost less to service, are simply more valuable to a company than other customers. When we discuss CLV, we typically refer to the value of a single customer, whether that customer represents the typical customer overall or the average customer within a customer segment (for example, West coast customer vs. East coast customer).

The value of a customer or customer segment can be broken down as a function of four elements:

- NC: Number of customers

- NP: Number of times the average customer make a purchase each year

- CL: Average customer life (in years)

- PPS: Average profit per sale ([total sales revenue – costs]/ number of sales)

While there are other elements that are included in the calculation of the CLV that are not presented here (for example, future value of the dollar and risk factors), the four elements presented here are at the core of understanding how customer loyalty and customer value are related to each other. Using these elements, we can calculate the CLV for the entire customer base (or customer segment):

$$CLV = NC \times NP \times CL \times PPS$$

Increasing the Lifetime Value of the Customers

Organizations using this CLV model can now view customers as assets with a specified value that, in turn, becomes the basis for making business decisions. The goal for management, then, is to maximize the CLV to the company. To increase the lifetime value of customers, organizations can do one or more of the following four things:

- Increase size of the customer base (or customer segments)

- Increase the number of purchases customers make

- Increase the average customer life

- Increase profits per sale

We see that higher CLV equates to greater financial growth with respect to profits and a greater likelihood of long-term business success. It is important to note that because the CLV is a multiplicative function of four elements, a negative value of profits (costs are greater than revenue) results in a negative CLV no matter how large the other elements of the CLV become. Therefore, before trying to manage the loyalty of a particular customer segment, it is important to know if the customer segment is worth growing or even worth having. This step involves calculating the profits per sale.

Providing a value for profit is oftentimes a game of guesswork due to the lack of understanding of costs associated with a given customer relationship. Costs may be difficult to quantify due to the lack of available data needed to make such precise calculations, or costs may be overlooked due to a lack of understanding of the company resources necessary to maintain relationships with customers. The estimation procedure of the profit value should be transparent and shared across the organization to ensure assumptions about its calculation are reviewed by all interested parties.

While the concept of CLV has traditionally been applied in the *sales/marketing* field to understand the cost of attracting new customers, more comprehensive CLV models include costs associated with other phases of the customer life cycle. Consider the customer life cycle model in Figure 1.5. We see that a customer's tenure with a company involves three general phases: attraction (marketing), acquisition (sales), and service. Within each customer life cycle phase, company resources are required in order to maintain a relationship with the customer. Accordingly, to get a more accurate estimation of the CLV, organizations are now including the costs to *service* the customers.

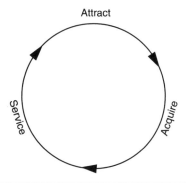

Figure 1.5   Customer life cycle.

Extending beyond the costs of attracting and acquiring customers, servicing costs expend organizational resources such as customer service staff costs and employee training costs, just to name a few. These service costs, along with sales/marketing costs, should be included in the estimation of profit per sale.

Once the costs associated with a given customer group are established, the lifetime value of that customer group can be determined. While some customer segments could be very profitable, other customer segments might not be profitable at all.

After identifying the extent to which a customer segment is profitable or not, the organization must decide whether to invest in that customer segment to increase the lifetime value of the customers in that segment. Clearly, a customer segment that costs more to maintain than the revenue it generates should raise red flags across the organization. In this situation, the organization can either attempt to decrease the costs of maintaining these relationships or simply attrite these relationships. For a customer segment that is profitable, the organization can determine how best to increase the lifetime value of that segment through loyalty management.

While there is much talk about how companies use CFPs to improve customer loyalty, there is little talk about how CFPs can be used to increase CLV. The lack of application is probably due to the notion that customer loyalty is often thought of as a single entity. Sole use of the NPS, for example, supports the idea that customer loyalty management is simply an exercise in improving one single metric. CLV underscores the concept that customer loyalty consists of three distinct components, each reflecting a particular kind of customer loyalty:

1. Size of the customer base (advocacy loyalty)

2. Number of purchases customers make (purchasing loyalty)

3. Average customer life (retention loyalty)

Advocacy loyalty reflects the degree to which customers will be advocates of the company and can be used to increase the size of the customer base. *Purchasing loyalty* reflects the degree to which customers will increase their purchasing behavior and can be used to increase the number of purchases by customers. Finally, *retention loyalty* reflects the degree to which customers will remain with a given company and can be used to increase the average customer life.

Increasing the lifetime value of customers, then, requires the effective management of all three types of loyalty of the customer base. By measuring each type of customer loyalty, executives can more effectively manage their customer relationships. To improve the CLV, companies need to apply loyalty management to all three types of customer loyalty: new customer growth, purchase behavior, and customer retention. Business decisions can now be targeted to address specific types of loyalty concerns.

The problem of loyalty management now becomes a measurement problem. Companies need to be able to reliably and accurately assess these three types of customer loyalty. The first step is to develop measures.

DEVELOPMENT OF THE ADVOCACY, PURCHASING, AND RETENTION LOYALTY INDICES

A series of three studies was undertaken to determine if the three components of customer loyalty could be reliably measured using customer surveys. The objective of the studies was to create reliable loyalty indices and determine if they could predict important business outcomes.

Studies 1 and 2

Two separate studies were conducted, each within a specific industry—wireless service providers and personal computer manufacturers. A sample of about 1000 general consumers ages 18 and older were surveyed in June and July 2007 regarding their attitudes toward their wireless service provider or personal computer manufacturer, respectively. All respondents were interviewed to ensure they met the profiling criteria, and an incentive was offered to reward respondents for filling out the survey. The survey data for this study were collected by GMI.

Seven loyalty items were included in the wireless service provider sample:

- Overall satisfaction

- Likelihood to choose again

- Likelihood to recommend

- Likelihood to continue purchasing same products/services

- Likelihood to purchase different products/services

- Likelihood to increase frequency of purchasing

- Likelihood to switch to a different provider

For the PC manufacturer sample, the "likelihood to switch" question was replaced with another loyalty question: likelihood to increase the amount or product/services purchased. For each study, a factor analysis was conducted on the set of loyalty questions.

Factor analysis, in statistical terms, is a data reduction technique that explains the statistical relationships among a given set of variables using fewer unobserved variables (factors). In simpler terms, a factor analysis tells us two things: (1) the number of factors (construct) being measured by the set of questions and (2) which questions are related to which factors.

Specifically, for our problem, a factor analysis will help us determine if the set of seven original loyalty questions is actually measuring fewer constructs (factors). It is important to note that an exploratory factor analysis involves some form of judgment when determining the number of factors as well as which variables are related to the smaller set of factors. A full discussion is beyond the scope of this chapter, but the interested reader can read more about this topic in Appendix K.

The elements in the factor pattern matrix are called factor loadings and essentially reflect the correlation between each item and the three factors. Higher factor loadings indicate a stronger relationship between the item and the underlying factor.

The results of the factor analysis suggest that there was considerable overlap among some of the loyalty items. In fact, the results suggest that the seven items measured fewer constructs (three constructs for the wireless sample and two for the PC sample). Figures 1.6 and 1.7 represent the factor pattern

		Factor*		
		1 **(Advocacy)**	**2** **(Purchasing)**	**3** **(Retention)**
Question (item)	Overall satisfaction	**.79**	.34	.35
	Choose again	**.71**	.41	.43
	Recommend	**.78**	.40	.39
	Purchase same	**.61**	.37	.58
	Purchase different	.29	**.75**	.23
	Purchase increase	.26	**.76**	.09
	Switch to another provider†	.32	.12	**.68**

*Based on a factor analysis with Varimax rotation.
†Reverse coded—higher scores mean lower likelihood of switching.

Figure 1.6 Factor pattern matrix of the seven loyalty questions for the wireless service provider study.

		Factor*	
		1 (Advocacy)	2 (Purchasing)
Question (item)	Overall satisfaction	**.77**	.32
	Choose again	**.81**	.35
	Recommend	**.90**	.34
	Purchase same	**.81**	.39
	Purchase different	.49	**.54**
	Purchase increase	.35	**.92**
	Purchase frequency	.32	**.79**

*Based on a factor analysis with Varimax rotation.

Figure 1.7   Factor pattern matrix of the seven loyalty questions for the PC manufacturer study.

matrices. As we can see in Figure 1.6, the factor analysis resulted in a clear three-factor solution; the factor loadings show that some of the loyalty questions were highly related to the underlying factors. Specifically, the first four questions were highly correlated with the first factor. Questions 5 and 6 were highly correlated with the second factor, and the last question was highly correlated with the third factor. This result demonstrates that the set of seven questions can be more easily described by three factors.

As we can see in Figure 1.7, the factor analysis resulted in a clear two-factor solution; again, the factor loadings show that some of the loyalty questions were highly related to the underlying factors. Specifically, the first four questions were highly correlated with the first factor. The last three questions, on the other hand, were highly correlated with the second factor. This result demonstrates that the set of seven questions can be more easily described by two factors.

Study 3

A third study was conducted to verify the initial research findings. For this study, surveys were fielded in September 2008 asking a sample of about 1000 general consumers in the United States ages 18 and older about their attitudes toward their wireless service provider. All respondents were interviewed to ensure they met the profiling criteria, and an incentive was offered to reward respondents for filling out the survey. The survey data for this study were collected by MSI (MSI International).

In this study, 11 loyalty questions were included in the survey:

- Overall satisfaction

- Choose again

- Recommend

- Purchase again

- Purchase different products/services

- Purchase more expensive

- Purchase more often

- Purchase larger

- Purchase from competitors

- Stop purchasing

- Switch to another provider

The results of the factor analysis suggest that there was considerable overlap among some of the loyalty items. In fact, the results suggest that the 11 items measured three constructs. Figure 1.8 represents the factor pattern matrix.

As we can see in Figure 1.8, the factor analysis resulted in a clear three-factor solution; the factor pattern matrix shows that

		Factor*		
		1 (Advocacy)	2 (Purchasing)	3 (Retention)
Question (item)	Overall satisfaction	**.85**	.41	.38
	Choose again	**.93**	.43	.41
	Recommend	**.94**	.45	.38
	Purchase again	**.92**	.42	.44
	Purchase different products/ services	.47	**.82**	−.06
	Purchase more expensive	.35	**.89**	−.17
	Purchase more often	.49	**.86**	−.05
	Purchase larger	.41	**.95**	−.14
	Purchase from competitors[†]	.21	−.31	**.72**
	Stop purchasing[†]	.41	−.06	**.88**
	Switch to another provider[†]	.47	.02	**.85**

*Based on a factor analysis with Varimax rotation.
[†]Reverse coded—higher scores mean lower likelihood of switching.

Figure 1.8 Factor pattern matrix of the 11 loyalty questions for the wireless service provider study.

some of the loyalty questions were highly related to the underlying factors. The first four questions were highly correlated with the first factor. Questions 5–8 were highly correlated with the second factor, and the last three questions were highly correlated with the third factor. This result demonstrates that the set of 11 seemingly different questions can be more easily described by three factors; that is, these 11 questions were not really measuring 11 constructs. The first four questions were measuring one underlying construct, the next four questions were measuring another underlying construct, and the final three questions were measuring yet another underlying construct.

ADVOCACY, PURCHASING, AND RETENTION LOYALTY

The labeling of the factors involves examining the content of the items that have high factor loadings. The naming of factors in a factor analysis involves some level of creativity and subjectivity. Other researchers might label the factors with different, but probably similar, words; the underlying construct being measured, however, remains the same.

The items that load on the first factor appear to have a strong emotional component, reflecting the extent to which customers advocate for the company. Consequently, this factor was labeled advocacy loyalty. The items that load on the second factor, labeled purchasing loyalty, reflect specific purchasing behaviors. For the wireless service provider sample, the item that represents the third factor reflects retention (opposite of switching) and was therefore labeled retention loyalty.

Results suggest that there are three types of customer loyalty: advocacy, purchasing, and retention. The following loyalty indices can be calculated by averaging the loyalty items that load highly on the same factor:

- **Advocacy Loyalty Index (ALI):** Reflects the degree to which customers will be advocates of the company (average across satisfaction, recommend, choose again, purchase same)

- **Purchasing Loyalty Index (PLI):** Reflects the degree to which customers will increase their purchasing behavior (average across purchase different, purchase increase, purchase frequency)

- **Retention Loyalty Index (RLI):** Reflects the degree to which customers will remain with a given company (single defection item—reverse coded)

DESCRIPTIVE STATISTICS, CORRELATIONS, AND RELIABILITIES OF LOYALTY INDICES

Descriptive statistics for and correlations among the three indices are reported in Table 1.1. Additionally, reliability estimates were calculated for each of the loyalty indices. Reliability deals with the extent to which measurement is free from random error. For Study 3, the wireless service provider sample, the reliability (Cronbach's alpha) of the ALI was .95, the reli-

Table 1.1 Descriptive statistics of the three customer loyalty indices and their intercorrelations and reliability estimates.

			Correlation		
Loyalty index	**Mean**	**SD**	**ALI**	**PLI**	**RLI**
ALI	8.00	2.12	(.95)		
PLI	5.06	2.78	.46	(.93)	
RLI	6.67	2.71	.41	−.11	(.85)

ability estimate (Cronbach's alpha) for the PLI was .93, and the reliability of the RLI was .85. These levels of reliability are considered very good for attitude research (Nunnally 1978; 0 = no reliability, 1 = perfect reliability).

These results show three interesting aspects of customer loyalty. First, the extent to which a customer will recommend a company measures the same thing as overall satisfaction. These two items (along with two other questions) load on the same factor, suggesting that these items measure the same underlying construct.

Second, the ALI, the PLI, and the RLI each measure something that is quite different from the other measures. Each is not highly related to the other measures, suggesting that a given customer can show a high level of one type of loyalty yet report a low level of another type of loyalty; that is, a customer could indicate low levels of advocacy for a given company yet show high levels of purchasing loyalty toward that company.

Third, it appears that customers, in general, are more likely to be advocates of their company than they are to buy additional products from that company. It seems that it is much easier to advocate for a company than it is to purchase more often from it.

IMPACT OF CUSTOMER EXPERIENCE ON CUSTOMER LOYALTY DIFFERS ACROSS COMPONENTS OF CUSTOMER LOYALTY

Customer experience has a large impact on the three components of customer loyalty. For Study 3, the loyalty indices were calculated for each company that had ample data. Additionally, a measure of the quality of customer experience was calculated by taking the average rating of three survey questions (product quality, service quality, and reputation). Higher scores indicate better customer experience. As we see in Figure 1.9, individuals who reported having a better customer experience also reported

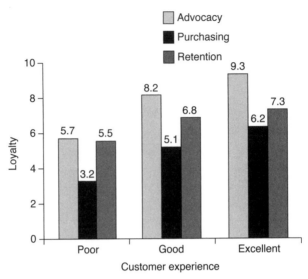

Note: Customer experience is the average rating of three questions (product quality, service quality, reputation), each rated on a 1–5 scale; poor experience = less than 3.5; good experience = 3.5–4.49; excellent experience = 4.5–5.0.

Analysis based on respondents who indicated they are responsible for paying for the wireless service plan themselves.

Figure 1.9   Relationship between customer experience and the three components of customer loyalty.

higher levels of customer loyalty. Customer experience had a stronger impact on advocacy loyalty (eta^2 = .44) than the other components of customer loyalty (purchasing loyalty: eta^2 = .16; retention loyalty: eta^2 = .07). It appears that advocacy loyalty was more highly influenced by the customer experience, suggesting that, while improving the customer experience will have an impact on improving purchasing and retention loyalty, it will have a far greater impact on improving advocacy loyalty.

CUSTOMER LOYALTY AND AMOUNT OF SPEND

To be useful to companies, loyalty indices need to be related to financial metrics. In Study 3, respondents were asked to indi-

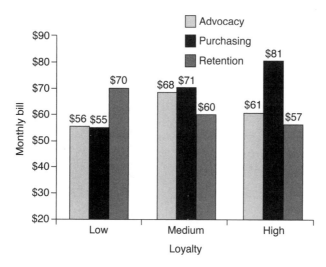

Figure 1.10   The relationship between customer loyalty components and amount of spend.

cate the total monthly dollar amount of their wireless plans. Results show that customer loyalty indices were related to the total monthly dollar amount of the wireless service plan. As seen in Figure 1.10, customers with higher levels of advocacy loyalty spend somewhat more than customers with lower levels of advocacy loyalty. On the other hand, customers with higher levels of purchasing loyalty spend much more than customers with lower levels of purchasing loyalty. Surprisingly, customers with higher levels of retention loyalty spend *less* than customers with lower levels of retention loyalty. These results suggest that improving purchasing loyalty would have the greatest impact on increasing the amount of money customers spend.

RANKING COMPANIES ON LOYALTY

The loyalty indices were able to detect meaningful differences across wireless service providers. Figure 1.11 contains the average loyalty indices for the wireless service providers. The

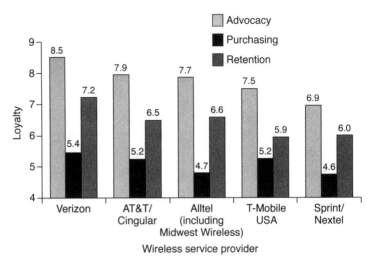

Note: Data were collected before Verizon's purchase of Alltel.

Figure 1.11   Bar graph of loyalty scores for wireless service providers.

analysis shows that the loyalty indices—ALI, PLI, and RLI—are sensitive enough to detect differences across the companies; it appears that the measurement precision of each loyalty scale can detect meaningful differences across the companies, allowing researchers and practitioners to reliably study different types of loyalty across different groups of customers.

ALI, PLI, AND RLI PREDICT BUSINESS GROWTH

To understand how well the ALI and the PLI predict future growth, objective loyalty measures for the wireless service providers were collected for Q3 2007 (fiercewireless.com and quarterly reports from the provider's respective Web site).

Each loyalty index was correlated with each of the following objective loyalty measures that were collected in Study 1, Q3 2007 (see Table 1.2 for values):

- Average revenue per user (ARPU) growth (Q2–Q3 2007)

- Churn for Q3 2007 (reverse coded—higher scores reflect better retention)

Table 1.2 Objective loyalty measures for wireless service providers.

	ARPU growth*	Churn[†]	Total new customer growth*
Alltel	$1.86	1.9%	3.7%
AT&T	$0.19	1.7%	4.7%
Sprint/Nextel	–$1.00	2.3%	2.3%
T-Mobile	$2.60	2.9%	5.9%
Verizon Wireless	$0.33	1.2%	6.8%

*Q2–Q3 2007
[†]Q3 2007

- % total of new customer growth (Q2–Q3 2007)— estimated from churn rate and net new customers

The correlations for each of the loyalty indices with each of the objective loyalty measures are located in Figure 1.12. As we can see, the loyalty indices (Q2 2007) were differentially related to the objective loyalty measures (Q3 2007).

The ALI had its greatest impact on new customer growth; companies that had higher ALI scores experienced greater new customer growth than companies that had lower ALI scores. Figure 1.13 illustrates the relationship between the ALI and new customer growth.

The PLI, however, was highly predictive of ARPU growth; companies that had higher PLI scores also experienced greater ARPU growth than companies that had lower PLI scores. Figure 1.14 illustrates the relationship between the PLI and ARPU growth.

Finally, the RLI was the best predictor of actual churn rates for wireless service providers; companies that had higher RLI scores had lower churn rates than companies that had lower RLI scores. Figure 1.15 illustrates the relationship between the RLI and churn rate.

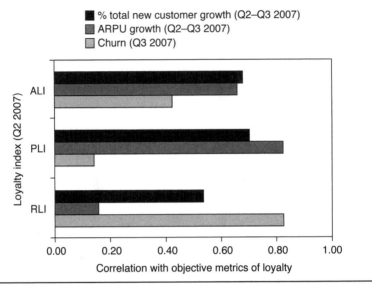

Figure 1.12 Impact of each loyalty index on objective loyalty measures.

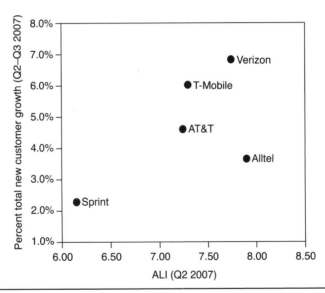

Figure 1.13 Relationship between ALI and new customer growth.

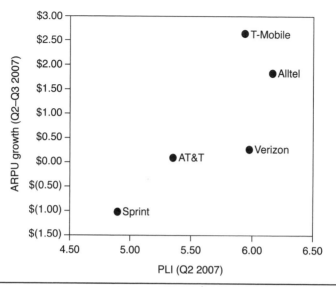

Figure 1.14 Relationship between PLI and ARPU growth.

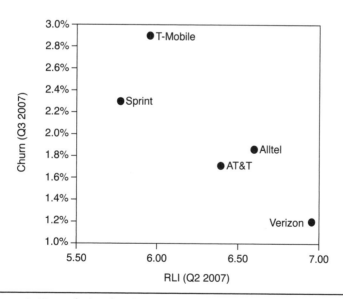

Figure 1.15 Relationship between RLI and churn rate.

The results show that loyalty indices are predictive of future business growth through new customers (new customer growth) and existing customers (ARPU), suggesting that the ALI, the PLI, and the RLI are useful measurement instruments in managing customer loyalty and business growth. While the present results are based only on the wireless industry, the findings showing the predictive power of the ALI and the PLI are very compelling. Future research in other industries can help verify and extend the current findings.

SPECIFICITY VS. GENERALITY OF MEASUREMENT

Predictability is improved when the specificity in the predictor and the outcome are the same (see Figure 1.16). That is, specific outcomes are best predicted by specific measures. As an example, an employee's intention to quit his job is a better predictor of whether that employee actually quits than general measures of employee satisfaction. Conversely, general outcomes are best predicted by general measures.

In Figure 1.17, we see that the ALI (general predictor) is better than "likelihood to switch" (specific predictor) in pre-

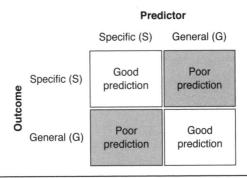

Figure 1.16   Specificity of predictors and outcomes, and the quality of prediction.

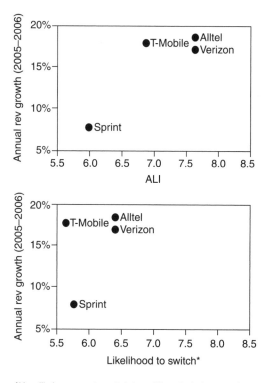

*How likely are you to switch to a different wireless service provider within the next 12 months? Ratings on a scale from 0 (not at all likely) to 10 (extremely likely). For analysis purposes, ratings are reverse coded—higher scores indicate lower likelihood to switch.

Figure 1.17   Predicting a general outcome with general and specific predictors.

dicting revenue growth (general outcome). Revenue growth is impacted by more than just customers' likelihood to switch. Advocacy loyalty, however, predicts growth better because of its general nature.

When we predict a more specific outcome, we see a different pattern of results (see Figure 1.18). "Likelihood to switch" (specific predictor) is better than the ALI (general predictor) in predicting the defection rate (specific outcome). "Likelihood to

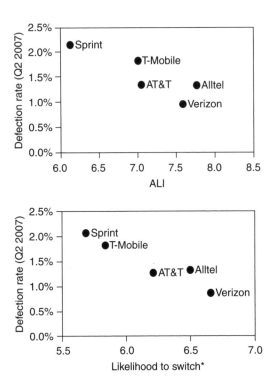

Figure 1.18   Predicting a specific outcome with general and specific predictors.

switch" is a better predictor because it is specific and targeted to the outcome of interest.

Advocacy loyalty, however, encompasses aspects that are not related to whether customers stay or leave. Companies need to examine their business metrics closely and then select the appropriate loyalty metrics that best match them. Managing important customer outcomes goes far beyond a single, ultimate question.

HAYES LOYALTY GRID

The ALI and the PLI assess the types of potential business growth that companies are likely to experience in the future. The ALI assesses new customer growth, and the PLI assesses purchasing growth. The Hayes Loyalty Grid charts the ALI and the PLI, which helps companies understand where they rank in the competitive landscape with respect to predicted business growth. Figure 1.19 is an example of the Hayes Loyalty Grid for the PC industry, and Figure 1.20 is an example of the Hayes Loyalty Grid for the wireless service provider industry.

As is seen in Figure 1.19, there is considerable variability across PC manufacturers with respect to their growth potential. Clearly, Apple Computers has high levels of both advocacy loyalty and purchasing loyalty. Compared to other PC manufacturers, it should expect to see faster growth with respect to acquiring new customers and increasing the purchase behavior of existing customers.

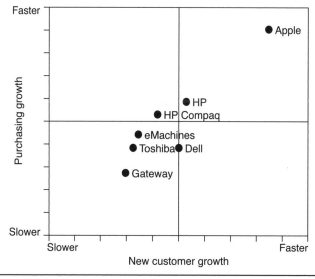

Figure 1.19 Hayes Loyalty Grid for the PC industry.

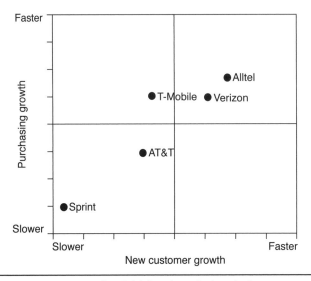

Figure 1.20   Hayes Loyalty Grid for the wireless industry.

Apple appears in the upper right quadrant, suggesting that it is poised to experience faster growth with respect to customer acquisition and increased purchases from existing customers. HP's (Compaq) and Dell's growth potential are on par with the industry average. Located in the lower left quadrant, Gateway, Toshiba, and eMachines, relative to their competitors, are expected to experience slower growth in both customer acquisition and increased purchases from existing customers.

As you can see in Figure 1.20, Alltel and Verizon appear in the upper right quadrant, suggesting that they are poised to experience faster growth with respect to customer acquisition and increased purchases from existing customers. Additionally, T-Mobile customers indicate that they are likely to increase their purchase behavior at a rate comparable to Alltel and Verizon customers.

AT&T's new customer growth potential is on par with the industry average. Located in the lower left quadrant, Sprint/Nextel, relative to its competitors, will experience slower growth in both customer acquisition and increased purchases from existing customers.

SUMMARY

The NPS is not the best predictor of business performance measures. Other conventional loyalty questions are equally good at predicting revenue growth. Reichheld's claims are grossly overstated with regard to the merits of the NPS. Reichheld and the other codevelopers do not address these criticisms about the quality of the research (or lack thereof) behind their claims.

General loyalty questions, including "likelihood to recommend," measure one general construct, customer loyalty. Consequently, it is not surprising that many researchers find similar results across these loyalty questions when predicting revenue growth. Because single survey questions have inherent measurement error, aggregating responses across general loyalty questions (for example, overall satisfaction, recommend, repurchase, choose again) is a useful way to create reliable loyalty metrics.

Customer loyalty is best conceptualized as consisting of three components: advocacy loyalty, purchasing loyalty, and retention loyalty. How well we are able to predict business performance measures depends on the match between the business outcome and the component of loyalty. Retention loyalty, for example, is useful for predicting defection rates. Advocacy loyalty, on the other hand, is useful for predicting revenue.

Companies need to do their research to fully understand how different loyalty measures correspond to specific business outcomes. Single, simple metrics are fraught with error and can lead to the mismanagement of customers and, ultimately, loss of revenue. Growing a business requires more than using a single question to manage customer relationships. To grow companies, executives need to understand more than just whether their customers will recommend the company. Companies can measure retention, advocacy, and purchasing loyalty to ensure different components of customer loyalty are properly managed and at-risk customers are identified in a variety of ways. By managing all three types of customer loyalty, executives can increase business growth through new and existing customers. Figure 1.21 presents the three general ways a company can grow business with the necessary business outcomes, customer behaviors, and loyalty measures needed to accomplish each type of business growth. Executives can understand all three dimensions of customer loyalty to improve CRM throughout the customer life cycle and maximize *all* potential revenue opportunities.

The success of any company relies on more than simply asking the right loyalty questions. The process of asking customers about their level of loyalty is embedded into a larger, more complex process of gathering customer feedback. Companies rely on CFPs to help them collect and then use the responses to these loyalty questions to effectively manage customer relationships. The next chapter introduces CFPs and discusses the general components that make up these programs. We will take a high-level overview of CFPs next and dive deeper into each component in subsequent chapters. As you will see, there are many moving parts to a CFP, each playing an important role in determining the program's success. The measurement of customer loyalty is only one part of a company's CFP; focusing only on this aspect minimizes the importance of the entire feedback program and all of its elements.

	Outcome	Behavior	Measure
Revenue growth	Increase length of customer life	Decrease churn/ defection rate	**Retention loyalty**
	Increase size of customer base	Increase number of referrals	**Advocacy loyalty**
	Increase number of purchases	Increase purchase behavior	**Purchasing loyalty**

Figure 1.21   Three ways to grow business.

2

The Structure of Customer Feedback Programs

ELEMENTS OF CFPs

A CFP, like any company program, has many components that influence its success. The various elements of the CFP are necessarily interrelated, and the proposed dimensions can be used as a heuristic to examine the broad components of the program. These components can be broken down into five major areas:

1. Strategy/Governance

2. Business process integration

3. Method

4. Reporting

5. Research

MODEL OF CFPs

Figure 2.1 reflects a general model summarizing the major components of CFPs. The proposed model helps us better understand how the different areas are related to and support one another. Overall, a CFP consists of two overarching areas that need to be addressed to ensure program success: (1) managerial and (2) operational. The managerial area, which encompasses

Strategy
Vision, value, culture

Governance
Executive ownership, decision making, accountability, compensation

Integrated business processes
Automated, closed-looped, customer relationship management and business intelligence integration, life cycle management, communication

Method	Reporting	Research
Data collection, contact management, sampling methodology, survey questions	Analysis, benchmarking micro and macro improvements, dissemination practices	Business impact; financial, operational, and constituency linkages; use of customer information

Figure 2.1   Elements of a CFP.

the strategy, governance, and integration of the program into the business system, rests at the top of the CFP. The strategy sets the tone for the company in which the CFP is embedded.

In the development of the strategy, company executives incorporate the customer and customer needs into the company's vision and help establish a customer-centric culture. Governance of the program reflects the manner by which the CFP is managed. Through executive ownership of the CFP, decision making, and compensation, governance of the CFP is essentially the extension of the corporate strategy by dictating how the CFP will be managed, supporting the importance of the customer and the customer's needs throughout the company. The integration of the CFP into the company business processes helps support objectives set forth by the strategy.

The operational area of the CFP includes components that are directly responsible for the daily workings of the CFP, which encompasses the method, reporting, and applied customer research. These three areas at the base of the CFP model support the strategy and help sustain the integration of customer feedback throughout the business processes. Next, I will cover each element of the CFP in detail.

STRATEGY/GOVERNANCE

Strategy reflects the overarching, long-term plan of a company that is designed to help the company attain a specific goal. For customer-centric companies, the strategy is directed at improving the customer experience. Improving the customer experience presupposes the belief that improving the customer experience leads to business growth and financial success. Customer-centric companies necessarily include the customer in the formation, implementation, evaluation, and modification of their strategy. This strategy is the process in which the company spells out its vision and values and develops policies and operating procedures to map out its general course toward becoming a customer-centric company.

Strategic management occurs at the highest level of the company and, therefore, is usually directed by the chief executive officer and supported by other top company executives. Top management provides the overall direction to the company and controls the resources needed to achieve the company objectives. Consequently, a successful CFP is highly dependent on the support of top management.

Top management sets the general culture of the company, typically in the form of a formal mission statement. Company mission statements that include the importance of the customer and the customer's needs help maintain a customer-centric culture and instill a set of values and implicit standards about meeting customers' needs. The company's culture encompasses a set of attitudes, beliefs, and values. The combined attitudes and opinions shared among the employees of the organization act as guidelines or expectations with respect to the behaviors that are expected of the employees. The governance of the CFP helps instill a customer-centric culture by establishing a set of expected behaviors on the part of all of the company's constituents, including the senior executives, middle managers, and frontline employees. In a customer-centric company, the work-related behaviors of each constituency are aimed at satisfying customers' needs. To have a successful CFP, the customer-centric company has as its goal to bring a sense of urgency and necessity of the customer to the fore of the company values. In order to instill a customer-centric culture throughout the entire company, corporate governance needs to contain elements of the CFP.

Governance can be defined as a system by which companies are directed and controlled. By establishing governance around the CFP, the company provides the structure through which the objectives of the CFP are set, and the means of attaining those objectives and monitoring performance toward those objectives. The success of a CFP, like any corporate program, requires support from the top management of the organization. With a corporate-driven program come the necessary guidelines as to how the program will be supported by and implemented throughout the company. CFPs necessarily extend across organizational lines, functional areas, and job levels. Because of the CFP's far-reaching impact throughout the company, it is especially dependent on effective governance.

There are three areas that need to be addressed in developing governance for a CFP. While there is some overlap among these areas, this structure is useful for discussing best practices of CFPs. These three areas, presented in Figure 2.2, are:

1. *Guidelines and rules.* CFPs, as we will see, impact decisions across the entire organization. To ensure the CFP runs efficiently and effectively, rules around the program need to be established. These guidelines and

Figure 2.2 Three areas of customer feedback governance.

rules reflect the set of processes, customs, policies, and laws affecting the way the CFP is directed, administered, or controlled. Specifically, guidelines can include the way the feedback data from CFPs are used in the business decision-making process. For example, customer feedback data can be used in a variety of ways, ranging from making company-wide decisions that impact an entire customer segment to decisions that impact a single customer. Decision-making policies around the use of the customer feedback data will have an impact on the success of the program. Vague policies regarding how the CFP is executed, including analytical methods and goals, dissemination of results, and data usage of the customer feedback data, will ultimately lead to less than optimal effectiveness of the program. The procedure for how business decisions using the CFP data are made and by whom is one of the most crucial elements of the CFP.

2. *Definition of roles and responsibilities.* Corporate governance of the CFP defines the responsibilities among constituencies in the company, such as the

board, executives, managers, and frontline employees. Because CFPs have far-reaching effects (across departments and organizational levels), establishing a set of policies around the responsibilities of the various stakeholders is critical for the program's success. Outlining the roles and responsibilities involves setting standards not only for employees directly related to the CFP but also for employees who use the CFP results. Therefore, communication of the roles and responsibilities is crucial to ensure consistent application of the CFP throughout the entire company.

3. *Procedures for changing CFPs.* CFPs change over time. There are two general types of changes: (1) managerial and (2) operational. Managerial changes are typically driven by the changing needs of the organization and/or marketplace and involve changes in the strategy, governance, and integration of the CFP into the business processes. For example, the introduction of a new corporate strategy, new marketing plans, and changing business processes require attention at the highest level of the company. Operational changes impact the daily operations of the CFP, including the survey method (for example, question modification, sampling methodology) and reporting of results. Operational changes are typically driven by new product/service offerings, company acquisitions, and the need for specific types of customer feedback data. As a result, these changes can require a lot of additional resources, ranging from additional employee time to direct financial costs for third-party feedback vendors. In either type of change, governance of the CFP needs to include considerations of how such program changes occur.

INTEGRATED BUSINESS PROCESSES

The area of integrated business processes addresses the extent to which the organization embeds elements of the CFP (including processes and data) into the daily business operations. The integration of the CFP into the daily business processes facilitates both the management processes and the operational processes to support the needs of the customers. You might think of the integration of the CFP into the business processes as ensuring that customer feedback is used at all levels of the organization, from top management to frontline employees. First, this integration helps ensure that customer feedback is delivered to top executives in order for them monitor the success of their strategy and modify it if needed. Second, this integration helps operationalize the governance of the program and ensures employees adhere to the guidelines and rules surrounding the program itself. By incorporating key elements of the CFP directly into the daily business processes, the organization is able to ensure customers' needs are met.

For the customer-centric company, CFPs play an important role in the management of the business. The extent to which a company integrates the CFP into the business processes can help reinforce a corporate culture of customer centricity. The integration of customer feedback into the daily operations keeps the customers' needs in the fore of the management and frontline employees' minds. The integration of the CFP into the business processes encompasses many elements, from communication of the CFP elements throughout the company to the use of the customer feedback data in resolving customer complaints.

Technological advances (CRM systems, Internet) have greatly impacted the extent to which CFPs can be integrated into the daily business processes. The effective integration of the CFP into the business processes (for example, customer problem resolution, CRM activities) can improve the customer experience by helping the company more effectively manage the customer relationship across the customer life cycle. Companies incorporating the CFP as part of their CRM system are able to use both objective data (sales/service history) and attitudinal data (satisfaction) to get a comprehensive picture of the quality of the customer relationship.

METHOD

The method of customer feedback data collection addresses the means by which the organization collects the data. There are various methods by which customer feedback data can be collected and customers can be surveyed. The process typically involves formal data collection via a survey that asks standardized questions about the customer's experience with service/ products. The surveys contain both rating questions (for example, 1–5 or 0–10 scales) that allow the customers to indicate their attitudes through a quantitative rating (higher is typically better) and open-ended questions that allow the customers to provide free-flowing feedback in their own words.

Surveys generally are of two types: relationship and transactional. *Relationship surveys* focus on assessing the quality of the overall relationship with the customer. Thus, delivery of the survey itself is not time-dependent; survey administration is done at the company's discretion and can occur at any time during the customer life cycle (marketing, sales, or service). Relationship surveys include questions about specific areas of the customer experience across the entire life cycle as well as questions assessing the customer's overall perceptions/attitudes of his or her relationship with the company. Ratings of the customer experience reflect levels of satisfaction or perceived quality.

Transactional surveys focus on specific customer transactions/ interactions and allow the customer to provide feedback. Thus, delivery of the transactional survey is time-dependent on the occurrence of the transaction. Like relationship surveys, transactional surveys include questions about the customer experience of the specific transaction in question and can include overall questions that measure customer loyalty. Ratings of the customer experience reflect levels of satisfaction of the experience or the perceived quality of the experience.

Other factors that must be considered with respect to how customer feedback data are collected include the types of survey vehicles that can be used and the types of questions to include in surveys. Are Web-based surveys more effective for collecting customer feedback? How should companies measure customer loyalty?

REPORTING

The quality of the CFP does not stop at the collection of the customer feedback. The company needs to know how to best summarize and present the customer feedback so that it can make useful business decisions. Customer feedback data can be viewed and analyzed in a variety of ways using spreadsheets, sophisticated software, and graphical presentation programs. As a general rule, reporting of the customer feedback results needs to be guided by the overarching strategy of the company as well as the survey objectives of improving customer loyalty. Improving customer loyalty requires specific business responses that are designed to impact the customer experience. The analyses and reporting of the results need to assist executives and frontline employees in making business decisions that will improve the customer experience.

CFPs are capable of generating large amounts of data. Consider this example from Oracle Corporation. Its semiannual global relationship survey includes roughly 100 rated questions (the survey is role-based, so only a percentage of all questions are visible to any given respondent). In one survey period,

Oracle received over 14,000 completed relationship surveys from its customers. The combination of over 100 demographic attributes associated with responding contacts and accounts equates to over 2.8 million data points! It is clear that extracting information from a vast sea of customer feedback data can be overwhelming.

Companies seek guidance regarding how to best report vast amounts of customer feedback results. The basic service delivery model (presented earlier) will be used to help guide data analysis. The use of the service delivery model will help you understand that analysis of the data is focused on maximizing customer loyalty. Best practices focus on all aspects of the reporting process, from summarizing the customer feedback data to disseminating the customer feedback results.

Reporting of customer feedback data helps management make better customer-centric business decisions. To report results effectively, companies must consider the collection, integration, analysis, and distribution of customer feedback data. These components of reporting apply directly to the area of business intelligence (BI). BI, through the application of technology and systems in the reporting process, is directly relevant to the integration of customer feedback data into business processes. The reporting of customer feedback data, as we will see, is a key component to the integration of the CFP into the business processes of the company via its business applications (for example, CRM system).

RESEARCH

Some companies develop comprehensive research programs to help unlock the potential of their customer survey data. Maximizing the value of their CFPs is often the result of conducting in-depth satisfaction and loyalty research. This research helps them gain superior customer insight that is necessary to accelerate business growth. With a substantive research program, companies transform themselves into customer-centric businesses by:

- Validating customer survey programs

- Creating reliable, valid, and useful business metrics for executive dashboards

- Quantifying the impact of customer loyalty on business performance measures (for example, revenue growth, sales volume, defection rate)

- Identifying business areas that significantly impact customer loyalty

- Evaluating the effectiveness of company-wide programs

- Identifying the important elements of employee and partner satisfaction that will improve customer loyalty

- Determining customer satisfaction and loyalty criteria for incentive compensation programs

- Building customer-centric operational metrics to align employees

- Benchmarking best practices across the company

- Developing employee training programs that impact the customer experience

While there are many different kinds of research methods (for example, case studies, historical, scientific), the focus of this book is not to make distinctions among the different types of research methods. The focus of this chapter is on the application of rigorous statistical analyses to the customer feedback data. The goal of this type of research is to draw conclusions about the entire population of customers of interest based on analysis of a sample of the population, the survey respondents.

Applied customer research can take many forms. For example, to understand the value of the CFP, companies quantify the degree to which customer satisfaction/loyalty is empirically linked to revenue and profitability. Also, to determine how specific variables (for example, geography, warranty status, employee satisfaction, partner satisfaction) impact customer satisfaction and loyalty, companies compare customer groups to better understand how customer satisfaction/loyalty differs across key customer segments (for example, across regions, across different warranty programs). Customer research can be structured to answer specific questions about the customer experience. Questions that can be addressed through research using customer feedback data are, What is the impact of employee training on customer satisfaction? How does customer satisfaction change throughout the customer life cycle?

CFPs often produce a plethora of data. This seemingly excessive amount of data can be attributed to the use of the Web, which facilitates the data collection process. Customer surveys can now be easily distributed, and, as a result, customer feedback databases are updated continuously.

Most companies rely solely on standard reports provided by their survey vendors or in-house survey teams. These reports, as we saw in Chapter 1, reflect a basic summary of the data (for example, averages, frequency of satisfied customers, drivers of loyalty). While this information is helpful in understanding the customer experience, some companies take advantage of their large customer feedback databases by conducting additional, in-depth research using supplemental analyses that go far beyond what is available through typical reporting sites. This type of research, often referred to as applied research, is aimed at garnering additional insight about the customer relationship that cannot be achieved through basic feedback reporting sites. This additional insight, it is hoped, will translate into improved customer relationships and higher levels of customer loyalty.

Applied research can address some very important questions:

1. To what degree is customer satisfaction related to objective measures of customer loyalty (for example, sale amount, churn rates, up-selling/cross-selling)?

2. What elements of employee satisfaction are most related to customer satisfaction and loyalty?

3. Which dimensions of partner satisfaction lead to customer satisfaction and loyalty of joint customers?

4. Which current operational metrics are good predictors of customer satisfaction/loyalty?

5. Can a company discover/create new operational metrics that are linked to customer satisfaction and loyalty?

Answering these types of questions can help a company better understand the customer relationship and identify factors that impact business success. The first question provides needed evidence to upper management that, indeed, customers' attitudes are important to business growth; this research provides support for management's investments into areas that improve the customer experience. Answers to the second and third questions help management understand the determinants of customer loyalty that go beyond the insights gained through analysis of the customer feedback data alone. Improving both employee and partner relationships can result in better customer relationships. The answers to the last questions will help identify and create operational metrics that impact customers' perception of the customer experience. While it has been shown that customer loyalty is the leading indicator of financial success and growth, it is the operational metrics, in turn, that are the leading indicator of customer loyalty. The operational metrics, therefore, can be a means by which management can improve company growth. Identifying the operational metrics that are linked to customer satisfaction and loyalty helps companies understand how they can change their business processes in ways that will improve the customer experience.

Despite the apparent benefits of conducting applied research, it is, however, not utilized in most CFPs. In fact, only 39% of companies with a CFP indicated that they regularly conduct applied research using their customer feedback data. Additionally, when asked about specific applied research practices (for example, linking customer feedback data to other sources of company business data), companies report similar and low adoption rates.

SUMMARY

CFPs are multifaceted business practices whose impact on the success of a company depends on many elements. The strategy and corporate governance guide the overarching structure of the program. The integration of customer feedback into the company's business processes helps ensure the program and all its elements are embedded into the company's daily operations. Additionally, the measurement system needs to be structured in a way that provides reliable and valid information about the customers' perceptions. The reporting of the customer feedback results ensures the company receives the information needed to make effective business decisions. Finally, customer-focused research using the customer feedback data provides additional insight into the needs of the customer base and increases the overall value of the CFP.

The next chapter summarizes the study approach used to explore a couple of questions regarding CFPs. First, this study helped identify how companies typically structure their CFPs. Basic knowledge of the business landscape with respect to CFPs is identified and can help a company understand where it fits relative to other companies that have CFPs. Second, this study helped identify which element or elements of the program impact the success of the overall CFP. While a company may want to know its relative standing with respect to how it structures its CFP, improving its program may involve targeting areas that are more likely to lead to higher levels of customer loyalty. The study approach was designed to address these questions and provide needed information in a company's pursuit of developing a new CFP or improving an existing one.

3

Customer Feedback Programs and Best Practices Study

BEST PRACTICES

The phrase "best practices" is often used when describing essential characteristics of CFPs. These espoused "best practices" are commonly in line with popular beliefs regarding their merit. For example, conventional wisdom says that best practices include such things as getting upper management's support of the program and sharing customer feedback results with all employees. Companies that adopt these best practices in their CFPs, so it is thought, will have a greater chance of being successful than companies that do not adopt these practices. The list of best practices is typically determined by case studies of handpicked companies that adopt specific practices. While case studies are a good first start in identifying potential best practices, they need to be verified using a more rigorous method.

In general terms, a *best practice* is a technique, process, or method that is more effective or efficient in delivering a desired outcome than other techniques, processes, or methods. Practitioners use the term "best practices" when illustrating techniques and methods, despite having no real or even assumed outcomes in mind. While there are much-cited case studies that establish lists of best practices for CFPs, there is no conclusive research that quantifies whether specific business practices impact customer satisfaction and loyalty. Toward that end, to help verify conventionally accepted best practices, a scientific approach to study CFP practices was undertaken using a variety of companies.

BEST PRACTICES SURVEY

I developed a survey to allow companies to provide input on how they structure their CFPs and use data from them. The survey questions were generated based on my professional experience in the field of customer satisfaction/loyalty research and based on the aforementioned conventional wisdom of customer satisfaction best practices. For each survey question, respondents were asked to indicate the degree to which the statement described their current CFP. Although I used the term "customer feedback program" in the survey, I asked respondents to complete the survey with respect to their formal customer feedback collection process no matter the nomenclature they employ for their program.

There were two main goals of the survey. The first goal was designed to help identify the frequency with which business practices are adopted in CFPs. Respondents were asked about how their company structures their CFP and how the data are used to manage their customer relationships. The questions reflected a wide range of issues that generally supported the "people, process, and technology" framework of successful business change. For further clarification of this framework, five major categories were used to represent the survey questions:

- **Strategy/Governance:** Addresses the organization's policies around the customer satisfaction program and uses of the customer feedback data

- **Process:** Addresses the extent to which the organization embeds customer feedback data into the business processes

- **Method:** Addresses how the organization collects customer feedback data

- **Reporting:** Addresses the elements around the reporting of the customer feedback data

- **Research:** Addresses the extent to which the organization engages in and disseminates customer satisfaction research (for example, segmentation, linkage analysis)

The second goal of the survey was to identify which business practices had an impact on key outcome variables. The two variables selected for study were the company's customer loyalty score and the company's satisfaction with its CFP in helping it manage customer relationships. Customer loyalty was selected as a key outcome variable because of the plethora of research showing it as a leading indicator of a company's financial success. A company's customer loyalty scores, however, are dependent on more than just the success of the CFP. Loyalty is dependent on organizational factors (for example, human resources, marketing, and training) and market factors outside the control of the CFP that may ameliorate its impact on customer loyalty. CFPs are often used to help companies manage customer relationships. Therefore, another outcome variable used in this study was the satisfaction with which the CFP helped in managing customer relationships.

Toward that end, two additional survey questions were crafted that allowed respondents to (1) indicate where their company ranked relative to industry competitors with respect to customer loyalty (respondents provided a percentile estimate) and (2) indicate their satisfaction with the CFP in helping them manage customer relationships. These questions were used to identify which of the "best practices" actually predicted customer loyalty scores and satisfaction with the CFP in helping manage customer relationships, respectively.

Finally, respondents were asked to indicate their company's biggest roadblock to increasing customer loyalty. This open-ended question allowed respondents to indicate, in their own words, what hinders improvements in customer loyalty.

Additional survey questions were included that allowed segmentation of the respondent/organizations:

• Job role of respondent in the CFP

• Level of knowledge of the respondent about the CFP

• Size of company (number of employees)

• Type of company (B2B, B2C, or both; single vs. multiple locations)

• Location of company (region)

• Industry of company

Survey administration was conducted using a Web-based survey tool provided by GMI. Respondents were provided by CustomerThink.com and the American Society for Quality (http://www.asq.org), and through the author's professional network. Members were sent an e-mail with an invitation to take the survey.

SURVEY RESULTS

A total of 277 respondents completed the survey. Demographic information of the respondents appears in Table 3.1. About 70% of the respondents indicated that their company has a formal CFP. Of those respondents, a majority indicated that their role is related to the company's CFP (63%). Nearly all of the respondents indicated that they have a good understanding of

Table 3.1 Demographic information of respondents.

CFP	Company has formal CFP	70%
	No formal CFP	22%
	Not sure company has CFP	8%
Job role	Senior exec of CFP	12%
	Director of CFP	16%
	Manager of CFP	12%
	Individual contributor of CFP	18%
	External consultant of CFP	5%
	Other	37%
Knowledge of CFP	No understanding	0%
	A little understanding	5%
	Some understanding	22%
	Much understanding	37%
	Complete understanding	36%
Company size	Don't know	1%
	Fewer than 10 employees	14%
	10–99 employees	13%
	100–999 employees	36%
	1,000–4,999 employees	13%
	5,000–19,999 employees	13%
	20,000–49,999 employees	2%
	50,000+ employees	8%

(Continued)

Table 3.1   Demographic information of respondents. (Continued)

Company type	B2B	50%
	B2C	14%
	B2B and B2C	36%
	One location	31%
	Multiple locations	69%
Region	North America	80%
	Europe, Middle East, Africa	9%
	Asia	9%
	Latin/Central America	2%
Industry	Services	54%
	Manufacturing	33%
	Other	13%

the company's CFP (95% indicated they have at least some understanding of the CFP).

Respondents came from both small and large companies (number of employees). A majority of the respondents (64%) work in companies with fewer than 1000 employees. Most of the companies consider their customers to be businesses. Specifically, half the respondents work for B2B companies (50%), while 36% of the companies have customers who are businesses and individuals. Considering 69% of the companies have multiple locations, the companies in the study could be considered somewhat complex with respect to managing multiple locations. Most of the companies are headquartered in North America (80%), and most are in the service industry (54%).

The impact of business practices on the success of Cfps likely varies across organizational variables. The governance component, for example, might be more difficult in large companies than in small companies. The reporting of customer feedback data is likely more complex in companies with multiple locations than in companies with one location. Due to sample size limitations in the current study, however, the impact of these organizational variables could not be examined. Future studies could pursue this type of research to shed more light on the impact of organizational variables on the success of Cfps.

TYPICAL Cfps

Of those companies that have formal Cfps, only 44% of the respondents provided their company's percentile industry customer loyalty ranking. Thirty-seven percent did not know their company's ranking, and 19% indicated that this information was confidential. Of the respondents who provided a percentile ranking, the average ranking was 67%, indicating that the loyalty ranking of the typical respondent's company was higher than 67% of its competitors.

About 64% of the respondents were satisfied with their Cfps in helping them manage their customer relationships (rating of 6–10), and about 11% of the respondents were very satisfied (ratings of 9 and 10). Again, the typical respondent was generally satisfied with the company's CFP in helping manage the customer relationship.

Table 3.2 contains the percentages of respondents who indicated their company follows the specific business practice related to their CFP. As can be seen in the table, the adoption rate of different CFP business practices varies greatly. Some business practices are adopted by many, while others are not.

Table 3.2 Of companies with a CFP, percentage that has adopted specific CFP business practices.

Area	Customer business practice	Adoption rate
Strategy/ Governance	Customer feedback used in strategic vision/goals	86%
Strategy/ Governance	Customer feedback as important as financial measures	59%
Strategy/ Governance	Executive is champion of CFP	86%
Strategy/ Governance	Customer feedback used in executive compensation	65%
Strategy/ Governance	Customer feedback used in employee compensation	74%
Process	Customer feedback included in executive dashboards	78%
Process	CFP integrated into business processes	73%
Process	CFP process/goals communicated to entire company	58%
Process	Resolution of customer issues integrated into CRM	51%
Method	Survey delivery is automated	59%
Method	Web surveys used	76%
Method	Multiple methods of collecting customer feedback	86%
Method	Contact management integrated into CRM	58%
Method	Telephone surveys used	62%
Method	Paper-and-pencil surveys used	46%
Method	Interviews used	60%
Method	Surveys done in-house	52%

(Continued)

Table 3.2 Of companies with a CFP, percentage that has adopted specific CFP business practices. (Continued)

Reporting	Web-based reporting tools used to report results	48%
Reporting	Customer feedback results shared only at executive level*	66%
Reporting	Customer feedback results shared throughout company	71%
Reporting	Customer feedback research presented internally	58%
Reporting	Customer feedback research presented externally	39%
Reporting	Customer feedback results benchmarked	53%
Research	Existing customer information used	73%
Research	Linkage between customer feedback and business metrics established	48%
Research	Linkage between customer feedback and operational metrics established	50%
Research	Linkage between customer feedback and constituency attitudes established	40%
Research	Applied research regularly conducted	39%

*Reverse coded.

Commonly adopted CFP business practices (adopted by 85% or more of companies) include the following:

• Executive is champion of CFP

• Customer feedback is used in strategic vision/goals

• Multiple methods of collecting customer feedback

CFP business practices that are not commonly adopted (adopted by 50% or less of the companies) are the following:

- Applied research regularly conducted

- Customer feedback research presented externally

- Linkage between customer feedback and constituency attitudes established

- Linkage between customer feedback and business metrics established

- Linkage between customer feedback and operational metrics established

- Web-based reporting tools used to report results

- Paper-and-pencil surveys used

The survey results show that there was much variability with respect to the adoption of CFP business practices across different business practices. Many of the conventionally accepted CFP best practices were adopted by many companies. For example, 86% of all respondents indicated that their company uses customer feedback in its strategic vision/goals, and reported that an executive is a champion of their company's CFP. Additionally, 74% of all respondents indicated that customer feedback is used in employee compensation, and 71% indicated that customer feedback results are shared throughout the company.

Conversely, there were several customer feedback practices that were not widely adopted. Specifically, a little over a third of all respondents (39%) indicated that their company adopted applied research practices as part of their CFPs. Furthermore, only about half of all respondents indicated that their company establishes statistical linkages between customer feedback data and business metrics (48%), operational metrics (50%), or other constituency's attitudes (40%).

Table 3.3 summarizes the most frequently adopted and least frequently adopted CFP business practices. The results show that most companies are able to demonstrate top support (via strategic visions/goals and executive champions) of CFPs.

Table 3.3 Most and least popular CFP business practices.

Area	Most popular CFP business practice	Adoption rate
Strategy/ Governance	Customer feedback used in strategic vision/goals	86%
Strategy/ Governance	Executive is champion of CFP	86%
Method	Multiple methods of collecting customer feedback	86%
Process	Customer feedback included in executive dashboards	78%
Method	Web surveys used	76%

Area	Least popular CFP business practice	Adoption rate
Research	Linkage between customer feedback and operational metrics established	50%
Reporting	Web-based reporting tools used to report results	48%
Research	Linkage between customer feedback and business metrics established	48%
Method	Paper-and-pencil surveys used	46%
Research	Linkage between customer feedback and constituency attitudes established	40%
Reporting	Customer feedback research presented externally	39%
Research	Applied research regularly conducted	39%

On the other hand, only a small number of companies invest in research practices using customer feedback data.

IDENTIFYING CFP BEST PRACTICES

Two analytical approaches were taken to identify CFP best practices. The first method compared adoption rates of CFP business practices for companies with high customer loyalty scores (Loyalty Leaders) with adoption rates of CFP business practices for companies with low customer loyalty scores (Loyalty Laggers). Comparing adoption rates of specific business practices across these two groups allows us to identify how Loyalty Leaders differ from Loyalty Laggers. Loyalty Leaders might adopt certain CFP business practices at a greater rate than Loyalty Laggers. CFP business practices more highly adopted by Loyalty Leaders (compared to Loyalty Laggers) would reflect best practices. *Loyalty Leaders* were defined as companies whose industry percentile ranking of customer loyalty scores was 70 or higher. *Loyalty Laggers* were defined as companies whose industry percentile ranking of customer loyalty was below 70.

The second method compared customer loyalty percentile rankings of companies that adopted a specific CFP business practice with customer loyalty percentile rankings of companies that did not adopt a specific CFP business practice. Examining each CFP business practice in this manner allows us to identify if the adoption of a specific practice is related to the company's customer loyalty percentile ranking. The next set of analyses was conducted to identify the degree to which each CFP business practice was related to customer loyalty scores.

Identifying the degree of impact each business practice had on customer loyalty was a two-step process. In the first step, for each business practice, companies were divided into two groups: those that adopted the business practice and those that did not adopt the business practice. For the second step, the customer loyalty percentile ranking was compared for the two groups.

These two methods provide a slightly different look at the study data and result in different types of information. The first method helps us describe the components of the CFPs of Loyalty Leaders as well as helps us identify why they may have higher customer loyalty scores than their Loyalty Lagger counterparts. The second method allows us to quantify the impact that a CFP business practice has on a company's level of customer loyalty.

In the subsequent chapters, survey results for the six areas of a CFP will be presented in detail. The order in which the survey results are presented reflects the basic structure of CFPs, starting with the management processes and concluding with the operational processes. The order of presentation does not necessarily reflect the importance of each of the CFP elements; the order simply reflects a logical progression from the higher-level management functions of CFPs to the operational processes necessary to support the program.

PART II

Best Practices of Customer Feedback Programs— Management Processes

4

Strategy and Corporate Governance

S trategy and corporate governance focus on the organization's guidelines concerning the CFP. Strategy and governance provide general direction for the CFP, which impacts all other areas of the program. The guidelines set the tone of the entire program, ultimately impacting how the program will be integrated into the daily operations of the business as well as the operational processes specific to the CFP.

ADOPTION RATES FOR STRATEGY/ GOVERNANCE-RELATED BUSINESS PRACTICES

The adoption rates for CFP business practices that are related to strategy/governance suggest that Loyalty Leaders, compared to Loyalty Laggers, tend to adopt certain types of practices at a much greater rate. The comparisons across the two groups appear in Figure 4.1.

Establishing a customer-centric culture is thought to be an important element of any CFP. In line with this common belief, the survey results show that Loyalty Leaders adopt strategic/ governance practices at a much greater rate than Loyalty Laggers. Specifically, the results show that 100% of Loyalty Leaders use customer feedback in their strategic visions/goals, while only about 70% of Loyalty Laggers do. Furthermore, 75% of

Strategy/Governance-related business practice	Adoption rate		
	Loyalty Leaders	Loyalty Laggers	Loyalty unknown
Customer feedback is included in the company's strategic vision, mission and goals	**100%**	71%	85%
Customer feedback results are as important as financial measures in making business decisions	**83%**	42%	56%
A top executive (for example, CEO, VP) is a champion of the CFP	**88%**	85%	86%
Customer feedback results are used in executives' objectives and incentive compensation	**75%**	50%	66%
Customer feedback results are used in frontline employees' objectives and incentive compensation	**91%**	83%	66%

Figure 4.1   Adoption rates of strategy/governance-related CFP business practices for Loyalty Leaders and Loyalty Laggers.

Loyalty Leaders, compared to 50% of Loyalty Laggers, use customer feedback in executives' objectives and incentive compensation. Additionally, nearly twice as many Loyalty Leaders (83% adoption rate) as Loyalty Laggers (42% adoption rate) think that customer feedback is as important as financial measures in making business decisions.

Surprisingly, the adoption rate of two elements of strategy/governance, commonly thought of as best practices, did not distinguish between Loyalty Leaders and Loyalty Laggers. Including a top executive (for example, CEO, VP) as a champion of the CFP and using customer feedback results in employee compensation did not seem to enhance the effectiveness of the CFP in increasing customer loyalty. We see that both Loyalty Leaders and Loyalty Laggers adopted these two business practices at a comparable rate.

STRATEGY/GOVERNANCE-RELATED CFP BUSINESS PRACTICES THAT IMPACT CUSTOMER LOYALTY AND SATISFACTION WITH THE CFP

The next set of analyses was focused on quantifying the impact of the strategy/governance-related CFP business practices on customer loyalty and satisfaction with the CFP. In general, the results (see Figures 4.2 and 4.3) show that certain aspects of strategy/governance had a substantial impact on the success of CFPs, whether success is defined as increased customer loyalty or satisfaction with the CFP in managing customer relationships.

The survey results show that strategy/governance-related business practices of CFPs had a substantial impact on customer loyalty scores as well as the satisfaction with the CFP in helping manage customer relationships. Companies that believe customer feedback is as important as financial measures in making business decisions reported far higher customer loyalty ratings (percentile ranking of 73) than companies that do not believe this (percentile ranking of 53). Additionally, companies that include customer feedback in their strategic visions, missions, and goals had higher levels of customer loyalty (percentile ranking of 68) than companies that do not do this (percentile ranking of 50). Finally, companies that use customer feedback results for executive objectives and incentive compensation reported higher levels

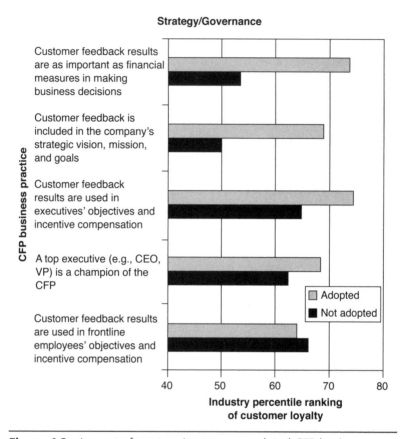

Figure 4.2   Impact of strategy/governance-related CFP business practices on customer loyalty.

of customer loyalty (percentile ranking of 75) than companies that do not do this.

While not all CFP business practices related to strategy/ governance had a substantial impact on the company's satisfaction with its CFP, a few business practices did. Specifically, the results show that satisfaction with the CFP in helping manage the customer relationship was significantly higher for companies that use customer feedback in their strategic visions (88% satisfied) and include it in executive compensation (92% satis-

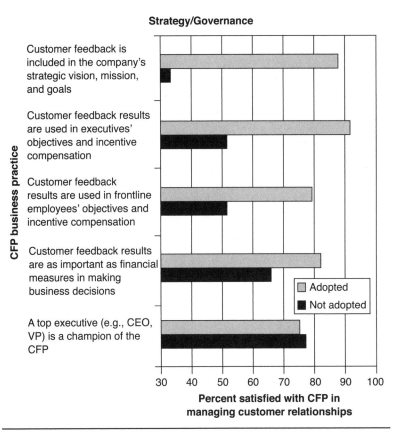

Figure 4.3   Impact of strategy/governance-related CFP business practices on satisfaction with the CFP in managing customer relationships.

fied) than for companies that do not use customer feedback in those specific ways (32% and 52%, respectively). Additionally, the importance of customer feedback results in making business decisions greatly improved the satisfaction with the CFP in managing customer relationships (83% vs. 64% are satisfied). Finally, companies that use the CFP for frontline employee objectives and compensation were more satisfied (80% satisfied) with their CFPs than companies that do not use customer feedback to incentivize frontline employees (53% satisfied).

STRATEGY AND GOVERNANCE DRIVE A CUSTOMER-CENTRIC CULTURE

Corporate governance as it relates to the CFP refers to the rules, processes, or laws by which the CFP is operated, regulated, and controlled. Clearly defined and enforced corporate governance of the CFP provides a structure that benefits everyone concerned by ensuring that the company and all its parts adhere to operating standards and best practices surrounding the program. Corporate governance around the CFP addresses the organization's specific policies in a wide variety of areas that essentially help establish the organizational culture around the customer, help reinforce the importance of the customer, and set the tenor for the entire organization.

Harris Stratex Networks

Harris Stratex Networks understands the importance of support from top management in the success of its CFP. Stephanie Ekins-Parnell, program director of customer satisfaction, says, "Customer satisfaction is instilled into the company from the top down and is clearly illustrated by the inclusion of customer satisfaction in many forms of corporate communications to employees." In fact, Harris Stratex Networks' company mission statement includes specific terms around the customer:

"To meet and exceed stakeholder expectations among:

- **Customers.** Build lasting relationships by listening. Deliver innovative solutions. Focus on our customer's evolving business goals. Be a partner in their success.

- **Employees.** Respect, motivate and reward. Enable all of us to win together.

- **Partners.** Act ethically and professionally. Pursue mutually beneficial business goals.

- **Investors.** Commit to profitable growth. Build value by maximizing our return in everything we do.

- **The world outside our company.** Advance global communications. Minimize our impact on the environment. Give back to our communities.

Finally, Harris Stratex Networks' company values include an emphasis on customers. The following are included in its list of values:

- Our customer is first

- We lead with innovation

- Our integrity is unquestioned

- We embrace change

- We excel together

- We attack to win

From the company's formal vision and mission statements to its company values, Harris Stratex Networks has thoroughly incorporated the customer into the company's corporate strategy. Harris Stratex Networks' customer-centric strategy helps the company communicate the importance of the customer to all stakeholders and improves the likelihood that the CFP will be successful.

BUILDING A CUSTOMER-CENTRIC CULTURE: AN EXAMPLE

While clear company policy regarding strategy and governance practices around customer-related issues is an effective means toward instilling a customer-centric culture, other examples for driving a customer-centric culture are also necessary. Companies have adopted a variety of methods, both mundane and unique, in establishing a customer-centric culture. These practices are designed to pervade all aspects of the company. Developing this customer-centric culture involves establishing business practices that ensure the customers' needs are at the forefront of all of the company's practices. These business practices impact both management decisions and frontline employee behaviors. Table 4.1 contains many of the specific business practices that were at the core of Siebel Systems' customer-centric culture.[3]

Table 4.1 Strategy and governance practices used at Siebel Systems.

- The CEO referred to himself as the "chief customer satisfaction officer."
- Customer satisfaction was included as a core value in the employee handbook. The core value handbook couched this aspect of the company in the following terms: "100 percent customer satisfaction is our overriding priority."
- Employee performance management included customer satisfaction as a key performance area across all levels of the organization, from executive vice presidents to frontline employees.
- Quarterly executive meetings started with reviews of customer satisfaction survey results to examine trends in customer loyalty across different customer segments (for example, regions and product lines). Additionally, executives used customer issues identified from the survey to craft corrective action plans that were regularly monitored.
- Employee incentive compensation was tied to customer satisfaction measurements across the entire company, from executive management to frontline support staff.
- All conference rooms were named after customers.
- Artwork in company offices reflected customer-related content. Specifically, annual reports of customers as well as letters from customers were formally presented (in high-quality frames) that highlight their success (business growth) and satisfaction with the company's products and services.
- Customers were spotlighted in all forms of advertisements, from print to television.
- The company shared its satisfaction measurement methodology with its customers to help them improve their customer relationships.

---

[3] Siebel Systems no longer exists. The company was purchased by Oracle.

INCENTIVE PROGRAMS

Cfps provide a rich source of customer data on which to build an incentive program around customer-related issues. This focus on the customer helps the company improve how it manages customer relationships and increases customer loyalty. Using customer feedback as part of the incentive program reinforces the company's customer-centric culture. Additionally, incentive programs help employees focus on improving their customer feedback, which encourages and enhances long-term positive relationships between employees and customers. Companies that use customer metrics from CFPs to incentivize employees need to consider many factors.

First, customer metrics used in the incentive program need to support the corporate objectives associated with the customer requirements. Corporate objectives, acting as a guide for the entire organization, help set the manner by which the progress of those objectives is assessed. When the goal of the company objectives is to improve the customer experience and customer loyalty, the company's incentive program needs to include customer metrics that assess the customer experience and customer loyalty.

Second, companies need to clearly communicate the incentive plan to employees as early as possible. Clear communication not only helps ensure employees understand the requirements needed to obtain the incentives but also helps employees understand how the incentive program is linked to corporate objectives. A company-wide program that is clearly articulated will have a greater likelihood of being accepted by the employees, improving the chances of a successful program.

Third, employees must have the power to effect change on the metrics on which they are incentivized. While a customer loyalty index may be the key metric used to incentivize executives, frontline employees can also be incentivized on customer metrics more closely linked to their daily performance. The technical support department can be incentivized on customer feedback related directly to technical support quality (for example, technical support knowledge, timeliness). Account managers, on the other hand, can be incentivized on customer feedback related directly to account management activities (for example, ease of doing business, sales responsiveness, and account management knowledge). While the ultimate goal of the company may be to improve customer loyalty, frontline employees effect change by improving the customer experience at various touch points for which they are responsible. Improvements in the customer experience will, in turn, increase customer loyalty.

Finally, companies need to use customer metrics in conjunction with other internal operational metrics. Companies may already be tracking operational metrics as part of their standard operating procedures. For example, call wait time, response time, and number of call transfers are commonly used to assess and track the quality of the technical support department. Some companies have, in fact, found that these operational metrics are related to customer satisfaction and customer loyalty. A company can investigate whether its operational metrics are, in fact, statistically related to customer satisfaction. Additionally, a company can identify new operational metrics that are statistically related to customer satisfaction/loyalty and use them to incentivize employees. This process of discovery involves linkage analysis in which operational metrics (for example, hold time, turnaround time, and number of transfers) are associated with attitudinal measures (for example, satisfaction ratings of overall support quality and support responsiveness). Operational metrics that are linked to customer feedback metrics will show a relationship to each other—as call time (operational metric) goes down, customer satisfaction with call center (customer metric) goes up.

The goal is to determine which of the operational metrics best predicts customer satisfaction. Do customers with a quicker turnaround time report higher satisfaction with responsiveness than customers with a slower turnaround time? Once the customer-centric operational measures are identified, they can be used for purposes of goal setting. As we will see later, companies that link their operational metrics to customer feedback have higher customer loyalty scores than companies that do not perform this sort of linkage analysis.

CUSTOMER LOYALTY AND GOAL SETTING

Companies that use customer loyalty surveys strive to see increases in their customer loyalty scores, as improving customer loyalty has a positive impact on business results and long-term business success. Toward that end, executives implement various programs, including incentive programs, in the hope that customer loyalty scores will improve.

One common method for improving performance is goal setting. Goal setting in the business setting is a process in which a company establishes specific and measurable objectives or performance levels. It is often used in conjunction with an incentive program. Incentives are paid out when a certain level of performance (goal) is reached. In the area of customer satisfaction, for example, what typically occurs is that management sees that its customer loyalty score is 7.0 (on a 0–10 scale) at the start of the fiscal year. It then sets a customer loyalty goal of 8.0 for the end of the year. At the end of the year, however, the score remains about 7.0. While its intentions are good, management does not see the increases in loyalty scores that it set out to attain. What went wrong? How can this company effectively use goal setting to improve its customer loyalty scores?

There is a plethora of research on the effectiveness of goal setting in improving performance. Here are a few characteristics of goals that need to be considered when using the goal-setting method:

- *Specific.* Goals need to be specific and clearly define what behaviors/actions are going to be taken to achieve the goal and in what time frame or frequency these behaviors/actions should take place. For example, a goal stating "decrease the number of contacts a customer must make with the company to resolve an issue" does little to help employees focus their efforts, because there is no mention of a rate/frequency associated with the decrease. A better goal would be, "resolve customer issues in three or fewer contacts."

- *Measurable.* A measurement system needs to be in place to track/monitor progress toward the goal. The measurement system is used to determine whether the goal has been achieved and provides a feedback loop to the employees who are achieving the goal. A common problem with using customer loyalty scores as the metric to track or monitor improvements is that satisfaction goals are still vague with respect to what the employees can actually do to impact the scores. Telling the technical support department that the company's customer loyalty goal is 8.0 provides no input on how those employees can affect that score. A better measure for the technical support department would be "satisfaction with technical support" or other technical support questions on the survey (for example, "technical support responsiveness," "technical support availability"). We know that satisfaction with technical support is positively related to customer loyalty. Using these survey questions for goal setting has a greater impact on changing customers' behaviors than using vague loyalty questions. Because satisfaction with technical support is related to customer loyalty, improvements in technical support satisfaction should lead to improvements in loyalty scores.

- *Difficult but attainable.* Research has shown that difficult goals lead to better performance than goals that are easy. Difficult goals focus attention on the problem at hand. Avoid setting goals that are too difficult and, consequently, not achievable. One way to set difficult but attainable goals is to use historical performance data to determine the likelihood of achieving different performance levels. As we will see, setting difficult but attainable goals must consider a few factors.

- *Relevant.* The goal should be important to both the employee and the organization. An effective way to ensure that the goal is important to both parties is to make sure it is in line with the organizational strategy. Organizationally aligned goals help facilitate the management of employees' performance throughout the management hierarchy. The goals for the employees should be appropriate for their roles. To attain goals, the employee needs to have the ability and responsibility to impact the goal. Holding employees responsible for goals outside their control is unfair and can lead to low morale. For example, technical support representatives need to be responsible for goals related to technical support satisfaction; product managers need to be held responsible for product quality.

- *Accepted (or mutually set).* For goal setting to increase performance, employees should be allowed to participate in setting their goals. Goals that are not accepted by the recipient are not likely to be internalized and motivating. A good approach is to get employees involved early in the goal-setting process. Let them help in identifying the problem, selecting (or understanding) the key measures to track, and setting the goal.

- *Factors affecting customer loyalty.* One of the most difficult aspects of using customer feedback in incentive programs is the process of setting the customer satisfaction/ loyalty goal. While we know that difficult goals result in improved performance, they also run the risk of being too difficult for the company to attain and are often so unrealistic that they become demoralizing to employees. While improvements in customer loyalty are possible, increases in customer loyalty ratings are typically small and take considerable time to occur.

We know that many factors impact customer loyalty ratings. There are two major factors you should consider when trying to set customer feedback goals. The first is the consistency of customer ratings over time. The second is the fact that, to realize long-term improvements in customer loyalty ratings, systemic changes to business processes must occur.

Customers tend to provide similar feedback ratings over time. That is, customers who report low levels of loyalty at time 1 tend to report low levels of loyalty at time 2; conversely, customers who report high levels of loyalty at time 1 tend to report high levels of loyalty at time 2. While this stability in ratings could be the result of a consistent customer experience over time, research has shown that personal characteristics of people (for example, negative affectivity) determine their attitudes. It appears that some customers are simply easier to satisfy than other customers. While the level of service may vary over time, customers will perceive it in a consistent way that is in line with how they view the world. Also, research has shown that customer satisfaction early in the customer life cycle (for example, marketing and sales) is highly correlated with customer satisfaction in later phases of the customer life cycle (for example, service). It appears that once a customer's attitude toward a company is established, that attitude is difficult to change.

Realizing a shift in the mean of any distribution requires that systemic changes be made to the process or processes driving the mean. Therefore, to see improvements in the mean score of customer loyalty scores requires systemic changes in many underlying business processes that impact customer loyalty. Improving the business processes is designed to change the customer experience for that specific business process. We know, however, that customer loyalty is simultaneously impacted by a variety of business processes (for example, sales, support, marketing, product quality). Consequently, a substantial improvement in one business process may not necessarily result in improvements in customer loyalty scores, because of the other, unchanged business processes.

Take, for example, a company that is using goal setting to incentivize and monitor organizational performance. This company reports customer loyalty scores only at the company level. Improvements in technical support quality result in improvements in customer satisfaction scores for technical support survey questions. Sales improvement efforts, however, fall short; as a result, sales satisfaction scores remain stagnant. As a consequence, overall customer loyalty (which is impacted by both sales satisfaction and technical support satisfaction) does not show any improvements. Reporting only customer loyalty metrics, therefore, masks improvement made in technical support.

The attainment of specific goals for a given business area (for example, technical support) is more likely to be observed when the measures of success are targeted to that specific area. Reporting customer feedback results for specific business areas can help detect successes that can be missed when more general measures of customer loyalty are used to monitor improvements.

Setting Appropriate Goals

In addition to the prior factors that are necessary in goal setting, a company needs to consider two practical aspects of using goals when incentivizing employees: (1) the probability of employees attaining the goal, and (2) the company's ability to reward employees who attain the goal. Rewards for incentive programs are at the company's discretion and vary from one company to another. Some companies have more discretionary money with which to incentivize employees than other companies. Companies need to ensure they are able to pay out rewards (whatever their form) to all employees who achieve the goal. Setting goals that are too easy will not lead to improvements in customer satisfaction, and it could also result in a large payout by the company because all employees are able to attain their customer satisfaction goals.

One way to set goals is to examine historical customer satisfaction data. The distribution of customer feedback ratings (along with the descriptive statistics) can help you understand the probability of reaching a specified goal or goals. Take, for example, the customer satisfaction data in Figure 4.4. The data represent customer sales satisfaction ratings for 100 sales associates for a given quarter. The mean of the ratings is 6.11 and the standard deviation is 2.3. Because the best predictor of future performance is past performance, the historical data give you the best picture of what to expect in the future. Given that this company does not make any systemic changes in the business processes, we would expect that future customer sales satisfaction ratings would be the same (distributions will look the same, with similar means and standard deviations). We see that, while the average rating is around 6.0, there is consid-

Figure 4.4   Distribution of customer loyalty ratings.

erable variability, with some sales associates receiving high marks and others receiving low marks.

The company decides to use an incentive program to improve customer loyalty. The company can use these data to set appropriate goals by estimating the percentage of employees who would attain a given customer loyalty rating in the next survey period. Using simple calculations, we know that about half the sales associates will be able to attain a rating of 6.0 (half the distribution is above the mean, and half is below the mean). Also, we know that 16% of the sales associates will be able to attain an average satisfaction rating of 8.0, and about 35% of the employees will be able to attain a goal of 7.0.

The company can use this analysis to guide its decision in setting appropriate goals for the sales team. Depending on the structure of the incentive program, some sales associates might not receive much, if any, bonus. For example, is a customer loyalty goal of 8.0 for the overall company reasonable? If a single goal of 8.0 is used, we would expect roughly 16% of sales associates to receive a bonus. Considering the degree to which customers' attitudes are consistent over time as well as the broad systemic changes that are needed to improve customer loyalty, moving the customer loyalty needle by 2.0 seems rather difficult to attain.

Setting customer feedback goals now becomes a performance management exercise that needs to incorporate performance history and the company's financial ability to reward those who achieve the goals. Following is one company's approach to setting goals in a customer-centric incentive program.

EXAMPLE OF INCENTIVE COMPENSATION PROGRAM FOR PROFESSIONAL TECHNICAL SUPPORT

Company ABC is well known for its focus on customer satisfaction. It states in its marketing material and on the company Web site that it stresses customer satisfaction as an important business practice. In fact, it includes "customer satisfaction" as part of the core values. Company ABC instituted a customer satisfaction incentive program to help ensure employees are focused on customer issues.

The Professional Technical Support (PTS) division of Company ABC was receiving low satisfaction ratings on its performance. Human resources believed customer satisfaction ratings could be increased through an incentive program. After all, customer feedback data showed that performance across the support staff did vary substantially; some technical support employees received high customer satisfaction ratings while others received low ratings.

Incentive Program Structure

The customer satisfaction bonus is based 50% on the Customer Satisfaction Index (CSI) and 50% on the Customer Loyalty Index (CLI) for each PTS region (Europe, the Middle East, and Africa [EMEA]; Asia Pacific [APAC]; Latin America and Central America [LACA]; and North America [NA]).

The bonus is earned at the end of the semiannual period. Three caveats are included as part of the incentive program. First, while bonuses are based on individual employee performance, the customer satisfaction bonus is based on the CSI and the CLI at the next most appropriate level of the services organization as determined by the senior vice president of technical services when the following situations occur:

- No customers in the employee's area are surveyed

- Company ABC is unable to identify responses from customers in the PTS area (for example, customer responds anonymously)

Second, if all accounts in the PTS area are surveyed (or should be surveyed) but no survey responses are received, then the PTS area is not eligible for a customer satisfaction bonus. Third, if the overall gross margin of the PTS area is not in line with expectations, the customer satisfaction bonus will not exceed 100%.

Customer Feedback Data

Company ABC conducted a customer survey quarterly in which 25% of the customer base was surveyed. Customer responses and nonresponses to a survey were used to calculate the indices for the customer satisfaction bonus. Possible ratings could range from 0 (low) to 10 (high). Higher scores reflect higher levels of customer satisfaction/loyalty.

CSI

The *CSI* is the average satisfaction rating obtained from customer responses and nonresponses on the business unit–specific questions. For the PTS organization, because there is only one question, the CSI is the satisfaction rating for the following question:

- Company ABC's PTS overall effectiveness

CLI

Customer responses to the customer satisfaction survey were used to calculate a CLI for each area. The CLI can range from 0 to 10 and is calculated as the average score obtained from customer responses and from the following four questions:

- Overall satisfaction with Company ABC (0 = extremely dissatisfied; 10 = extremely satisfied)
- Likelihood to continue purchasing (0 = not at all likely; 10 = extremely likely)
- Likelihood to recommend (0 = not at all likely; 10 = extremely likely)
- Likelihood to choose again (0 = not at all likely; 10 = extremely likely)

Instead of using individual loyalty questions, the CLI was used, as it is more reliable than any single question used alone.

Payout Criteria for Bonuses

The goal structure for Company ABC provided bonus amounts based on different levels of goal attainment of the employees. Rather than using an all-or-nothing approach to incentivize employees, Company ABC recognized that employees might not be incentivized to focus on customer issues if they felt they would not be able to achieve a single goal level. The company looked at historical customer feedback data to determine the probability of employees reaching certain satisfaction scores. Using these historical data and the financial health of the company, human resources established different levels of bonus payouts that were dependent on the customer satisfaction received and were within the financial constraints (for example, available pool of incentive compensation money).

CSI Payout

Eligible accounts that do not respond to the survey (no customer contacts respond to the survey) will be assigned a penalty score of 5.99 (on a 0–10 scale, 5.99 translates into 0% of payout). The employee will receive different bonus payouts depending on the level of CSI achieved.

CSI criteria	CSI payout
≥7.75 and <8.5	100% of goal
≥7.0 and <7.75	75% of goal
≥6.0 and <7.0	50% of goal
<6.0	0% of goal

The customer feedback data for the survey period resulted in the following payout by region. The gradient payout schedule, working as planned, allowed each region to receive a bonus for its performance on the CSI even though it did not achieve the highest level of performance.

Region	CSI for region	N	SD	CSI payout
Asia	7.74	62	1.86	75%
EMEA	7.69	242	1.67	75%
LACA	8.10	29	2.06	100%
NA East	8.07	131	1.66	100%
NA West	8.15	204	1.79	100%

CLI Payout

Eligible customers who do not respond to the survey (no customer contacts respond to the survey) will be assigned a 6.99 CLI (this level resulted in no bonus payout). The employee will receive different bonus payouts depending on the level of CLI achieved.

CSI criteria	CSI payout
≥8.0	75% of goal
≥7.5 and <8.0	50% of goal
≥7.0 and <7.5	25% of goal
<7.0	0% of goal

The customer feedback data for the survey period resulted in the following payout by region. Again, the gradient payout

schedule allowed each region to receive a bonus for its performance on the CLI.

Region	CLI for region	N	SD	CLI payout
Asia	7.48	72	2.22	25%
EMEA	7.35	288	1.53	25%
LACA	7.62	31	1.89	50%
NA East	7.48	160	1.52	25%
NA West	7.55	238	1.53	50%

SUMMARY

Corporate strategy and governance of the CFP can be exhibited
in a variety of ways, from resource allocation in supporting
customer initiatives to the use of public forums to communicate the company's vision and mission to its constituents. Some
examples of these areas are included in Table 4.2.

Executive support and use of customer feedback data as
well as communication of the program goals and the customer
feedback results help embed the customer-centric culture into
the company milieu. Executive use of customer feedback in setting strategic goals helps keep the company customer-focused
from the top. Additionally, using customer feedback in executive dashboards and for executive compensation solidifies the
importance of customers as a key business metric.

The strategy/governance of the CFP provides a high-level
direction for the company. This high-level management process creates an atmosphere in which the company's attention is
directed at customers and their needs. The next chapter examines how companies can support these higher-level management
processes through integration of the CFP into the business.

Table 4.2   Summary of strategy/governance-related CFP best practices.

Best practice	Important points
Customer feedback used in strategic visions/ goals	• Present customer-related information (e.g., satisfaction/loyalty goals) in employee handbook • Use customer feedback in setting company goals • Incorporate customer focus in mission statement • Address customer requirements
Establish ownership of the CFP (executive, senior VP ownership)	• CEO owns CFP • Executives evangelize CFP
Customer feedback as important as financial measures in making business decisions	• Present customer feedback results in company meetings and official documents • Use driver analysis to identify where improvements would have the biggest impact on customer loyalty • Include customer metrics in balanced scorecard (use customer indices—see Chapter 8, "Applied Research")
Customer feedback used in executive objectives and incentive compensation	• Use key performance indicators and customer loyalty metric
Include a top executive (e.g., CEO, VP) as a champion of the CFP	• Executive responsible for reporting customer feedback results at executive meetings
Build accountability for customer satisfaction/ loyalty goals into the company	• Make customer loyalty/satisfaction a key performance area for all employees (built into performance management system) • Employees set customer satisfaction goals as part of their performance objectives
Customer feedback used in frontline employee objectives and incentive compensation	• Use customer feedback data to manage performance for frontline employees • Use customer feedback metrics that can be impacted by employee behavior • Use objective business metrics that are linked to customer satisfaction (see Chapter 8, "Applied Research") as key indicators on which to build employee incentive programs

5

Business Process Integration

The integration of the CFP into the daily operational business processes ensures that the program and its elements penetrate all aspects of the business. Thus, to ensure employees support the corporate strategy of customer centricity, companies create work processes that include elements of the CFP, from communication of program goals and objectives to use of customer feedback data.

ADOPTION RATES FOR PROCESS-RELATED BUSINESS PRACTICES

The adoption rates for CFP business practices that are related to business process integration suggest that Loyalty Leaders, compared to Loyalty Laggers, tend to adopt certain types of practices at a much greater rate. The comparisons appear in Figure 5.1.

Integration of the CFP into daily business processes is an important element of the program. In line with this common thinking, the survey results confirm that Loyalty Leaders, compared to Loyalty Laggers, adopt at a much greater rate those practices that strengthen the integration between the CFP and business processes. Specifically, we see that 100% of Loyalty Leaders include the use of customer feedback in executive dashboards, while only 69% of Loyalty Laggers do. Also, 85% of

Process-related business practice	Adoption rate		
	Loyalty Leaders	Loyalty Laggers	Loyalty unknown
CFP is integrated into business processes and technology (e.g., CRM system)	**93%**	64%	68%
Customer feedback results are included in the company/executive dashboards	**100%**	69%	72%
All areas of the CFP (e.g., process and goals) are communicated regularly to the entire company	**86%**	64%	43%
The resolution of customer issues identified by the CFP is integrated into the company's CRM system	**75%**	60%	40%

Figure 5.1   Adoption rates of process-related CFP business practices for Loyalty Leaders and Loyalty Laggers.

Loyalty Leaders, compared to 62% of Loyalty Laggers, regularly communicate CFP processes/goals to the entire company. Additionally, over 90% of Loyalty Leaders have their CFPs integrated into their business processes and technology, compared to only 64% of Loyalty Laggers.

PROCESS-RELATED CFP BUSINESS PRACTICES THAT IMPACT CUSTOMER LOYALTY AND SATISFACTION WITH THE CFP

The next set of analyses was focused on quantifying the impact of the process-related CFP business practices on customer loyalty and satisfaction with the CFP. The results (see Figures 5.2

Process

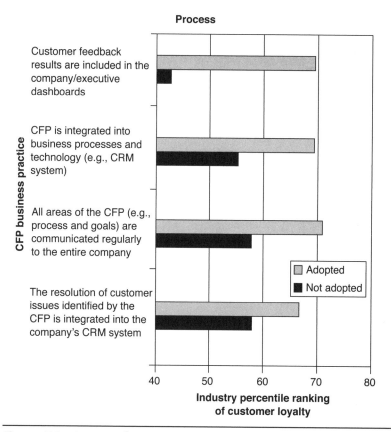

Figure 5.2   Impact of process-related CFP business practices on customer loyalty.

and 5.3) show that certain business practices had a substantial impact on the key outcome variables (customer loyalty and satisfaction with CFP in managing customer relationships).

The survey results show that process-related business practices of CFPs had an impact on customer loyalty scores. Business attributes that had the largest impact on customer loyalty are related to the use of the customer feedback data. For example, companies that use customer feedback in executive dashboards had higher customer loyalty scores (percentile ranking of 70) than companies that do not use customer feedback in

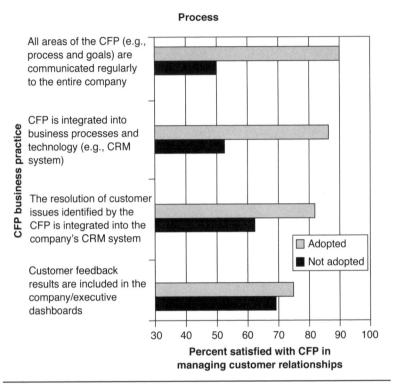

Figure 5.3   Impact of process-related CFP business practices on satisfaction with CFP in managing customer relationships.

executive dashboards (percentile ranking of 43). Additionally, companies that integrate their CFP into their business processes and technology had higher levels of customer loyalty (percentile ranking of 69) than companies that do not (percentile ranking of 56). Finally, companies that communicate all aspects of their CFPs to the entire organization reported higher levels of customer loyalty (percentile ranking of 72) than companies that do not communicate the elements of their CFP throughout the organization.

Satisfaction with the CFP was also enhanced by the adoption of process-related business attributes. Companies that regularly communicate the CFP process and goals were more satisfied with the feedback program (90% were satisfied) than companies that do not regularly communicate the CFP process and goals (50% were satisfied). Also, companies that integrate their CFPs into their business processes and technology were more satisfied with their CFPs (87% were satisfied) than companies whose CFPs are not integrated into their business processes and technology (52% were satisfied). Finally, companies that incorporate the resolution process into their CRM system were more satisfied (82% were satisfied) than companies that do not incorporate the resolution process into their CRM system (62% were satisfied).

CUSTOMER FEEDBACK IN EXECUTIVE DASHBOARDS

Integration of the CFP into the business processes needs to start at the top of the organization. An effective way to demonstrate this integration at the upper level of a company is to incorporate customer feedback data into the executive dashboard. Stephanie Ekins-Parnell, of Harris Stratex Networks, says, "Using customer feedback in our executive dashboard ensures that our executives keep a consistent focus on customer issues and also strengthens the customer-centric culture of the company by demonstrating to the employees the importance of customers to management."

The benefits of incorporating customer feedback metrics into the executive dashboards are matched by the variety of purposes for which the metrics can be used:

- Drive customer-centric strategy execution

- Clarify customer strategy and make the strategy operational

- Identify and align customer-related strategic initiatives

- Link budget with customer strategy

- Align the organization with customer strategy

- Conduct periodic customer strategic performance reviews to learn about and improve the strategy

The concept of the balanced scorecard is very applicable when considering including customer metrics as part of the executive dashboard. A balanced scorecard allows executives to track and monitor a variety of metrics (for example, financial, internal processes, innovation, and learning) to ensure strategic objectives and goals are attained. For companies that are Loyalty Leaders, a comprehensive balanced scorecard includes customer feedback metrics to monitor and track the customer-centric strategy. The simple practice of incorporating customer feedback metrics in executive dashboards increases the likelihood that customer-centric metrics will be on par with other business metrics used in executive decision making (best practices in strategy/governance).

CRM AND CFPs

CRM is considered a business strategy that is designed to align the company around the customer. Traditional CRM systems generally track operational metrics related to marketing and sales and service processes. These operational metrics include sales volumes, response times to service requests, and success statistics for marketing campaigns. These metrics are then intelligently used to customize business processes to meet customers' needs.

Integrating CFP into Business Processes and Technology

Early in its growth, Siebel Systems found that its customers received greater value from their CRM implementation when they also had a CFP. That is, customers who had both a customer feedback system and a CRM system reported greater revenue increases and greater employee productivity increases than customers with just a CRM system. It appeared that a complete CRM solution needed to include the integration of a CFP. CRM solutions, using both attitudinal data and operational data of customers, can provide a comprehensive picture of customers' attitudes and behaviors to help companies maximize customer loyalty and financial performance.

The integration of a company's CFP into its CRM system improves the company's performance in account management activities. For example, account managers, armed with customer information regarding their needs and prior activities, can be more effective in their account management activities. In addition to knowing the history of the account's business activities (for example, purchasing behavior and service requests), account managers can now understand if the account was satisfied or dissatisfied with these business activities. Account managers would be better prepared to anticipate the needs of the account. The attitudinal metrics and objective metrics regarding account quality could be used together to better manage the account (for example, knowing that an account recently gave low quality marks to a recently purchased product, the sales representative could hold off on cross-selling the account on a new product).

Resolving Customer Issues

Improving the customer experience is a process in which not only company-wide systemic changes are made but also individual customer level changes are made. Take, for example, a company with a high mean customer satisfaction rating. While this rating suggests the business process underlying the ratings is sound, there will inevitably be special, unforeseen events/situations (for example, a missed returned phone call; a new, untrained employee not totally conversant on company policies) that will result in substandard performance for a few customers. These "outliers" are the result of special causes and need to be dealt with individually.

For these dissatisfied customers, companies must address the customers' specific needs and resolve their issues. CFPs can be an effective tool for identifying dissatisfied customers and help companies retain their loyalty. Companies that merge this problem resolution process with their CRM system receive much benefit in the way of customer loyalty and improved CRM. "Integrating the customer resolution process into the company's formal CRM process allows us to seamlessly manage customer issues from inception to resolution. Addressing customer issues in a timely manner ensures these at-risk customers remain loyal," says Ekins-Parnell. Companies understand the importance of closing the customer feedback loop by acting on, and resolving, customer issues. Loyalty Leaders understand the importance of formally integrating this resolution process into their overall CRM strategy.

The problem resolution process of specific customer complaints contains four general steps, each facilitated with the integration of the customer feedback system into the CRM system. These four steps are identifying the customer issue, notifying the responsible party, integrating the negative response into the CRM system, and resolving the issue. They are explained in greater detail in the following list:

1. *Negative response*—Each organization has its own definition of a negative response. Typically, a negative survey response is a rating below the midpoint of the scale. For example, a rating of 4 on an 11-point scale, where 0 is "extremely dissatisfied" and 10 is "extremely satisfied," could be used as the criterion for a negative response. A more conservative approach to defining a negative response would be to increase the criterion to a rating of 5 or 7. A more liberal approach would be to decrease the criterion to a rating of 2 or 3. When deter-

mining the level at which the criterion is set, not only should the definition of "negative" to the customer be considered but also the amount of negative responses the survey generates. If 90% of the survey responses are deemed negative, it might overwhelm the resolution process. Taxing the resolution process might result in more dissatisfied customers. Set the negative criterion at a point where the company can effectively deal with the quantity of negative responses.

2. *Notify responsible party*—The responsible party needs to be notified of the negative response. The responsible party is the one who is able to resolve the customer issue. The customer problem should be matched with the department that is best equipped to resolve the problem. For a technical support problem, for example, the technical support department is notified. For a product-related problem, the product marketing department is notified. Before the survey is administered, each survey question is associated with a given department (or person within the department) so each department understands that it is responsible for a given question.

   An important element in the notification process is the speed with which the responsible party is notified of the customer complaint. Because response time is a key determinant of customer satisfaction, the responsible party to the customer problem should be notified immediately when a complaint is made. Notification speed is improved when a Web-based survey (another best practice) is used to collect customer feedback. The sophistication of Web-based surveys allows for automated e-mails to be sent to responsible parties when a predetermined response is given by a respondent to a given question or questions. When an automated e-mail notification is not possible, the survey manager (somebody who has access to all customer responses) can triage the negative responses to the responsible parties. This method, due to the time-consuming nature of sorting and sending negative responses, slows the overall response time to address and resolve the customer issue.

3. *Negative response housed in CRM system*—Whether the notification process is manual or automatic, a key component to the success of a CFP is to ensure that notification of the customer complaint is incorporated into the company's formal CRM process. Harris Stratex Networks created a process in which customer issues are housed in a formal management system. This system requires that all customer issues be assigned ownership, that all issues can be escalated, and that all issues have a published action plan. Account teams are able to access the management system to view the customer complaint and understand its status.

4. *Problem resolved* (customer is notified and satisfied)— The customer complaint process concludes with notifying the customer that the problem has been addressed to his or her satisfaction. This step of the process, again, is enhanced when the customer issue can be housed in a formal CRM system or process.

Each company will have its own unique criteria for problem resolution and will know when it has reached the end of the resolution process. The issue at hand is the company's ability to monitor the status of the customer complaint from the beginning of the problem to its resolution. Automating this end-to-end process with the assistance of business systems allows the company to easily monitor and resolve customer issues.

COMMUNICATION OF CFP PROCESS AND GOALS

The communication of company strategies and policies for corporate, company-wide programs to all employees is essential to their success. The reliance on communication of a CFP initiative to the entire company is no different. A CFP has many moving parts and therefore requires much coordination among different constituencies. Additionally, the program impacts the daily activities of all employees. Therefore, communication of the program's process and goals to the entire company is essential to its success.

A comprehensive communication plan helps with program success for two reasons. First, communication of program processes improves the probability that employees will adhere to governance aspects of the CFP. Employee observance to the roles and responsibilities of the administration aspects of the CFP helps it run smoothly. A seamlessly run program helps improve the effectiveness with which the program is administered.

Second, communication of the program helps clarify the performance expectations of the employees to reinforce the importance of the customer in their daily activities. Customer satisfaction expectations help executive management translate the corporate customer strategy into tangible targets for specific employees or employee groups. These targets are used in employee incentive programs to help motivate employees to engage in behaviors that help improve the customer experience.

Companies use a variety of methods to communicate the CFP processes. Information about the program can be included in regularly published company newsletters. A special section dedicated solely to the CFP ensures important customer-related stories (for example, changes in the program, quarterly reports, applied research findings, program success, and employee awards) reach employees. Communication of the program can also come directly from the CEO in the form of a company-wide e-mail; this method is likely the most effective means of communicating the program goals, as employees will read messages from the CEO. Additionally, company intranet sites are an effective means of communicating all aspects of the CFP, and they are good repositories of information (from corporate strategy to detailed survey results) that all employees (new and existing) can easily access to learn about the importance of the CFP's processes and goals.

While there are really no set methods for how to distribute information about the CFP (for example, Webinars, face-to-face meetings), what is important is that the information is consistent across all methods of distribution. Consequently, the governance model of the CFP needs to include rules and regulations regarding the actual content of the communication.

SUMMARY

The CFP best practices for business process integration are summarized in Table 5.1. Company adherence to the policies of the CFP is accomplished by regularly communicating the goals and processes to all employees. Additionally, building the CFP into the company's CRM system ensures that each employee has access to customer feedback data and operational data for each customer. Executives need to understand how the company is meeting its customer-centered objectives. Including customer feedback data in executive dashboards is an effective means toward that end.

Integrating the CFP into the company's business processes and systems has a large impact on the company's customer loyalty scores. This integration helps provide support for the com-

Table 5.1 Summary of process-related CFP best practices.

Best practice	Important points
Customer feedback included in executive dashboards	• Summary scores used to track loyalty/business attributes
Integrate the CFP into business processes and technology (e.g., CRM system)	• Company needs a CRM system that includes both objective and attitudinal metrics of the quality of the customer relationships
Regularly communicate all areas of the CFP (e.g., process and goals) to the entire company	• Develop a customer feedback portal on company intranet site to house all content related to CFPs • Summarize survey methodology • Present research findings
Integrate into the company's CRM system the resolution of customer issues that are identified using the CFP	• This approach deals with issues that are unique to a given customer • Survey responses housed directly in the CRM system • Customer feedback data, used to help resolve specific customer's issues

pany's strategy around the customer and improves adherence to the governance model.

The next section of the book includes survey results regarding three major operational processes of the CFP that support the management processes of the program: survey method, reporting, and applied research. While these three areas impact one another, each area will be examined separately for simplicity's sake.

PART III

Best Practices of Customer Feedback Programs— Operational Processes

6

Survey Method

The success of the CFP does not rest solely on the management processes that support the program. In addition to the corporate strategy and business process integration, the CFP is made up of operational processes that include the measurement of customer feedback. The overall effectiveness of the program is only as good as the quality of the customer feedback data that are captured. The measurement system needs to be structured in a way that provides reliable and valid information about the customer's perceptions. The following section summarizes the key ingredients needed for a successful measurement strategy of a CFP.

ADOPTION RATES FOR METHOD-RELATED BUSINESS PRACTICES

The adoption rates for CFP business practices that are related to method suggest that Loyalty Leaders, compared to Loyalty Laggers, tend to adopt certain types of practices at a much greater rate. The comparisons appear in Figure 6.1.

Specifically, we see that 85% of Loyalty Leaders use Web surveys to collect customer feedback, while only 60% of Loyalty Laggers do. Similarly, 67% of Loyalty Leaders said that their survey delivery process is automated, while only 46% of

Method-related business practice	Adoption rate		
	Loyalty Leaders	Loyalty Laggers	Loyalty unknown
Multiple methods of collecting customer feedback are used (e.g., relationship survey, transactional survey, Web site survey)	**93%**	80%	86%
Customer contact management process (e.g., identifying who gets surveyed) for the feedback process is integrated with the company's CRM system	67%	67%	52%
Survey delivery is an automated process	**67%**	46%	62%
Web surveys are used to collect customer feedback	**85%**	60%	79%
Telephone surveys are used to collect customer feedback	**64%**	67%	58%
Paper-and-pencil surveys are used to collect customer feedback	**73%**	54%	30%
In-person interviews are used to collect customer feedback	**71%**	62%	55%
Customer satisfaction surveys are conducted by the company's own employees using tools developed in-house	**57%**	47%	52%

Figure 6.1 Adoption rates of method-related CFP business practices for Loyalty Leaders and Loyalty Laggers.

Loyalty Laggers indicated this. Finally, 73% of Loyalty Leaders use paper-and-pencil surveys to collect customer feedback, while only about 54% of Loyalty Laggers do.

There was no substantial difference in adoption rates for many of the method attributes, such as the use of in-house employees to conduct surveys, use of interviews or telephones to collect customer feedback, and use of a CRM system to manage survey contacts. The survey shows that both Loyalty Leaders and Loyalty Laggers adopted these practices at comparable rates.

METHOD-RELATED CFP BUSINESS PRACTICES THAT IMPACT CUSTOMER LOYALTY AND SATISFACTION WITH THE CFP

The next set of analyses was focused on quantifying the impact of the method-related CFP business practices on customer loyalty and satisfaction with the CFP. The results (see Figures 6.2 and 6.3) show that only a few business practices had an impact on these key outcome variables.

The only practice that seemed to impact customer loyalty was the adoption of Web-based surveys; that is, companies that use Web surveys to collect customer feedback had higher customer loyalty scores (percentile ranking of 68) than companies that do not use Web surveys to collect customer feedback (percentile ranking of 52).

Satisfaction with the CFP in helping manage the customer relationship was impacted by three business practices. Specifically, companies that incorporate the customer contact management for the CFP into the CRM system were more satisfied with their CFPs (82% were satisfied) than companies that do not adopt this practice (60% were satisfied).

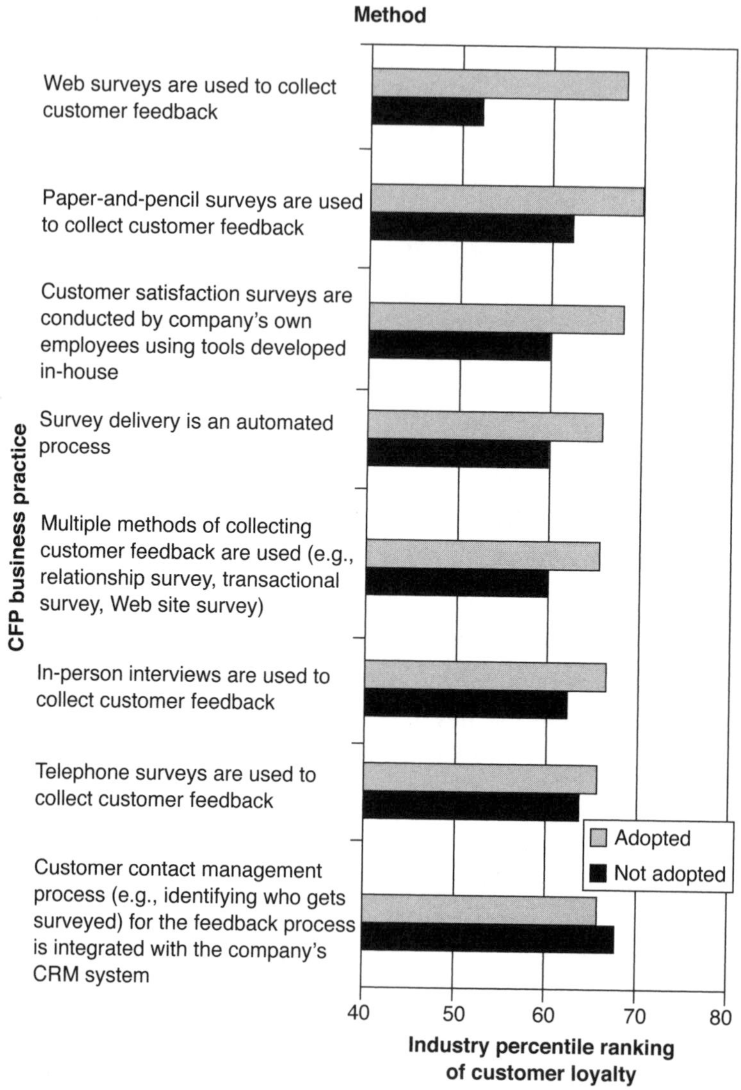

Figure 6.2   Impact of method-related CFP business practices on customer loyalty.

Method

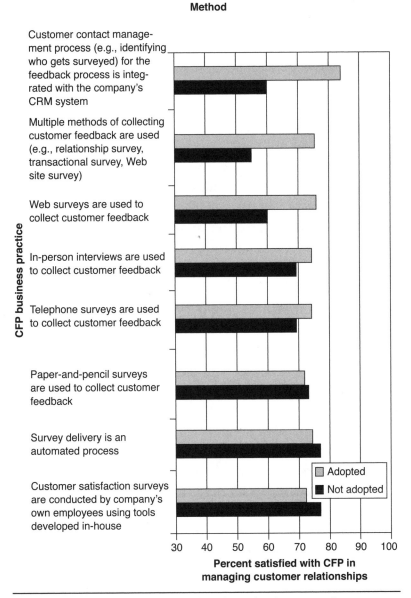

Figure 6.3 Impact of method-related CFP business practices on satisfaction with CFP in managing customer relationships.

Also, companies that use multiple methods of collecting customer feedback (for example, relationship surveys, transactional surveys, Web site surveys) were more satisfied with their programs (76% were satisfied) than companies that do not use multiple methods (55% were satisfied).

Finally, companies that use Web-based surveys were more satisfied with the feedback program in helping them manage customer relationships (76% were satisfied) than companies that do not use Web-based surveys (60% were satisfied). The use of Web-based surveys facilitates the CRM process through the ease with which the survey data can be incorporated into the CRM process and system. The effective management of relationships within the business setting (customer, employee, and partner) is dependent on both objective and attitudinal measures.

MULTIPLE SURVEY METHODS

The use of different survey methods had a large positive impact on the satisfaction with the CFP. The use of relationship and transactional survey methods helps companies more fully understand how to effectively manage customer relationships at both a strategic and tactical level, respectively. Jeremy Whyte, director of customer feedback and reporting for Oracle, says of the benefits of using multiple methods to collect customer feedback, "To ensure Oracle captures the right type of feedback from the right contacts at the right time without over-surveying, we use an integrated survey program featuring a portfolio of relationship, transactional and targeted surveys."

For Oracle, the customer relationship survey highlights the overall customer experience and identifies the drivers of customer loyalty across different, yet cumulative, contact experiences. Transactional surveys allow Oracle to measure the service quality of each organizational unit, which leads to improvements to enhance operational effectiveness. Finally, the use of targeted surveys (surveys designed for special projects) complements the relationship and transactional surveys by helping Oracle dive deeper into identifying solutions to problems uncovered by other survey or feedback approaches.

WEB-BASED CUSTOMER SURVEYS

Web-based surveys, according to the survey results, are the most popular and effective method for collecting customer feedback data. Companies truly benefit from using Web-based customer surveys. The reasons for the popularity of Web-based surveys (for example, speed of implementation, speed of receiving customer feedback, flexibility to perform more complex logic inexpensively) likely contribute to their effectiveness in improving the company's customer loyalty scores and the company's satisfaction with the CFP.

Web surveys provide many benefits compared to other types of customer surveys (see Table 6.1 for benefits and disadvantages of different survey methods). Web surveys can be quickly implemented and can gather thousands of responses within a matter of hours. Additionally, they are relatively inexpensive compared to other methods of data collection (after initial setup). The cosmetics of the survey can be enhanced with the use of varying colors, fonts, and formatting options that include videos, pictures, and audio. Also, Web surveys can incorporate complex question-skipping logic and randomizations of question order. The resulting quality of data from Web-based surveys is also richer with detail, as respondents typically provide longer answers to open-ended questions on the Web than they do on other kinds of self-administered surveys.

The reason why Web surveys result in higher customer loyalty scores is likely due to their ability to facilitate CRM. Across many industries, a key determinant of customer loyalty

Table 6.1   Advantages and disadvantages of different customer survey methods.

Advantage/ Disadvantage	Survey type			
	Web	**Telephone**	**Paper-and-pencil**	**Face-to-face**
Cost	Inexpensive (initial setup costs high; low recurring costs)	Expensive (interviewer)	Expensive (printing and postage; data entry)	Expensive (interviewer)
Response rate	High	Low	Lowest	Low
Ease of data management	High: Few concerns, as responses are easily incorporated into statistical analysis tools	Low: Manual upload of data into systems introduces possible error	Low: Manual upload of data into systems introduces possible error	Low: Manual upload of data into systems introduces possible error
Utilize Web capabilities	Facilitate real-time results; easy segmentation of data; worldwide teams have access to information	No	No	No
CRM integration	Easy	Difficult	Difficult	Difficult
Questions	Can add logic to surveys (exclude irrelevant questions)	Can add logic to surveys (exclude irrelevant questions)	Cannot add logic to surveys (all questions asked)	Can add logic to surveys (exclude irrelevant questions)
Response detail	More detail to open-ended questions	Less detail to open-ended questions	Less detail to open-ended questions	Less detail to open-ended questions
Interviewer bias	None	Potential	None	Potential
Sample bias	Only reach customers with Web access	Only reach customers with phones	Low	Low

is responsiveness. Customers who feel their needs are met in a timely manner are typically more loyal than customers whose needs are not met in a timely manner. With Web surveys, because the customer feedback data are already in digital format, results can be more quickly integrated into a company's CRM system, resulting in a more timely response to individual customer concerns. Additionally, the digitized customer feedback data can be quickly analyzed, summarized, and presented, allowing the company to address systemic issues impacting a large group of customers. Finally, data from Web-based surveys can be easily and quickly imported into statistical packages for additional analyses to provide deeper insight into factors impacting the customer experience and customer loyalty.

MEASURING CUSTOMER LOYALTY

Customer loyalty has been shown to be a leading indicator of business performance metrics. Researchers have demonstrated a link between customer loyalty and financial success/growth. For example, Reichheld and Sasser (1990) demonstrated that decreasing customer defections by 5% increases profits from 25% to 85% across a variety of industries. While they focused on rates of defections, there are several objective measures of customer loyalty that show a relationship with financial performance:

- Number of referrals
- Word of mouth/word of mouse
- Purchase again
- Purchase different products
- Increase purchase size
- Customer retention/defection rates

Based on the objective measures of customer loyalty, we can see how company financial growth can occur through the increase in customer loyalty. Through the referral process, companies can grow by acquiring new customers. The idea is that the customer acquisition process relies on existing customers to promote/recommend the company to their friends, who, in turn, become customers. Another way of strengthening the financial growth of a company is through increased purchasing behavior of existing customers (for example, increase amount of purchases, purchase different products/services). Finally, company growth is dependent on the company not losing existing customers at a rate faster than it acquires them. For example, customer defection rate is an important metric in the wireless service industry, where customer defections are common.

WHAT DO CUSTOMER FEEDBACK PROFESSIONALS THINK ABOUT THE NPS?

As part of the CFP best practices survey, respondents were asked their opinion on the NPS methodology. Specifically, respondents were asked to indicate the degree to which they agreed or disagreed with the following two statements:

1. The Net Promoter Score ("recommend" intentions) is a better predictor of growth compared to other loyalty questions (for example, satisfaction, repurchase intentions).

2. The Net Promoter Score ("recommend" intentions) is a better predictor of growth compared to other loyalty indices (aggregate of recommend, satisfaction, repurchase intentions).

Over 80 customer feedback professionals answered the two NPS questions (see Table 6.2). When asked to compare the NPS with other loyalty questions/items, only 26% of the customer

Table 6.2 Percentage of respondents who agreed that the NPS is better than other loyalty items or indices.

	Overall sample	Loyalty Laggers*	Loyalty Leaders[†]
NPS better than other items	26%	28%	23%
NPS better than other indices	26%	42%	14%

*Industry loyalty percentile ranking <70%.
[†]Industry loyalty percentile ranking ≥70%.

feedback professionals agreed that the NPS is a better predictor of growth. When asked to compare the NPS with other loyalty indices, again only 26% of the customer feedback professionals agreed that the NPS is a better predictor of growth.

When we examine the difference between the Loyalty Leaders and the Loyalty Laggers, the results are much different. More Loyalty Laggers (42%) than Loyalty Leaders (14%) believe the NPS is better than other loyalty indices.

The results clearly show that the NPS claims are not widely supported by customer feedback professionals. This finding is more remarkable for customer feedback professionals from companies that are Loyalty Leaders.

Yes, the NPS is a simple metric, but the issue regarding its merits is much deeper. The simplicity of the NPS does not make it the right solution and does not minimize the problems (for example, research bias) of the NPS research as well as the codevelopers' misleading claims regarding the superiority of the NPS over other loyalty metrics. Customer feedback professionals seem to be aware of the limits of the NPS claims. They need to share their concerns (along with the recent research on the NPS) with their CEOs and CMOs.

Regarding the measurement of customer loyalty, Jeremy Whyte, director of Oracle customer feedback and reporting, says, "Our research has repeatedly shown that the Customer Loyalty Index (CLI), compared to any of the individual loyalty questions, is a more reliable and better predictor of objective metrics of customer loyalty and business growth. The use of multiple loyalty questions allows us to calculate a highly reliable CLI and identify at-risk customers in a variety of ways."

SURVEYS AND CUSTOMER LOYALTY

Customer loyalty, when measured through surveys, is typically assessed through the use of standard questions or items, mirroring the objective measures listed earlier. As we will see later in this section, customer loyalty can be conceptualized or defined in three ways, each requiring a different set of questions for measurement.

Each customer loyalty item provides an indication of the customer's level of affinity for, endorsement of, and approval of a company or brand. The items usually ask the customer to provide a rating that reflects the likelihood that the customer will exhibit positive behaviors toward a company. Commonly used customer loyalty survey questions include the following items:

- Overall satisfaction

- Likelihood to choose again

- Likelihood to recommend

- Likelihood to continue purchasing same products/services

- Likelihood to purchase different products/services

- Likelihood to increase frequency of purchasing

- Likelihood to switch to a different provider

The first question is rated on a "satisfaction" scale (for example, 0 is "extremely dissatisfied" and 10 is "extremely satisfied"). The remaining questions are rated on a "likelihood" scale, which allows respondents to indicate their likelihood of behaving in different ways toward the company or brand (for example, 0 is "not at all likely" and 10 is "extremely likely"). Higher ratings reflect higher levels of customer loyalty.

Customer loyalty questions should appear at the start of the survey, before business attribute questions are presented. Presenting the questions in this manner ensures that the responses reflect the respondents' general perceptions regarding their relationship with the company. If questions about specific business attributes (for example, specific customer experience questions) are asked at the start of the survey (before the loyalty questions), the loyalty questions could be influenced by the specific questions asked and could impact the respondents' ratings of the subsequent loyalty questions.

STANDARDIZED LOYALTY QUESTIONS

Standardized customer loyalty questions have been used in many research studies across a variety of industries. Results have shown that these loyalty questions are reliable, valid, and useful measures of customer loyalty; that is, these loyalty questions appear to measure what we think they are measuring. Additionally, these loyalty questions are both theoretically and statistically linked to financial growth of companies across a variety of consumer groups; companies with higher customer loyalty scores on these measures also report higher levels of financial success than companies with lower customer loyalty scores on these measures. Responses to these loyalty questions help organizations understand their expected growth.

CUSTOMER SURVEYS AND CUSTOMER LOYALTY

Recall that results suggest that there are three types of customer loyalty: advocacy, purchasing, and retention. The following loyalty indices can be calculated by averaging the loyalty items that load highly on the same factor:

- **Advocacy Loyalty Index (ALI):** Reflects the degree to which customers will be advocates of the company (average across satisfaction, recommend, choose again, purchase same)

- **Purchasing Loyalty Index (PLI):** Reflects the degree to which customers will increase their purchasing behavior (average across purchase different, purchase increase, purchase frequency)

- **Retention Loyalty Index (RLI):** Reflects the degree to which customers will remain with a given company (single defection item—reverse coded)

Each type of loyalty is represented by a few survey questions. The customer loyalty dimensions and their respective questions appear in Table 6.3. As you can see, individual survey questions are grouped together to measure a given dimension of customer loyalty. Figure 6.4 illustrates the relationship between retention loyalty and the three survey questions that represent it.

Table 6.3   Three areas of customer loyalty and their respective survey questions.

- Advocacy loyalty
  - Overall satisfaction
  - Likelihood to choose again for the first time
  - Likelihood to recommend
  - Likelihood to continue purchasing same products/services
- Purchasing loyalty
  - Likelihood to purchase different products/services
  - Likelihood to purchase more expensive products/services
  - Likelihood to increase amount of purchases
  - Likelihood to make larger purchases
- Retention loyalty
  - Likelihood to purchase from competitor
  - Likelihood to stop purchasing
  - Likelihood to switch to a different provider

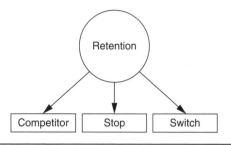

Figure 6.4   Relationship between retention loyalty and the three customer loyalty questions.

RELIABILITY OF LOYALTY INDICES

Reliability deals with the extent to which measurement is free from random error. Reliability estimates were calculated for each of the loyalty indices across two separate studies using the survey questions. Using the wireless service provider sample, the reliability estimate (Cronbach's alpha) of the ALI was .92, and the reliability estimate (Cronbach's alpha) of the PLI was .82. Using the personal computer manufacturer sample, the reliability estimate of the ALI was .94, and the reliability estimate of the PLI was .87. These levels of reliability are considered very good for attitude research (Nunnally 1978; 0 = no reliability, 1 = perfect reliability). So, while individual questions can be used to measure customer loyalty, their composite score is a much more reliable measure of customer loyalty.

SINGLE-ITEM MEASURES OR AGGREGATED METRICS

Recall that research found that single-item measures are less reliable than multiple-item measures (see Chapter 1). Customer loyalty is a multidimensional construct that contains three components: advocacy, purchasing, and retention. Research has shown that measuring the complexities of customer loyalty is impossible using only a single question.

The trouble with using only one question as the single best measure of customer loyalty is clearly illustrated in the preceding example. Capturing the meaning and complexities of customer loyalty far exceeds the capability of a single item. The answer in using the correct customer loyalty items lies in the customer behaviors you want to maximize. One company may want to focus on a specific type of customer loyalty while another company may want to focus on a different type of customer loyalty. To suggest that companies use just one type of customer loyalty would limit their ability to effectively measure other types of customer loyalty that are important for their specific need or industry.

CUSTOMER LOYALTY QUESTIONS FOR MONOPOLIES

The usefulness of these loyalty questions in predicting financial success is not intended to prevent you from developing your own loyalty questions for your particular industry or organization. In some monopolistic industries, such as utilities or regulatory agencies, customers do not have a choice in who they use (for example, to get power, they are required to use the local utility; to practice medicine, physicians need to be certified by a regulatory agency). In these circumstances, the organization or industry needs to conceptualize loyalty in nontraditional ways that extend beyond purchasing behavior. In a noncompetitive environment, we need to redefine what we mean by customer loyalty.

Monopolistic industries are generally concerned with two types of loyalty behaviors of customers: (1) operative and (2) advocacy. *Operative loyalty* reflects the likelihood that constituents request and utilize the company's advice, direction, and expertise and then change self-behaviors. For example, operative loyalty could reflect the degree to which constituents look to companies to provide guidance on issues or the degree to which constituents seek help from companies in order to do their jobs. *Advocacy loyalty* reflects the likelihood that constituents promote/support the company's position on important matters and thus change the behaviors of others. For example, advocacy loyalty could reflect the degree to which constituents speak positively (not speak negatively) about the company or the degree to which constituents openly support the company.

The following are examples of operative loyalty:

- Signing up for programs that help constituents do their job more effectively

- Using company as a consultant when selecting products/ services from a third party

- Seeking company's advice/expertise on issues

- Accepting company's endorsement for third-party contractors

- Complying with/influenced by agency's advice or opinion

- Providing personal information (to better serve customers)

The following are examples of advocacy loyalty:

- Supporting company's position or action on issues impacting the public

- Supporting company's issues on policy changes

  — Changing licensing processes, like new tests

  — Changing usage policies around energy use

- Providing testimonials about positive experiences with the company

The key is that companies need to identify loyalty questions that best suit their needs. When determining which customer loyalty questions to include in your CFP, you need to identify the desired customer behaviors in which you want your customers to engage. Some specific questions you can answer are:

- What types of behaviors do we want from our customers?

- How can our customers support the company's mission?

- What can customers do to help the company better serve them?

- What can customers do to help the company minimize the cost of doing business?

Using these questions and the examples of operative and advocacy loyalty in monopolies, here are some possible customer loyalty questions to tap these two dimensions of customer loyalty:

- How likely are you to speak favorably about the company to friends/family?

- How likely are you to sign up for different programs the company offers?

- How likely are you to use different services?

- How likely are you to comply with the company's advice in regulatory matters in your field?

- How likely are you to support the agency's position or action on licensing-related public issues?

WEB-BASED SURVEYS

There are a few benefits of using Web-based surveys to collect customer feedback compared to other traditional methods. First, Web-based surveys are relatively inexpensive to conduct. Unlike with paper-and-pencil methods, there are no costs associated with printing, stuffing envelopes, postage, or data entry. Additionally, no interviewer is needed with Web-based surveys. Response rates are typically higher with Web-based surveys compared to other methods because Web-based surveys are easier to complete and respondents can complete them at their convenience.

Dillman (2006) has listed other advantages of Web surveys, which include a faster response rate and the ease of sending reminders to participants. Because survey responses can be easily downloaded to a spreadsheet, database, or statistical analysis software program, data processing is greatly facilitated because there is no need for manual data entry.

Survey presentation and completion are greatly facilitated with the use of Web-based surveys compared to other forms of survey methods. Specifically, survey questions can be sorted in any order (for example, random order). Dynamic error checking (verifying responses are appropriate or valid) is also an advantage of Web-based surveys. Additionally, skip patterns for survey questions, where responses to a given question dictate future survey questions, are facilitated with Web-based surveys. (In a skip pattern, a respondent is asked, for example, if he or she received technical support. If yes, the respondent is asked additional questions about technical support. If no, the respondent is not asked these additional questions.) Web surveys allow for the inclusion of pop-up instructions for selected questions as well as multiple methods for answering questions (for example, check boxes and drop-down boxes).

BEST PRACTICES IN DESIGNING AN EFFECTIVE ONLINE SURVEY

An effective Web survey requires consideration of five important areas. These areas are not exclusive to Web surveys, and some principles apply equally well to other types of surveys, such as telephone surveys and interviews. The following section outlines essential steps needed to ensure the final customer survey delivers reliable and valid customer responses. For a more detailed discussion on the development of customer surveys, please see Hayes (2008b).

1. Determine Objectives and Goals of Survey

The first step in developing or evaluating a survey program is to determine the survey objectives and goals. The survey objectives provide the basis on which the remaining survey elements are constructed. The extent to which the company is able to clarify the survey goals will determine the specific survey questions. Typically, the objectives and goals of CFPs are to improve customer loyalty (ultimately, increased customer loyalty will improve the financial success of the company). With the goal of improving customer loyalty, some additional questions to be addressed are the following:

1. Will you be conducting a relationship survey or a transactional survey or both?

2. Which loyalty questions will be included in the survey? Are you trying to focus your efforts on improving one, two, or all three kinds of customer loyalty?

3. What specific business attributes will you include in the survey?

4. Are you trying to solve a specific organizational problem? If so, what organizational changes, if any, will you make based on the survey outcomes? Will organizational changes, if made, result in changes to your future survey results?

The survey objectives will also help determine the types of statistical analyses that will be conducted. The objectives and goals of the survey ensure that the questions remain focused and directed on specific issues. Without clear survey objectives, there is an increased likelihood that the final survey will be unfocused and will include unneeded questions.

2. Determine Customer Target to Survey

The next step in conducting an online customer feedback survey is to determine the customers to be surveyed. The objective or goal of the customer survey will likely determine the type of customers surveyed. For example, in a B2B setting, if the goal is to assess the customer loyalty of decision makers, the customer group to be surveyed should consist of those customers who make the buying decisions. These customers typically reflect executive-level respondents. If the objective of the survey is to assess differences in loyalty across customer segments (for example, differences across levels), it is imperative that all customer segments be represented in the sample of respondents (executives, directors, managers, individual contributors, and so forth). In a B2C setting, similar objectives would lead you to select customer groups that are needed to support the objective of the survey.

In survey research, it is important that an adequate sample size be used to ensure the survey conclusions reflect reliable results that are representative of the entire customer base. The sample size is determined through statistical estimation that takes into account the differences among customers. Basically, if your customers are very similar to one another, the required sample size is relatively small compared to situations in which customers vary greatly from one another; in the latter case you will need a larger sample of respondents if you want to have adequate confidence in your final results.

Reliability of results is not the only factor to consider when determining the sample of customers to survey. For B2B customers, it may be important to invite all accounts at least once per year; surveying accounts lets the customers know that they are important to the company. Also, when compensation for a given employee is dependent on survey results, it is important that the employee's score be based on an adequate sample size. Variable compensation purposes could require all customers to be surveyed regularly in order to get a sample size large enough on which to make compensation decisions for individual employees. Web surveys are relatively inexpensive to conduct and result in larger sample sizes very quickly; consequently, the size of the sample of customers to be surveyed does not greatly impact the survey budget. For customers from B2C companies, invite a sample of respondents, do not over survey, and opt in or opt out participants who do/do not want to be surveyed.

3. Determine Customer Requirements

The questions are the meat of every survey. Achieving the company's survey objectives and goals is accomplished through the development and use of a proper set of survey questions. Hayes (2008b) outlines the steps for developing survey questions. The first step in writing survey questions is to understand the customer requirements. Customer requirements are the business attributes that are important to customers. Establishing a list of customer requirements can be accomplished by two methods: (1) the use of subject matter experts and (2) the use of the critical incidents approach. Both methods provide an effective means by which to generate aspects of the business that are important to customers. A complete discussion of determining customer requirements can be found in Appendix A.

Subject Matter Experts

A *subject matter expert* is an individual who has expertise in a specific field. This individual holds special knowledge about the area being studied and can provide insight about the process being studied. Experts can include employees who have deep familiarity with the subject matter, such as directors of customer service, employees who have customer contact, and call center agents. The employee's job level is not necessarily important when selecting a subject matter expert; what is important is the employee's extent of experience in the area of interest. Soliciting help from employees from across all levels of the organization will likely result in a comprehensive picture of customer requirements. Additionally, seeking help from frontline employees improves the acceptance of the resulting CFP, as frontline employees help in the development of the customer feedback tool.

Subject matter experts can also come from outside the company. Academicians, researchers, and practitioners provide great insight through their vast experience in studying and working with a variety of companies and industries. They can consult directly with the company about a specific topic, or companies can gain knowledge through these experts' publications in trade and scientific journals.

Critical Incidents Approach

The *critical incidents approach* focuses on gathering information from customers about the services and products they receive. The strength of this approach is its utilization of customers in identifying customer requirements. Who else is in a better position to help you understand the needs of customers? Using employees as part of the item generation process is an effective method. Yet relying solely on members of the organization might lead to a less than exhaustive list of customer requirements or a list of customer requirements that do not really reflect customers' needs.

The critical incidents approach identifies specific performance examples that illustrate company performance related to the services or products it provides. The interview process is used to gather these examples from customers. The questions that are typically posed for this purpose are qualitative in nature.

The question to ask a small number of customers is, "Please provide two specific examples of good/poor customer service or product quality that you experienced. Please be specific." This question elicits a long list of examples that can then be grouped on the basis of their similarity to one another, resulting in a smaller group, each representing a customer requirement. By involving the customers in the development of customer requirements, you are ensured that the resulting survey questions are meaningful to the final set of customers who will be surveyed. Also, involving customers in this process ensures that the survey does not include needless questions, which prevents the survey from becoming unnecessarily long.

4. Develop Questions

Survey questions fall into two general categories: quantitative and qualitative. Both types of questions provide useful information for understanding customers' perceptions about the quality of the company as well as their level of satisfaction and loyalty toward the company. *Quantitative questions* involve the use of numeric rating scales that typically allow the customers to indicate their attitude along a continuum from low to high. The rating scale needs to match the question being asked. There are many different numeric rating scales, so selection of the correct scale is crucial to the effectiveness of the survey. Additionally, to improve the ease with which customers can answer the survey questions, the specific numeric rating scale needs to match the question being asked. For example, you would never use an agreement rating scale (1 = strongly disagree to 5 = strongly agree) for questions that ask about level of satisfaction (for example, How satisfied are you with the technical support?). And you would never use satisfaction rating scales (1 = extremely dissatisfied to 10 = extremely satisfied) for questions that require an agreement rating (for example, "Technical support staff are knowledgeable").

The proper scale range (for example, 1–4, 1–5, 1–7, 0–10) will match the needs of the survey and the ability of the respondent to make distinctions across the different scale values. A useful scale for measuring attitudes is the 0–10 rating scale. While there has been much research on the topic of appropriate scale length, there is no clear benefit of one method over another. What can be said about scale ranges is that with too few scale values, small differences among customers in their attitudes toward the company may not be detected. Too many scale values (0–100) may reflect too many distinctions, and customers may not be able to differentiate differences between scale values (for example, the difference between 45 and 46).

Qualitative questions allow the respondent to answer the question in his or her own words rather than being restricted to a predefined set of response options. Qualitative questions are an effective way of providing examples of customer issues that support the quantitative results of the survey. Open-ended responses can be used effectively in final survey reports to help illustrate the quantitative findings. Open-ended customer comments bring the survey results to life by personalizing the responses for the executives.

If necessary, additional survey questions can be added to collect important demographic and psychographic information, such as age, customer tenure, marital status, job title, income level, and educational status. These types of questions allow you to understand important customer segments needed to achieve the objectives of the survey.

5. Create E-mail Introduction to Survey

Customers do not provide feedback in a vacuum. When you are inviting your customers to complete a feedback form, you need to tell them why you are seeking their feedback. In the introductory invitation e-mail, introduce the survey itself and explain why you are conducting the survey (remember the survey objective).

Customers will be more responsive if they know why you are seeking their feedback. If you are seeking feedback for improvement purposes, let your customers know. Clarify why the survey is relevant to them and how their responses will help the company improve and create better products and services.

Remember to be honest in your e-mail. If you are capturing customer-sensitive data that are unique to a particular respondent, disclose this information up front so that the customer is aware that his or her responses are not anonymous. The responses, however, can still be confidential (for example, only the account team will know the responses and the data will be reported only in aggregate form).

In Web-based surveys, respondents are typically invited via an e-mail that contains a hyperlink that takes them directly to the survey. An example of an e-mail invitation appears in Figure 6.5.

Survey invitations have an embedded hyperlink that directs the respondent to the hosted survey. Some companies use surveys that provide unique hyperlinks for each respondent, the hyperlink identifying the respondent. In these cases, existing customer data (for example, product owned, service warranty levels, region, and age) can be matched to each respondent's survey responses for later segmentation. The existing customer data can be used to personalize the e-mail invitation and can help deliver the appropriate customer survey to the right person (for example, customer in the sales cycle receives the sales survey; customer in the service cycle receives the service survey). Additionally, the existing data help reduce the number of survey questions the respondent is asked.

The hyperlink sends the respondent to a survey located on the Web, where the respondent can provide feedback about the company (see Figure 6.6 for an example Web-based survey).

When sending the e-mail invitation to the target customer group, it is important to send the invitation at a time that results

Company ABC is interested in your opinions about our products and services. To that end, we have developed a survey enabling you to provide specific feedback on how you feel about our company. Your feedback will help us make improvements to ensure we deliver the best products and services to you.

Business Over Broadway is conducting this survey for us, and we would like to invite you to connect to the survey site and complete your response. To access the survey, please click on the URL below. The survey will remain open until <CLOSE DATE> and will take approximately 10 minutes to complete.

http://www.surveyhyperlinkgoeshere.com

Individual responses to this survey will remain strictly confidential. Results will be reported in aggregate form only.

Thank you for your time and feedback.

Sincerely,

John Doe
President, Company ABC
president@companyabc.com
http://www.companyabc.com

Figure 6.5   Sample e-mail invitation to Web-based survey.

http://www.surveyhyperlinkgoeshere.com

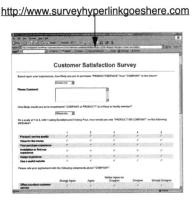

Figure 6.6   Hyperlink takes respondent directly to the Web-based survey.

in the highest response rates. As a general rule, e-mail invitations should be sent early in the week, preferably Monday morning. Customers are starting the week fresh and will have ample time throughout the week to complete the survey at their leisure. For B2C customers, survey invitations can also be sent at the end of the week, preferably Friday. B2C customers will have free time away from their workweek responsibilities and may be more likely to complete the survey over the weekend. While a response rate of 15–20% is considered acceptable for B2C customers, I have seen response rates in a B2B setting as high as 75%.

Individuals do not always respond to surveys when they are invited. While a nonresponse to a survey invitation might reflect a customer's lack of interest in giving feedback, a nonresponse might also reflect the customer's busy schedule; he or she may have overlooked the initial e-mail invitation or, thinking they will respond to the survey later, may have simply forgotten to respond to the survey. Thus, follow-up e-mail invitations are an effective method of reminding customers about the importance of the survey. In fact, follow-up reminder e-mails have been shown to improve overall survey response rates. Response rates typically jump several percentages immediately after a reminder e-mail is sent. An actual distribution of response rates (daily and cumulative) for a customer survey is presented in Figure 6.7. As can be seen in the figure, response rates jumped considerably on the day of the e-mail reminder and had a substantial impact on the overall response rate (64%). The projected response rate, if the e-mail reminders were not used, would be around 40%.

Individuals need to be given adequate time to respond to the survey. The company can usually keep the Web survey open for as long as it likes. The length of time a survey is open depends on a variety of factors, such as the type of survey (transactional or relationship) being conducted, the length of the survey, and

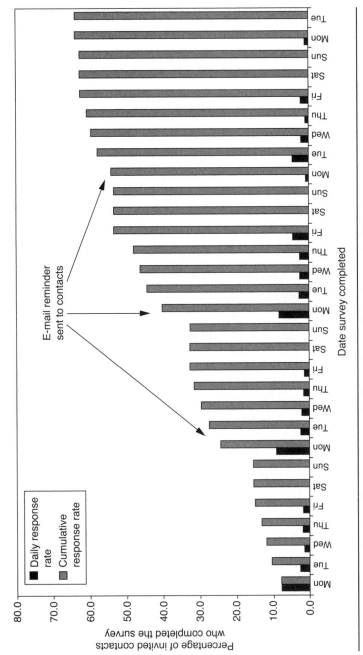

Figure 6.7 Distribution of response rate (daily and cumulative) over the life of a survey.

the needs of the company (Is segmentation needed? Are results needed quickly? How much variability is in the responses?).

Transactional surveys, because they are associated with a specific event, are open a shorter period of time than relationship surveys. A week or two will usually suffice. If the transactional survey is open too long, the respondent's memory might be impacted by other events that take place in between the original event and the administration of the survey. Also, if business decisions need to be made quickly, a survey may be open for only a week. Finally, if there is not much variability in responses, you will need fewer respondents to attain a high degree of confidence in the results, compared to situations where there is a high degree of variability in the responses. Response rates can be monitored on a daily basis to assist in decision making on the survey time period. If no more customers respond within a couple of days of receiving a reminder e-mail, it may be a good time to close the survey.

The e-mail invitation list can be generated from your current customer list. Companies that have incorporated their contact management process (for example, determining who gets surveyed) into their CRM system are significantly more satisfied with their CFP than companies that have not done this. Using the company's CRM system greatly facilitates this contact management process with respect to not only identifying recipients of the survey invitation but also helping the survey team manage follow-up e-mails to nonrespondents. Additionally, the customer feedback results can be easily matched to the customer's information so that the responses can be incorporated into the customer's profile. Customer information housed in CRM systems can be very extensive and can also facilitate future segmentation analysis; for example, CRM systems typically include such factors as number of service requests, types of products the customer purchases, geographical location of the customer, customer tenure, and other company-specific information (for example, value of the customer, type of service package held by the customer).

Providing an incentive has been shown to significantly improve the response rates to surveys. If your survey budget allows, and you want to improve your response rates, consider an incentive program for your survey. Incentives can be in the form of a nominal gift to each respondent or involve a lottery method in which one randomly selected respondent receives a substantial gift. You might even consider using the survey results themselves, in the form of a brief executive report, as an incentive for completing the survey. Some studies say up to 50% of participants feel incentivized when they are given the opportunity to view survey results.

Frequently, incentives are used to drive higher participation rates, particularly if the survey targets groups that traditionally are low responders. The need for incentives is dependent on how motivated the potential participants are to complete the survey. Experience indicates that if the survey is within an area of interest to the participants, an incentive is not necessary. If it is determined that a true incentive is needed, experience shows that the best incentives reward the individual directly. Entries in raffles and contests are less effective than purchase credits, discounts, and cash incentives. Recent research (see Dillman 2006, 168) has also shown that paying all potential respondents a nominal incentive ($1–$5) prior to participation is actually the most cost-effective recruitment method, creating a sense of obligation on the part of the recipient that results in a much greater likelihood of participation.

6. Item Selection and Testing the Survey

The next step is to examine the final set of items you have generated for your survey and select only those questions that are needed for the final survey. Oftentimes, the number of questions generated exceeds the number of questions needed to accomplish the survey objective. Hayes (2008b) gives two general approaches for selecting the final set of questions: (1) judgmental and (2) mathematical. In the judgmental process, you simply review the set of questions and remove those that are not needed. Is there too much redundancy in the questions? Can some questions be grouped into a smaller set of questions? Some redundancy in questions is fine and even expected, especially when trying to measure business areas (customer support) that are broad in content and contain many subcomponents (knowledgeable of products/services, responsiveness, overall quality, professionalism, understands business needs).

In the mathematical process, you administer the survey to a set of real customers and apply statistical analysis on the responses to the set of questions. This topic is beyond the scope of this book, but the interested reader can learn more about this method by reading Hayes (2008b). The bottom line is that the statistical analyses will pinpoint which items can be removed without sacrificing data integrity. Similar to the judgmental approach, the mathematical approach has as its goal to remove redundant questions from the survey.

With real customer responses, another useful approach to remove unneeded questions is to conduct some analyses using the existing responses. This approach will help you better understand the quality of the survey questions and verify whether the survey will meet the needs of the survey objective.

By using real customers to test the survey, you will be able to evaluate all phases of the survey, from survey objective to analysis and reporting. Testing a survey up front on a limited number of customers will help avoid administering a less-than-perfect survey to the entire customer base. Testing surveys can prevent such problems as poor data quality, failure in meeting survey objectives, adversely impacting the company brand through an inferior customer survey, and required additional rework on behalf of the survey team to respond to the host of problems arising out of the initially poor survey.

Additionally, when testing the survey, it is important to conduct statistical analyses and create a final report. This exercise will help clarify whether the questions are sufficient to address the survey objectives. If the questions are insufficient, new questions can be developed that will help achieve the survey objectives.

From the item selection process to the formalized testing of the customer survey, the mathematical methods applied in each approach require the consultation of an expert in survey construction and analysis, as the interpretation of the analyses (item analysis, reliability analysis, correlational analysis) is essential to the process of item selection and theory testing (Hayes 2008b).

Additionally, the testing process should also involve testing the Web survey on as many operating platforms and Web browsers as possible to ensure the look and feel of the survey are not adversely impacted by a particular configuration.

PRINCIPLES FOR DESIGNING WEB-BASED SURVEYS

Dillman, Tortora, and Bowker (1998) outlined several principles to consider when designing Web surveys:

1. Shorten the length of invitation and reminder messages.

2. At the start of the survey, provide all necessary information on why the respondent should complete the survey and how to do so. Specifically, introduce the survey with an initial screen that encourages the respondent to complete the questionnaire (for example, what's in it for them), tells how long it will take to complete the survey, and provides instructions on how to complete each question (different questions require different types of responses).

3. Begin with a question that is completely visible on the first screen of the survey and can be easily comprehended and answered by all respondents. Customer loyalty questions are excellent leadoff questions.

4. Be as straightforward as possible when writing the survey questions. Put the questions in a natural order or progression with logical transitions from one section to the next. Limit the line length of the questions to decrease the likelihood of a long line of text extending across the screen of the respondent's browser.

5. For each section of the survey, provide specific instructions on how to take each necessary computer action for responding to questionnaires. Some survey questions require checking a single response, while other questions require multiple responses for a single question. Still other survey responses might require a numerical response (for example, ranking, specific values) or a full-length text response.

6. Provide computer operation instructions as part of each question where the action is to be taken, not in a separate section prior to the beginning of the questionnaire.

7. Do not require respondents to answer each question before proceeding to subsequent questions. Doing so will increase dropout rates.

8. Inform the respondent of his or her survey completion status. You can use either graphical symbols or words to indicate how much of the survey has been completed.

9. Pilot test each survey with a variety of people using different browsers. Surveys may look different on different browsers.

SUMMARY

The CFP best practices for methods are summarized in Table 6.4. A Web-based survey approach, used across a variety of survey types (for example, transactional and relationship), that is incorporated into the CRM system helps companies easily and quickly understand different customer constituencies in a cost-effective manner.

To determine which questions to include in a survey, the company needs to understand customer requirements. Surveys need to include questions that tap factors that are important to customers. Establishing a list of these customer requirements will ultimately lead to better survey questions that measure essential elements of the customer relationship.

Customer surveys need to include customer loyalty questions that are best suited to the company's specific needs. Rather than relying on one single measure of loyalty (for example, likelihood to recommend), companies need to think critically regarding the type of loyalty or loyalties they want to improve. Relying on a single measure of customer loyalty leads to unreliable results, the mismanagement of customers, and, consequently, missed revenue opportunities.

The method by which customer feedback is collected plays a crucial role in the customer feedback process. The information resulting from the customer feedback method will impact the quality of the business decisions. An effective feedback method will result in good business decisions. Collecting reliable and valid customer feedback data is not enough; the company must analyze the data, transform the data into useful information, and disseminate this information throughout the company. The next chapter presents best practices in the reporting of customer feedback data.

Table 6.4   Summary of method-based CFP best practices.

Best practice	Important points
Use Web-based surveys to collect customer feedback	• Surveys are used to allow customers to provide feedback
Use multiple methods to collect customer feedback	• Relationship surveys are used to assess general attitudes about the quality of the overall relationship; transactional surveys are used to assess the quality of a specific interaction with the organization • Web-site surveys are used to assess customers' perceptions of a specific touch point
Incorporate customer contact management of the CFP into the CRM system	• Links survey to specific contact(s) within accounts. This greatly simplifies the survey program by streamlining the logistics behind the sampling of the customers. • Ensures right customers are surveyed
Determine reliability/ validity of customer survey	• Reliable/valid survey results lead to better business decisions • Builds comprehensive measurement system for customer experience (attitudinal measure and objective measures)
Identify customer requirements	• Helps executives understand what is important to customers • Helps in creating the right questions for the feedback tool
Survey different types of customers within a given account	• Obtain a comprehensive picture of all aspects of account quality
Use multiple measures of customer loyalty	• NPS is not the best predictor of growth • Understand what type of loyalty you want to maximize before choosing customer loyalty questions • Using multiple loyalty questions results in more reliable survey results • Customer loyalty is best conceptualized as consisting of three components (advocacy, purchasing, and retention)

7

Reporting

ADOPTION RATES FOR REPORTING-RELATED BUSINESS PRACTICES

Customer survey data become useful for management purposes when they are summarized and presented in a way that draws clear conclusions about company strengths and leads to specific actions that can be taken to address identified problems. While companies must ensure the method by which they collect their customer feedback results in reliable and valid data, attention to the data must not stop there. Companies need to adopt good business practices in the reporting of these data that help them extract value from the data. Best practices around the reporting process ensure organizations are able to effectively summarize the customer feedback data and disseminate the results to concerned parties in order to effectively manage customers and, ultimately, improve customer loyalty.

Organizations can maximize the value of their feedback data through appropriate reporting practices. The survey results identified key factors of the reporting process that will improve the effectiveness of the CFP. When examining the adoption rates of CFP business practices, we see that some reporting practices differ across Loyalty Leaders and Loyalty Laggers. The comparisons between the two groups appear in Figure 7.1.

Reporting-related business practice	Adoption rate		
	Loyalty Leaders	Loyalty Laggers	Loyalty unknown
Web-based reporting tools are used to report customer feedback results to employees	**67%**	38%	45%
Customer feedback results are shared only at executive/ management level*	64%	64%	**68%**
Customer feedback results are shared throughout the company	**85%**	80%	62%
Results of customer satisfaction research are presented internally (through employee portal, newsletters)	69%	**70%**	48%
Results of customer satisfaction research are presented externally (e.g., conferences, user groups, thought-leader events)	**64%**	43%	25%
Customer feedback results are benchmarked against competitors and industry averages	**69%**	62%	40%

*Reverse coded—higher percentage indicates more favorable responses.

Figure 7.1   Adoption rates of reporting-related CFP business practices for Loyalty Leaders and Loyalty Laggers.

Specifically, we see that 67% of Loyalty Leaders, compared to only 38% of Loyalty Laggers, use Web-based reporting tools to report customer feedback results to employees. With respect to sharing the customer feedback results, the survey results found that 64% of Loyalty Leaders present their customer feedback results externally (for example, conferences, user groups, thought-leader events), compared to only 43% of Loyalty Laggers that did the same.

REPORTING-RELATED CFP BUSINESS PRACTICES THAT IMPACT CUSTOMER LOYALTY AND SATISFACTION WITH THE CFP

The next set of analyses was focused on quantifying the impact of the reporting-related CFP business practices on customer loyalty and satisfaction with the CFP. The results (see Figures 7.2 and 7.3) show that reporting-related business practices had very little impact on improving customer loyalty. The only (and relatively small compared to other areas) impact was seen for the extent to which customer feedback is shared throughout the company. Companies that adopted this practice reported higher customer loyalty (percentile ranking of 69) than companies that did not adopt this practice (percentile ranking of 60).

The survey results show that reporting-related business practices of CFPs, however, had a substantial impact on the satisfaction with the CFP in helping manage customer relationships. Nearly all of the reporting-related practices were shown to have a substantial impact on improving the satisfaction with which the CFP helped the company manage customer relationships.

Results show that companies that adopted the following practices were substantially more satisfied with their CFPs in helping them manage their customer relationships than companies that did not adopt them: (1) customer feedback results presented internally via portals and newsletters (97% vs. 45% satisfied), (2) customer feedback results shared throughout company (90% vs. 52% satisfied), (3) customer feedback research results presented externally (for example, conferences, user groups, thought-leader events; 95% vs. 62% satisfied), (4) Web-based

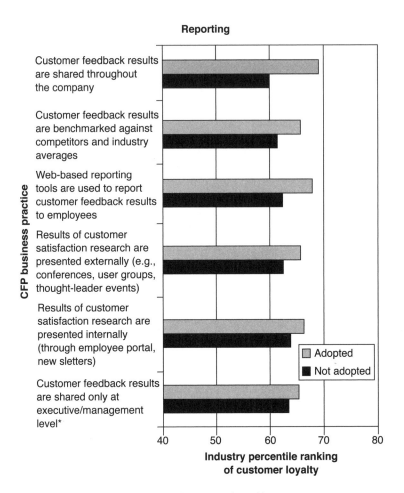

Figure 7.2   Impact of reporting-related CFP business practices on customer loyalty.

reporting tools used to report customer feedback data to employees (89% vs. 57% satisfied).

The analysis and reporting of customer feedback data are crucial to making the data useful to the company. Analysis of the data includes the application of statistical methods, both simple and complex. The analysis organizes the raw data into an interpretable form by putting structure around it. Business

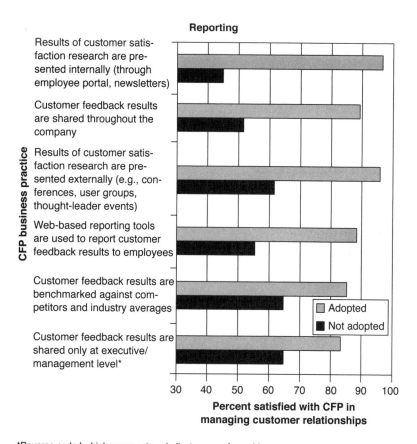

Figure 7.3 Impact of reporting-related CFP business practices on satisfaction with CFP in managing customer relationships.

models that include customer variables can be used to guide the types of analyses that help make sense of the sea of data. The next section includes a discussion on loyalty management, which will set the tone for the types of analyses that are effective in improving customer loyalty.

The use of customer feedback data to help manage customer relationships has received much technological innovation over the past decade. Web-based surveys provide an easy vehicle for customers to provide feedback. For example, in

B2B uses of Cfps, individual customer concerns are addressed through the use of automated prompts (typically in the form of an e-mail) to account team members who are responsible for quickly resolving specific causes of customer concerns. Additionally, organization-wide customer loyalty issues are identified through automated analyses (for example, driver analysis) that highlight common causes of customer loyalty/disloyalty. Furthermore, customer survey results are accessible 24/7 by all employees through Web-based reporting tools. Finally, companies link customer survey data to their CRM systems to enhance day-to-day account management with both attitudinal data and operational data. It is clear that efforts in the field of customer loyalty have simplified the process of data collection, analysis, reporting, and integration with existing business systems.

UNDERSTANDING CUSTOMER FEEDBACK DATA

Cfps can generate a lot of data. With thousands of customers and by using questionnaires with multiple questions, it is not uncommon to find that some enterprise companies have hundreds of thousands of pieces of customer information to consolidate. Understanding, aggregating, and analyzing customer feedback data starts with a business model. Because the nature of the data is customer-related, this business model needs to be customer-centric and service-oriented. This business model will help guide data analysis and will, ultimately, lead to customer-centric business decisions.

Service Delivery Model

The service delivery model, based on the work of researchers at Harvard Business School, illustrates how the CFP helps the company manage its customer relationships throughout the customer life cycle (see Figure 7.4). Supported by empirical

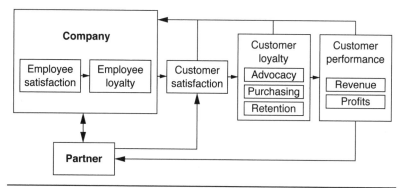

Figure 7.4 Service delivery model illustrating the relationship among key organizational variables.

Source: Adapted from Heskett, Sasser, and Schlesinger (1997).

research, the model states that profitability and growth are stimulated primarily by customer loyalty. Loyalty is a direct result of customer satisfaction, and satisfaction is largely influenced by the value of services provided to customers. Value is created by satisfied, loyal, and productive employees. Employee satisfaction, in turn, results primarily from high-quality support services and policies that enable employees to deliver results to customers. Partners also provide products and services to joint customers and help impact customer loyalty to the partnering company. The quality of the three relationships (customer, employee, and partner) impacts company financial success, and the key to business success is managing these three key relationships.

To maximize customer loyalty and increase the lifetime value of customers, companies must manage their customer relationships effectively throughout the entire customer life cycle. Successful companies know which business attributes have the largest impact on attracting new prospects and turning them into customers. Once new customers are acquired, the companies are able to provide these customers greater value, as they understand where to allocate their resources to improve customer loyalty. As customer loyalty increases, so does business success, specifically revenue, profitability, and market share.

CFPs provide the information the company needs to ensure the customer relationship is managed effectively.

CUSTOMER LOYALTY MANAGEMENT

The key, then, to business success is to increase customer loyalty. The company can take two general approaches to improve customer loyalty through customer loyalty management: (1) micro or individual approach and (2) macro or organizational approach.

Micro (Individual) Approach to Loyalty Management

The micro approach examines the customer relationship for a specific customer or survey respondent. In this approach, the organization identifies customers who are disloyal and intervenes to address the specific customer's concerns. This approach addresses special causes of disloyalty (those that fall outside normal variations) and is a short-term solution to customer concerns. Rather than focusing on improving the business process that resulted in this customer becoming at-risk, the organization focuses on addressing this at-risk customer's concerns. Improvements are targeted at disloyal customers to immediately address their specific needs.

In this approach, timely handling of unhappy, disloyal customers is key to ensuring their attitudes regarding the company do not ultimately result in disloyal behaviors (for example, defect, discontinue buying). Web-based surveys are an important ingredient in the micro approach to handling disloyal customers. The Web-based survey utilizes the power of the Internet to notify the organization regarding the specific customer's negative response(s). Trigger e-mail alerts are often used to notify employees that there are unhappy, disloyal customers.

During the development of the customer survey administration process, survey questions should be assigned to the individual or department responsible for those particular results.

Assignment of a survey question to a specific department should be based on that department's ability to change customers' ratings on that question. A survey question regarding the sales process, for example, should be assigned to the sales department. A survey question regarding technical support quality should be assigned to the technical support department. These two departments have influence on the quality of the sales process and the technical support process, respectively, and, consequently, are in the best position to address problems from these areas.

Trigger e-mails are activated from customers' responses to these key satisfaction and loyalty questions. For example, an organization may set up an automatic e-mail trigger to an account team member when his or her customer responds to an overall satisfaction question with a rating of 5 or below on a 0–10 scale. This low rating indicates that this customer is at risk for exhibiting disloyal behavior. The e-mail alert is sent to the account team member immediately after the respondent submits the survey responses.

The e-mail alert should include information necessary for the recipient to be able to take immediate action to contact the respondent to address any concerns identified in the e-mail. Typical information in the e-mail includes respondent's name, company name, product information, and the ratings on the key questions used as criteria for the trigger e-mail. An example of a trigger e-mail alert appears in Figure 7.5.

This micro approach to loyalty management requires that the respondent be identified after the completion of the survey. The trigger e-mail approach is not uncommon in B2B customer surveys. Most large-scale survey vendors possess this sort of sophisticated survey approach, allowing companies to identify respondents in order to address their individual concerns.

After the e-mail triggers are sent to the responsible party, the action taken to resolve the problem can be logged. Some companies that have incorporated the customer resolution process

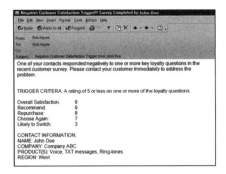

Note: Likely to switch <6, indicating defection is likely.

Figure 7.5 Trigger e-mail indicating an at-risk customer.

into their CRM system are able to keep track of the steps taken to resolve specific customer concerns. Not only does the tracking of the resolution process ensure a closed-loop process for customer-identified issues, but it also allows an easy analysis of how quickly customers' issues are being addressed. Companies can then trend the time it takes to resolve a problem to ensure the micro approach to customer loyalty management is effective. The micro approach is summarized in Table 7.1.

Macro (Organizational) Approach to Loyalty Management

The macro approach examines the customer relationship across all customers (or customer segment) in which data are analyzed as a whole. In doing so, the organization attempts to identify systemic reasons causing loyalty/disloyalty. The macro approach to loyalty management addresses common causes of disloyalty and focuses on improving systemic issues responsible for the disloyalty. Unlike the micro approach to loyalty management, which focuses on resolving a specific customer's unique concerns, the macro approach to loyalty management reflects organizational improvements targeted across a large group of customers (or at least large customer segments) and is aimed at improving the service delivery system. Systemic

Table 7.1   Summary of micro approach to customer loyalty
management.

• Understand the customer relationship for a specific survey respondent — Individual survey respondents • Identify customers who indicate they are disloyal — Threatened customer relationship • Target improvements on disloyal customers to address specific needs immediately — Action plan directed at impacting individual customers • Use trigger e-mails to identify disloyal customers — Negative responses to loyalty/satisfaction questions trigger notification to pre-determined employees and managers — Trigger email alerts enable employees to take immediate action on important customer issues • Incorporate micro approach into company's CRM system — Ensures closed-loop process for customer-identified issues to resolution — Analyze set of problems to determine trends

changes to business processes are designed to have a long-term impact on customer loyalty.

The macro or organizational approach to loyalty management begins with summarizing large sets of data; the goal of summarizing data is to draw general conclusions across a large segment of customers. There are various statistical methods of summarizing large sets of data, each with a different purpose. Some of these are presented below. For the interested reader, popular statistical analysis methods are presented in the appendices.

A key analytical method used for loyalty management is referred to as "loyalty driver analysis." Loyalty driver analysis combines a couple of the statistical analysis methods presented in the appendices and is a powerful method used in loyalty management. This method essentially identifies business areas that, when improved, will have a substantial impact on increasing customer loyalty. The macro approach is summarized in Table 7.2.

Table 7.2 Summary of macro approach to customer loyalty management.

• Understand the customer relationship across all customers 　—Analyze entire customer base • Identify systemic reasons causing loyalty/disloyalty 　—Software quality, technical support, staff knowledge • Target company-wide improvement programs directed at all customers • Help improve the service delivery system 　—Impacts how the work gets done • Conduct driver analysis to calculate degree of impact each business attribute has on customer loyalty 　—Derived importance is the correlation between satisfaction ratings of a business attribute and CLI 　—Business attributes typically vary from 0 (no relationship) to 1.0 (perfect positive relationship) • Identify top drivers of customer loyalty 　—These business attributes define what is important to the customers • Examine satisfaction and gap scores for top drivers 　—Large gaps and low satisfaction scores = focus improvements in these areas 　—Small gaps and high satisfaction scores = leverage as strengths

Summary of Micro vs. Macro Approach

The two approaches to survey-based loyalty management should not be viewed as competing types of loyalty management. Instead, the survey-based loyalty management system, by design, should work to help deal with specific customer complaints and identify systemic reasons for dissatisfaction/disloyalty. Table 7.3 summarizes the features of each type of loyalty management approach. The micro (individual) approach addresses special causes of customer loyalty and focuses on changing individual customer concerns with customer-specific improvements that are short-term solutions to improving customer loyalty. The macro (organizational) approach addresses common causes of loyalty and focuses on improving systemic issues with organization-wide improvements that are long-term solutions to improving customer loyalty.

Table 7.3 Summary of micro and macro approaches to loyalty management.

Micro approach	Macro approach
Addresses special causes of disloyalty	Addresses common causes of disloyalty
Focuses on changing individual issues	Focuses on improving systemic issues
Makes customer-specific improvements	Makes organization-wide improvements
Looks for short-term solutions	Looks for long-term solutions

LOYALTY DRIVER ANALYSIS

Loyalty driver analysis is a process in which we identify how best to improve customer loyalty. Two pieces of information are examined in a loyalty driver analysis: (1) derived importance, the degree of impact of each business attribute on customer loyalty, and (2) performance, the level of performance of each business attribute.

The *derived importance* of a business attribute is the correlation coefficient between satisfaction ratings for that business attribute and the measure of customer loyalty (see Appendix J for a description of correlation coefficients). The correlation between the satisfaction scores of a business attribute and the loyalty indicates the degree to which performance on the business attribute has an impact on customer loyalty behavior. *Performance* of a given business attribute is the average rating for that particular business attribute.

Loyalty Matrix

Each business attribute has a derived importance and a performance score associated with it. Using both the derived importance and the performance (for example, rating) of each business attribute, we can create a loyalty matrix (see Figure 7.6) that allows us to visually examine all business attributes at one time. This matrix allows us to understand how each business attribute affects customer loyalty.

The abscissa (x-axis) of the loyalty matrix is the performance rating (agreement, performance, satisfaction) of the business attributes. The ordinate (y-axis) of the loyalty matrix is the impact (derived importance) of the business attributes on customer loyalty. The loyalty matrix is divided into quadrants using the average score for each of the axes. Each of the business attributes will fall into one of the four quadrants. Loyalty

	Key drivers	Hidden drivers
High (Impact)	Invest in these areas. Improvement in these areas is predicted to attract new customers (advocacy), increase purchasing behavior (purchasing), or retain customers (retention).	Leverage as strengths in order to keep current customers loyal. Advertise as strengths in marketing collateral and sales presentations in order to attract new customers (advocacy), increase purchasing behavior (purchasing), or retain customers (retention).
Low	Consider as lowest priority for investment. These areas have relatively low impact on improving customer loyalty.	Advertise as strengths in marketing collateral and sales presentations in order to attract new customers. Evaluate as areas of potential over-investment.
	Weak drivers	*Visible drivers*
	Low Performance High	

Figure 7.6   Loyalty matrix.

management at the macro (organizational) level is a process of understanding this matrix and the types of business decisions that should be made to maximize customer loyalty.

Let us take a look at the loyalty matrix using the ALI. Using the PC manufacturer study, we can set up a loyalty matrix (see Figure 7.7). With this loyalty matrix, the organization can make business decisions that will have a positive impact on advocacy loyalty.

Key Drivers

Business attributes that appear in the upper left quadrant are often referred to as key drivers. *Key drivers* reflect business attributes that have both a large impact on advocacy loyalty and low performance ratings relative to the other business attributes. Business attributes that are key drivers reflect good areas for potential improvement that, when improved, should also

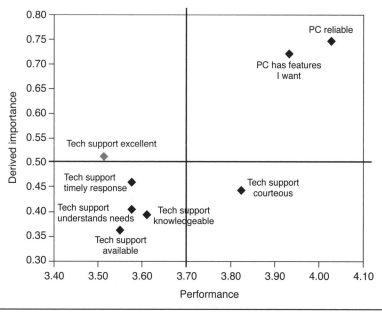

Figure 7.7   Driver analysis of advocacy loyalty—PC manufacturer.

improve the advocacy of their customers. Improving advocacy will improve new customer growth.

To see improvements in advocacy loyalty, the results of the driver analysis suggest this organization should examine the following business attribute:

- Tech support excellent

Hidden Drivers

Business attributes that appear in the upper right quadrant are referred to as hidden drivers. *Hidden drivers* reflect business attributes that have both a large impact on advocacy loyalty and high performance ratings relative to other business attributes. Business attributes that are hidden drivers reflect the company's strengths, which keeps the customer base advocating the product. These areas should be monitored regularly to ensure they remain high. These attributes could also be used in marketing material to attract new customers.

The following are the company's strengths:

- PC is reliable

- PC has features I want

Weak Drivers

Business attributes that appear in the lower left quadrant are referred to as weak drivers. *Weak drivers* reflect business attributes that have both a small impact on advocacy loyalty and low performance ratings relative to other business attributes. Business attributes that are weak drivers reflect the lowest-priority areas for investment. They are of low priority because, despite the fact that performance is also low in these areas, these areas do not have a substantial impact on whether customers will advocate the product/company.

The following areas do not have a large impact on whether your customers will advocate the product/company. If your resources are limited, improvement in these areas might take a back seat to improvements to your key drivers:

- Tech support understands needs
- Tech support timely response
- Tech support is available
- Tech support is knowledgeable

Visible Drivers

Business attributes that appear in the lower right quadrant are referred to as visible drivers. *Visible drivers* reflect business attributes that have both a low impact on advocacy loyalty and high performance ratings relative to other business attributes. Business attributes that are visible drivers reflect the company's strengths. These areas may not be responsible for encouraging customers to be advocates, but they do reflect high performance. These business attributes can be advertised as strengths in marketing collateral and sales presentations in order to attract new customers.

The following area does not have a large impact on advocacy loyalty, but its performance is good. The company might consider using this area in advertisements (sales and marketing) to attract new customers:

- Tech support is courteous

Because we have two customer loyalty indices, we can calculate multiple separate loyalty matrices. The PC manufacturer using the PLI appears in Figure 7.8.

With regard to purchasing loyalty, however, we see that many of the technical support attributes (excellence, timeliness, understands needs, availability) have a relatively big impact on purchasing loyalty. Interestingly, PC attributes do not have a big impact on purchasing loyalty.

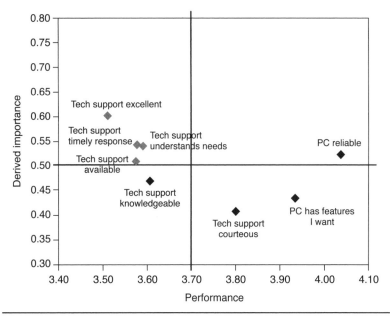

Figure 7.8   Driver analysis of purchasing loyalty—PC manufacturer.

Using the two loyalty matrices, we can draw some conclusions regarding how this particular PC manufacturer can increase advocacy loyalty and purchasing loyalty. To improve advocacy loyalty, the driver analysis appears inconclusive. While PC features are big determinants of advocacy, they are rated as relatively good. Consequently, there is not much room for improvement in these attributes. The technical support attributes, while rated as relatively low, do not have a large impact on advocacy loyalty.

If this PC manufacturer wants to improve purchasing loyalty, however, the results of the driver analysis indicate that the manufacturer should focus on improving technical support attributes, as these attributes have a relatively large impact on purchasing loyalty and have much room for improvement.

The different results from this analysis suggest that "improving customer loyalty" is more complex than simply using a single metric. If the company were to use only advocacy loyalty as a measure of loyalty (as is commonly done), it would not have identified ways in which it could improve purchasing loyalty of its customer base. Inclusion of the two different dimensions of customer loyalty ensures the company fully understands how to improve both advocacy loyalty and purchasing loyalty.

SUMMARIZING THE DATA

The customer satisfaction data are analyzed and summarized to help us understand the customer relationship of our entire customer base or large customer segments. These analyses summarize survey results to help identify overall company strengths and areas for improvement and identify ways to increase customer loyalty and, ultimately, financial success. Company executives are usually the first to see the results of these analyses.

The presentation of data is an important issue in the reporting process. The quality of the data obtained from the customer survey can be affected by the way in which they are summarized and presented. A reliable and valid CFP will be of little use if the data cannot be understood. There are several ways to summarize the data, some of which are presented in Table 7.4. But rather than focus on a detailed discussion here, the reader is directed to the appendices, which cover this topic in detail.

Frequency distributions or histograms can be used to summarize questions in the customer satisfaction data. A frequency table organizes the data by listing every possible score (including those not actually obtained in the sample) and indicating the number of times each score occurred. Frequencies can be used to summarize the following questions in the customer survey:

- Continue purchasing
- Recommend
- Overall satisfaction

Table 7.4.　Ways of summarizing data.

Method	Definition
Frequencies	The occurrence of a specific value, or how often that a given value occurs in the data
Percentages	The proportion of scores of a particular value
Histograms	Graphical representation of frequencies
Mean	Measure of central tendency: The arithmetic average of all scores in the data set, calculated by adding all scores in the data set and dividing by the total number of observations.
Median	Measure of central tendency: The score closest to the middle after the data have been ranked from low to high.
Mode	Measure of central tendency: Score that occurs most frequently.
Variance	Measure of variability
Standard deviation	Measure of variability

Descriptive statistics summarize the data by determining the middle point of a distribution of scores. Specifically, the mean is used to determine the center or middle point of ratings (for example, satisfaction, importance, and gap scores). The *mean* is the arithmetic average of scores across all contacts. The mean is calculated by adding all the scores and dividing by the number of contacts who answered that question. The mean is used to describe the general attitude of the customers as a group. For example, an average satisfaction score of 8.2 for a given question indicates that the customers, on the whole, are satisfied in that area. An average satisfaction score of 4.7 for a given question, however, indicates that the customers, on the whole, are not satisfied in that area. The average is used to summarize the responses to the following types of questions in the customer survey:

- Satisfaction indices
- Loyalty indices

Once averages are calculated for each question, they are used for such purposes as benchmarking and tracking customer satisfaction over time.

BENCHMARKING

Benchmarking is the search for the industry's best practices that lead to excellent performance. Camp (1989) outlined a process of benchmarking that includes identifying premier companies and determining their business practices. Once a company identifies these superior business practices, it may incorporate them into its own practices or change existing processes to conform to the ones identified. This change is designed to increase the organization's effectiveness in meeting customers' requirements.

Benchmarking can also occur across different customer segments within a given company. These different customer segments can be defined by a number of organizational variables, like department, region, or other important company segments. Take, for example, a company with multiple call centers in different regions (North, South, East, and West). Each call center is run independently from the others and has its own set of business processes. The company sets out to benchmark the call centers to determine which call center, if any, has the highest customer satisfaction ratings. Comparing customer satisfaction ratings across all call centers, the company determines that the call center located in the South has the highest ratings. As a result of this process, the company could adopt the business processes of the call center in the South.

Significance testing determines whether observed differences across customer segments are real or are just due to chance factors. These tests include *t*-tests and analysis of variance (ANOVA). For example, satisfaction scores are compared across regions, and these differences can be tested to determine their strength and reliability. Differences that are real should be examined further to identify the underlying reasons driving those differences.

It is important to determine whether the adoption of business processes has, in fact, led to increases in customer satisfaction. The company can use customer satisfaction indices to identify where customer satisfaction has improved. This goal is accomplished by examining customer satisfaction before and after the new processes have been implemented and noting any differences.

TRACKING CUSTOMER SATISFACTION OVER TIME

Average scores can be used to track changes in customer satisfaction over time. For example, once areas needing improvement are identified, action plans are developed and implemented to address these areas. Customer satisfaction scores can then be monitored over time to see if improvements are occurring and to determine the effectiveness of that action plan.

Trend charts are used for examining customers' ratings over a given time period. While different summary metrics can be used (for example, top box, bottom box), companies often use the average response of the question for their trend charts. These charts can help divisional managers keep track of their division's performance and help them understand the impact of organizational programs designed to impact change. At the executive level, trend charts help executive management keep track of their organizational goals.

COMMUNICATING RESULTS INTERNALLY

Improvement in performance rests on employee knowledge of current levels of performance. It is not surprising, then, that communication of customer feedback results to the entire company had the largest impact on a company's customer loyalty score. After the feedback data are summarized, they are distributed in a variety of ways to a wide range of employee groups:

- Senior executives receive results in quarterly review meetings
- Standard reports include overall high-level results
- Standard results appear along with other corporate results
- Board meeting/annual report includes section on customer feedback results
- Articles on CFP and results appear in the company newsletter or employee portal site
- Discussions in regular departmental meetings for customer-facing functions include reports on customer feedback

Distribution of the customer feedback results occurs across a variety of organizational departments and levels:

- Senior leadership/Executives
- Account/Sales senior managers
- Account/Sales teams
- Customer service/Order process managers
- Manufacturing/Operations
- Product management
- Strategic planning
- Technical support/Installation managers

Feedback targeted to specific employee groups needs to be tailored to the target group's specific information needs. Senior-level executives need to understand the state of the customers at a high level. This 30,000-foot view of customers' attitudes is best accomplished using the macro approach mentioned earlier. Also, at the executive level, results need to be conveyed that encourage comprehensive understanding of the customer landscape without resulting in information overload. Summarizing the customer feedback results regarding overall company performance can be accomplished by using summary indices (for example, scores that are the result of aggregating similar items). Presenting customer feedback results using customer indices is an effective and efficient way of presenting the results without loss of important information.

Frontline employees who interact with customers should receive more detailed results about their or their department's performance. The micro approach to reporting that was mentioned earlier is an effective way of presenting specific, detailed feedback necessary for performance improvement.

COMMUNICATING RESULTS EXTERNALLY

How are results communicated to customers?

- Program results are mentioned in general marketing communications

- Customers are informed of product and/or process improvement plans

- Individual customers are informed of planned action in response to results

How are results communicated to a larger community?

- Formal customer satisfaction conferences for customer feedback professionals

- Company's user groups
- Thought-leader events

WEB-BASED REPORTING TOOLS

The use of Web-based reporting tools provides many advantages to an organization. First, this method allows the organization to standardize the information that is delivered to all employees. With a Web-based delivery tool, the company can easily push consistent information across the entire organization, even in companies with multiple worldwide locations.

Additionally, in conjunction with the use of Web-based surveys for collecting customer feedback (another best practice), Web-based reporting tools provide up-to-date, live customer feedback results. With the use of both Web-based surveys and reporting tools, customer feedback reports contain timely results on which an organization can act to address time-sensitive customer issues.

Also, the Web-based reporting tools house all the verbatim comments made by the customers and provide quick access to this information by all employees. Finally, a Web-based reporting tool can include security features that allow only certain employee segments to view specific customer responses and prevent other employees from accessing customer responses.

Web-based reporting tools allow organizations to seamlessly integrate customer feedback reporting processes with other information systems, such as their CRM systems. Integrating customer attitudinal data with objective customer information (for example, marketing, sales, and service data) provides the organization a comprehensive picture of the quality of the customer relationship.

As was indicated in Chapter 4, the concurrent use of attitudinal data and objective data helps the company form a business strategy that is analogous to a CEM (customer experience management) approach. The CEM approach allows the company to understand how the perceptions, attitudes, and feelings of customers are related to their behaviors. Studying these types of linkages helps the company illustrate the relationship between the customer experience and customer loyalty.

SUMMARY

Simply conducting a customer survey is not sufficient to ensure success of the program. Analyzing, summarizing, and disseminating the customer feedback results are essential components into providing insight into the customer feedback data. Two general approaches to using the data in loyalty management were presented and reflect ways a company can improve customer loyalty at the individual customer level as well as at the company-wide level. The customer loyalty matrix provides direction into where the senior executives can make investments (in time and resources) if they want to improve customer loyalty (or maintain the loyalty currently experienced). Table 7.5 contains the best practices in reporting methods.

Figure 7.9 illustrates the operational processes of the CFP. From survey development to reporting, this figure places the content from the previous chapters in context to help you understand the complete picture of the operational steps needed to conduct a customer survey. The next chapter presents the findings regarding the types of applied research that can be conducted using customer feedback results.

While reporting of the customer feedback results did not greatly impact the success of CFPs, disseminating customer feedback results in specific ways will help improve the satisfaction with which the CFP helps in the management of customer relationships.

Table 7.5. Summary of reporting-related CFP best practices.

Best practice	Important points
Present customer feedback results throughout the company	• Build customer feedback portal on company's intranet site • Publish results in company newsletters
Present customer research results externally	• Attend thought-leader groups, user group forums, and professional associations • Research reflects company's deep understanding of its customers • Brands the company as customer-centric
Use Web-based tools to report customer feedback results	• Standardizes customer feedback reports • Coupled with Web-based surveys, reports contain timely results • Reports can be updated (and disseminated) quickly and efficiently
Share customer feedback results throughout the company	• Facilitates customer-centric culture • Keeps all employees focused on company's customer-centric goals
Benchmark customer feedback results against competitors and industry averages	• Helps executives understand competitive landscape • Helps identify best practices inside and outside the company's industry
Employ micro and macro reporting of results	• Improvement occurs at the individual customer level as well as at company-wide level
Use indices to summarize customer feedback results for macro reporting	• Indices are more reliable than single items • Helps in identifying organization-wide improvement opportunities • Account management will benefit
Use items to report customer feedback results to responsible parties	• Items provide detailed feedback for specific customer respondents

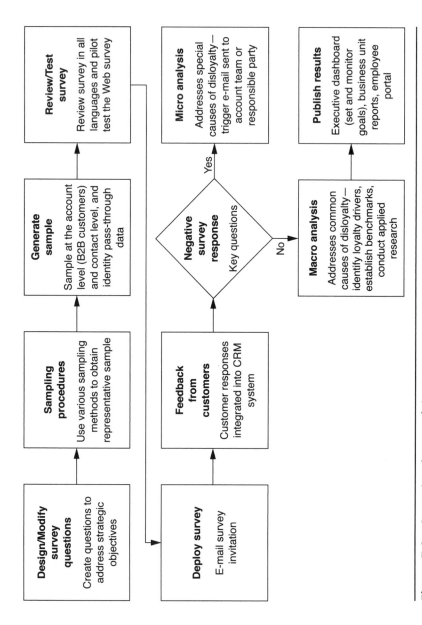

Figure 7.9 Operational steps of the CFP.

Companies regularly gather customer feedback to improve their customer loyalty and financial performance. Thousands of customers are surveyed annually in an attempt to better understand what determines their loyalty. However, little or no improvements are seen in their loyalty scores, and the company's financial metrics remain flat. Why?

The answers may be in how companies use their survey data. While companies use automated reporting tools (for example, online reporting sites) to help summarize and disseminate customer feedback results, these tools provide only a glimpse into the vast amount of information contained in the customer data. Analysis of customer feedback data can go well beyond descriptive statistics and driver analysis. The next chapter presents the results of best practices around the use of customer feedback data in customer research.

8

Applied Research

ADOPTION RATES FOR RESEARCH-RELATED BUSINESS PRACTICES

Customer-focused research using customer feedback data can provide additional insight into the needs of the customer base and increase the overall value of the CFP. Understanding the impact of this in-depth research on the effectiveness of the CFP can help companies appreciate the extent of information that can be extracted from the customer feedback data beyond what is found using simple reporting tools.

Examining the adoption rates of research-related practices between Loyalty Leaders and Loyalty Laggers, we see that Loyalty Leaders do, in fact, have a higher adoption rate of research practices than Loyalty Laggers. The comparisons appear in Figure 8.1.

Generally, the adoption of an applied research practice distinguishes Loyalty Leaders (80% adoption rate) from Laggers (63% adoption rate). It appears that the in-depth applied customer research helps Loyalty Leaders gain insight that helps them improve their customer relationships and, consequently, customer loyalty.

Additionally, the survey results show that Loyalty Leaders adopted specific applied research practices to a greater degree

Research-related business practice	Adoption rates		
	Loyalty Leaders	Loyalty Laggers	Loyalty unknown
Existing information from customer databases is used to help segment customer feedback data	**91%**	75%	65%
Statistical relationships are established between customer feedback data and business metrics (e.g., revenue, margin)	**75%**	50%	36%
Statistical relationships are established between customer feedback data and operational metrics (e.g., turnaround time, hold time)	**92%**	38%	36%
Statistical relationships are established between customer feedback data and other constituency metrics (e.g., employee satisfaction or partner satisfaction metrics)	**64%**	30%	33%
Applied research using customer feedback data is regularly conducted	**80%**	64%	24%

Figure 8.1 Adoption rates of research-related CFP business practices for Loyalty Leaders and Loyalty Laggers.

than Loyalty Laggers. Linkage analysis (the process of merging customer feedback data with other data sources, such as employee satisfaction, operational metrics, and financial metrics) is a very popular practice among Loyalty Leaders. Specifically, about 92% of Loyalty Leaders, compared to only 39% of Loyalty Laggers, have established a statistical relationship between customer feedback data and operational metrics (for example, turnaround time, hold time). The same pattern emerges when considering statistical relationships of customer feedback with other data sources: constituency metrics (63% vs. 30% adoption rate) and financial metrics (75% vs. 50% adoption rate).

RESEARCH-RELATED CFP BUSINESS PRACTICES THAT IMPACT CUSTOMER LOYALTY AND SATISFACTION WITH THE CFP

The next set of analyses was focused on quantifying the impact of the research-related CFP business practices on customer loyalty and satisfaction with the CFP. The results (see Figures 8.2 and 8.3) show that certain business practices had a substantial impact on these two key outcome variables.

The survey results show that research-related business practices of CFPs had a substantial impact on customer loyalty scores. Specifically, companies that conduct customer-centric research (for example, linking customer feedback data with operational metrics) had higher customer loyalty scores (percentile ranking of 72) than companies that do not conduct customer-centric research (percentile ranking of 50). Companies that regularly conduct applied research using customer feedback data had higher customer loyalty scores (68%) than companies that do not regularly conduct this type of research (57%).

The survey results show that research-related business practices of CFPs had a substantial impact on the satisfaction with the CFP in helping manage customer relationships. This finding is robust across nearly all the research-related practices that were studied. The practices of customer segmentation analysis, regularly conducted research, and linkage analyses all resulted in higher satisfaction with the management of the customer relationship.

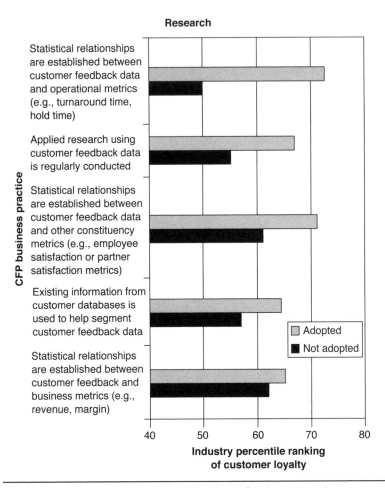

Figure 8.2   Impact of research-related CFP business practices on customer loyalty.

Applied customer feedback research extends well beyond the typical reporting of customer feedback results. Rather than simply reporting averages, top box results, driver analyses, and other basic statistics, customer feedback professionals can conduct in-depth research in order to mine insights that help the business better understand customer needs. Digging deeper into the causes of customer satisfaction/loyalty helps the company identify ways to improve these areas. While basic

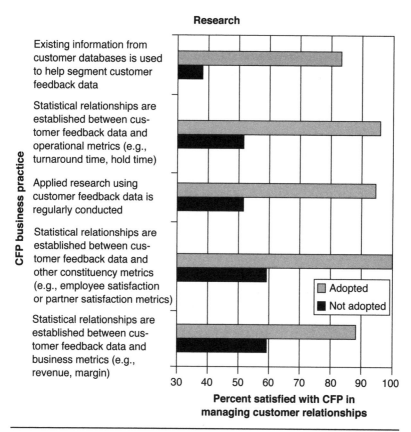

Figure 8.3 Impact of research-related CFP business practices on satisfaction with CFP in managing customer relationships.

statistics provide a useful summary of the customer feedback results, in-depth research extracts additional information from the customer feedback data, allowing companies to maximize the value of their CFPs.

REGULARLY CONDUCTED APPLIED RESEARCH

Companies that regularly conduct applied research using their customer feedback data had higher customer loyalty scores and were more satisfied with their CFPs than companies that do not regularly conduct applied research. Applied customer research can take many forms, yet the primary goal for conducting the research is to improve the customer experience to maximize customer loyalty. Applied research can help the company develop a deeper understanding of the customer relationship, enhance a customer-centric culture, ensure the business incorporates customer-centric metrics, and maximize the value of the CFP.

Applied research can be driven by corporate directives as well as CFP professionals who have access to the data and who might have hypotheses they would like to validate with the customer feedback data. In either case, the outcome of the research provides additional information that would not ordinarily have been obtained through basic reporting of the data. Applied research can take many forms. Examples include, but are not limited to, the following:

- An understanding of the impact of company-wide programs (for example, new business processes) on customer satisfaction

- Development of reliable metrics for a high-level corporate view of the customer experience

- Linkage analysis to identify operational metrics that are related to customer satisfaction

- Linkage analysis to quantify impact of improvements in satisfaction/loyalty on financial metrics

- Linkage analysis to identify employee- and partner-related variables (for example, training, satisfaction, loyalty) that are related to customer satisfaction

Microsoft

Business growth and financial success are never accomplished by accident. Microsoft's continued growth over the past 30 years has been guided by a dedication to technology coupled with a commitment to its customers and partners. Microsoft's feedback program allows it to conduct in-depth customer-centric research to better understand its customers' and partners' needs. This research provides deep insights that allow Microsoft to deliver the right solutions to its customers and partners.

Doug Doyle, director of market research, says, "Our fundamental approach to long-term growth relies on meeting the needs of our customers and partners. How do we get there? By making investments in the right opportunities, by delivering innovative products and services, by creating opportunities for the 700,000+ partners who work with us, and by improving customer satisfaction. Core to this is getting constructive feedback on whether we're on the right track in our efforts to improve customer satisfaction. Our research program is designed to do just that: to elicit feedback from all types of customers and partners on what they see us doing well, as well as identifying ways we can improve. That input becomes the foundation for all that we do."

VALIDATING THE CUSTOMER SURVEY PROGRAM

Validating the customer survey program should be the first research conducted on any survey program. Survey validation efforts are designed to provide an objective assessment of the quality of the program to ensure survey results reflect reliable, valid, and useful customer feedback. Because customer feedback can be used in making business decisions, survey results that are reliable and valid result in excellent business decisions. These business decisions include, but are not limited to, the following:

- Compensating employees

- Allocating company resources

- Changing business processes

- Benchmarking best practices

- Developing training programs

The use of customer survey data allows organizations to make business decisions that are customer-centric. A validation study of the survey program builds confidence that such decisions lead to improved customer loyalty and business success.

VALIDATION PROJECT DESCRIPTION

The procedure for validating the CFP consists of two general areas: (1) review documentation and (2) conduct statistical analyses on existing data.

Review of Documentation on Survey Process

First, the company needs to obtain and review all documentation that outlines implementation of the survey program(s). The goal of reviewing the survey process documentation is to understand the various elements of the process:

- How survey questions were developed

- How customers are sampled

- How data are reported and disseminated

This review is critical, as the method and procedure of data collection have a substantial impact on the quality of the data that stem from the survey process. Best practices in these three areas were reviewed in the previous chapters.

Statistical Analysis of Customer Survey Data

The second area in a validation study is to analyze existing data from the customer survey to understand the quality of scores that result from this survey process. The extent of analyses performed on the survey data will depend, in part, on the survey questions and the number of surveys being conducted. Generally, the statistical analyses focus on calculating indices that support the reliability and validity of survey programs.

Two general areas of survey quality will be addressed: reliability and validity. *Reliability* reflects the degree to which scores are free from random error and typically deals with measurement precision/consistency. *Validity* refers to the degree to which the scores measure what they are designed to measure and typically deals with the meaning of scores from the measurement system. These two areas, along with their meanings, are outlined here.

Reliability

1. Inter-rater reliability: Degree of agreement between two or more customers who are rating the same attribute

2. Test-retest reliability: Degree of agreement between the same measure/customer over two time periods

3. Internal consistency reliability: Degree of customer's consistency of ratings across survey questions within a measure

Validity

1. Content-related validity: Examining the customer survey questions to determine if they are a representative sample of the universe of all possible questions that could be asked of customers

2. Criterion-related validity: Correlating scores from the customer survey with other criteria (for example, objective measures of account quality)

3. Construct-related validity: Determining the relationship among key survey variables from the customer survey that support a theory of customer satisfaction

The ultimate goal of the preceding analysis is to provide qualitative and quantitative evidence that the customer survey is delivering precise, consistent, and meaningful scores regarding customers' attitudes about their relationship with the company. The extent of the statistical analyses depends on the quality and type of the survey data provided. Typically, the following types of analyses are conducted:

Reliability

1. *Inter-contact reliability:* The correlation (Pearson correlation coefficient) among different contacts within accounts can be calculated to identify the degree of agreement among respondents from different levels of the organization (for example, executive vs. director, director vs. manager) as well as different functions (for example, information technology [IT] vs. sales/marketing, finance vs. research and development [R&D]). There should be some degree of agreement among different constituencies within a given account but not so high as to be totally redundant. The purpose of surveying different constituencies from the same account is to obtain a comprehensive picture of account quality. We expect that there will be some differences in customer ratings depending on the role and/or level of the respondent. This analysis will essentially tell us the value of surveying different types of respondents within a given account.

2. *Test-retest reliability:* Test-retest reliability requires, at least, two time periods of survey administration across the same respondent group. The correlation (Pearson correlation coefficient) across the same respondent (or account, averaging across all respondents within accounts) will be calculated. There should be a good level of test-retest reliability because customer satis-

faction ratings should be consistent over time within an account. Customers who are very dissatisfied at time 1 will likely be dissatisfied at time 2; conversely, customers who are very satisfied at time 1 will likely be satisfied at time 2. The degree to which the rank order of customers (on satisfaction ratings) differs from time 1 to time 2, the test-retest reliability indices will be decreased.

3. *Internal consistency reliability:* Cronbach's alpha estimate can be used to gauge the degree of internal consistency of questions used in a summated scale; a *summated scale* is a score based on the sum or average of two or more questions. *Cronbach's alpha estimate* is a standard index used in psychological research that indicates the degree to which the questions in a summated scale measure the same thing (underlying construct). Summated scales should reflect a single concept (for example, technical support quality, consulting services quality). Summated scales are very useful for executive dashboards because a smaller number of variables can be used without having to present the results of each individual question. Minimizing the number of variables needing to be presented in an executive dashboard while not losing information allows the company to maximize the reporting efficiency of the CFP results.

Validity

1. *Content-related validity:* No single index is used to establish the content validity of a given survey process. Content validity is established when the questions in the customer survey are a representative sample of the important content domain of interest. The *important content domain* is the possible questions that could have been asked of the respondents. Two methods can be employed to understand the content-related validity

of the customer survey. First, the process by which the survey questions were generated can be reviewed. The review process would necessarily include documentation of the development of the survey questions. Survey questions could be generated from subject matter experts and/or actual customers themselves. Second, a random sample of open-ended comments from respondents can be reviewed and summarized to determine the general content of these verbatim comments. These general content areas will be compared with existing quantitative survey questions to discern the overlap between the two. The degree to which customers' verbatim comments match the content of the quantitative survey questions indicates some level of content validity.

2. *Criterion-related validity:* The relationship between survey ratings and some external criteria (not measured through the customer survey) is calculated to provide evidence of criterion-related validity. This relationship is typically indexed using the Pearson correlation coefficient, but other methods for establishing this form of validity can be used. For example, we can compare survey ratings across two *knowingly different groups* that should result in different satisfaction ratings. Specifically, satisfaction ratings should be distinguished across different "service warranty levels" and "account size." The different treatment of various customer groups should lead to different customer satisfaction results. In these types of comparisons, the ANOVA will be employed on the data. The ANOVA allows us to determine if the observed differences across the customer segments are due to chance factors or are real and meaningful.

3. *Construct-related validity:* Construct validity is usually considered the ultimate form of validity. All previ-

ously outlined methods are used to provide evidence of construct validity. The questions in the survey should be representative of all possible questions that could be asked (content-related validity), and survey ratings should be related to important criteria (criterion-related validity). The goal of construct-related validity is to show that the survey is measuring what it was designed to measure. Theoretical models are implicitly used to embed the constructs being measured (for example, satisfaction, loyalty) into a framework. In customer satisfaction research, it is widely accepted that customer satisfaction is a precursor to customer loyalty. Consequently, we can calculate the relationship (via Pearson correlation coefficient) between satisfaction ratings and measures of customer loyalty questions (for example, overall satisfaction, likelihood to recommend).

DEMONSTRATING THE IMPACT ON FINANCIALS

To grow additional support for the CFP and demonstrate the positive impact of nurturing customer relationships, Oracle illustrated the value of improving customer loyalty on the bottom line. Toward that end, Oracle examined the statistical relationship between customer loyalty and key measures of financial performance—such as license revenue, maintenance renewals, and maintenance cancellation rates—across customer segments. Results showed that customer loyalty was correlated with financial performance (see Figure 8.4). Specifically, customers with higher customer loyalty ratings had higher license revenues, higher maintenance renewal levels, and lower cancellation rates.

For confidentiality purposes, the customer segments have been generalized and loyalty identifiers have been removed.

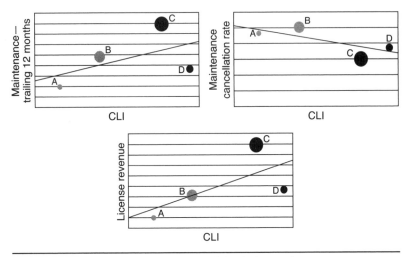

Figure 8.4   A general illustration of the linkages between customer loyalty and three key financial measures.

Examples of customer segments include account, account type, account size, geography, product line, and industry.

Each graph highlights three specific measures:

• Color: Identifies the loyalty level of the customer segment

• Size: Represents revenue of the customer segment

• Location: Intersection of the loyalty level and financial measure

CONDUCTING LINKAGE ANALYSIS

To conduct this linkage analysis, the attitudinal data were merged with the financial data. A general data model is illustrated in Figure 8.5. This model shows that, for each unit (in this case, a customer), we must have information about the attitude (for example, loyalty) and financial performance.

Financial linkages help establish the economic benefits of a CFP and can help determine the return on investment of such a program. Additionally, supported by a real statistical linkage

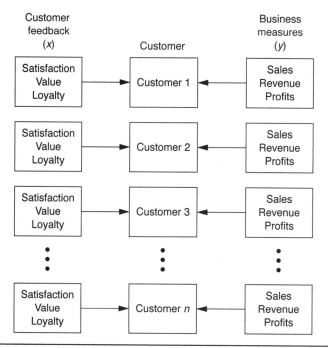

Figure 8.5 Illustration of the data model that links customer feedback (*x*) with business measures (*y*) at the customer level.

between customer feedback metrics and financial metrics, the use of customer feedback surveys reflects a valuable and practical means by which a company can improve its financial standing. The establishment of a linkage between customer feedback data and financial business metrics appears to have a lesser impact on customer loyalty scores compared to its impact on the satisfaction with the CFP in helping managing customer relationships.

Following are some guidelines around the linkage between customer feedback metrics and financial metrics:

1. *Use a variety of customer satisfaction and loyalty metrics.* Careful thought should be taken when uncovering relationships between customer satisfaction/loyalty metrics and financial metrics. For example, different customer loyalty metrics assess different expected future

customer behaviors. The three dimensions of customer loyalty—advocacy, purchasing, and retention—likely have different relationships to comparable business metrics (for example, new customer growth, sales rate, churn rate). We shouldn't expect that a single loyalty metric will be related to all financial metrics.

2. *Use reliable customer metrics.* The use of statistically reliable customer measures is better at uncovering relationships when these relationships truly exist. Using measures that are unreliable (those with a large degree of measurement error) could prevent you from finding real relationships between customer metrics and business metrics when they truly exist.

3. *Use different types of financial metrics.* A company's financial well-being is measured in a variety of ways. As suggested earlier, matching financial metrics to different components of customer loyalty may help companies identify alternate means of improving business growth through various ways of managing customer loyalty.

4. *Disseminate the essential results of the linkage studies.* As with other findings about the CFP, sharing the results of linkages with employees of the company can help support the benefit of the CFP on the bottom line. Only the fundamental findings of the study should be publicized; the results should not be bogged down by the complex analyses used to establish the relationships. The goal in the information is to show the benefits of the CFP.

LINKING CUSTOMER FEEDBACK DATA TO OPERATIONAL METRICS

Linking operational measures to customer feedback data appears to be a requisite element of an effective CFP. Linking customer feedback data to operational metrics has a bigger impact on improving customer loyalty and satisfaction with the CFP than linking customer feedback data to business metrics. Operational linkage analysis is typically conducted using results from a transactional survey. The ultimate goal is to identify operational metrics that are correlated with customer satisfaction/loyalty ratings. Demonstrating a statistical linkage between customer satisfaction and operational measures provides a company with insight into business processes that truly influence the customer experience. By identifying the operational metrics linked to customer attitudes, companies can use these metrics to manage customer satisfaction.

The general approach of linkage analysis is somewhat exploratory in nature. As an example, the concept of turnaround time can be defined in different ways: (1) the amount of time between when the technical support representative was dispatched and the problem was resolved, or (2) the amount of time between a customer's first service request and problem resolution. While a company may track many different operational measures in its call centers (for example, number of calls per service request, time between customer call and on-site arrival of technical support, number of times call is transferred, and time to answer call), linking operational metrics to customer feedback enables the company to understand which operational measures are related to customer satisfaction. Additionally, research that explores relationships of operational metrics to customer attitudes can help companies identify and/or create new operational measures related to customer satisfaction.

Operational Metrics and CRM

Executives implement various company-wide improvements in hopes that improvements in customer loyalty scores will follow. One common method for improving performance is goal setting. There is a plethora of research on the effectiveness of goal setting in improving performance. In the area of customer satisfaction, what typically occurs is that management sees that its customer loyalty score is 7.0 (on a 0–10 scale) at the start of the year and then sets a goal of 8.0 for the end of the fiscal year. What happens at the end of the year? The score remains about 7.0. While its intentions are good, management does not see the increases in loyalty scores that it set out to attain. What went wrong? How can this company effectively use goal setting to improve its customer loyalty scores?

A common problem with using customer loyalty scores as the metric to track or monitor improvements is that customer satisfaction/loyalty goals are still vague with respect to what the employees can actually do to impact satisfaction/loyalty scores. Instructing the technical support department to increase customer loyalty scores to 8.0 provides little direction in how employees can reach that score; there are multiple factors that drive customer loyalty, some of which are outside the direct control of the technical support staff. In fact, as we found earlier, employee incentive programs that use customer feedback results do not appear to improve customer loyalty or the satisfaction with CFPs.

Operational metrics linked to customer satisfaction can be helpful in managing customer relationships. Customer-centric operational metrics are a better metric with which to manage performance of frontline employees who interact directly with customers. The use of operational metrics in the employee incentive process would result in very specific and clearly defined behaviors/actions for employees. A goal stating, "Improve technical support availability by 1 point" does little to help employees focus their efforts, because there is no mention of a how to accomplish this goal. By using an operational metric that is linked to customer satisfaction, a more useful goal could be established: "Resolve customer issues in three or fewer contacts." This goal has a better chance of changing employees' behavior because it focuses the employees' attention on a specific behavior they can change. In fact, the use of operational metrics in setting goals for incentive programs satisfies four major tenets of goal setting:

1. *Specific.* Goals need to be specific and clearly define what behaviors/actions will be taken to achieve the goal and in what time frame or frequency these behaviors/ actions will take place. By their very nature, operational metrics are very specific and can be used to direct employees' energy toward achieving set goals.

2. *Measurable.* A measurement system needs to be in place to track/monitor progress toward the goal. The measurement system is used to determine whether the goal has been achieved and provides a feedback loop to the employees who are achieving the goal. Operational metrics are commonly tracked by the company's systems and are measurable in a straightforward manner.

3. *Difficult but attainable.* Research has shown that difficult goals lead to better performance compared to goals that are easy. A company's historical operational data can be used to determine the degree to which different goals are likely to be attained. Management can use this information to set and monitor goals accordingly.

4. *Relevant.* Goals for the employees should be appropriate for the employees' roles; can the employee impact the goal? Operational metrics have more face validity to the employees than customer feedback goals.

OPERATIONAL LINKAGES

Oracle regularly correlates operational data to survey results to identify internal key performance measures impacting the customer experience. "It is important to understand how the operational measures that we use to drive our business correlate to the satisfaction of our customers," says Jeb Dasteel, Oracle's senior vice president and chief customer officer. "Our studies have helped determine the areas of operational performance that are the key drivers of our customers' satisfaction. This has provided an opportunity to focus our improvement initiatives specifically on those areas that are of greatest importance to our customers."

Take, for example, a study around the support services experience. Oracle customers may ask for help in the form of service requests submitted via call centers or online. Oracle tracks both operational metrics and customer satisfaction metrics for each service request. Operational metrics include, but are not limited to, total time to resolve the service request (SR, defined as [close date – open date]), initial response time, and number of SR ownership changes. To keep all customer service employees focused on providing superior customer service, Oracle regularly surveys customers on their service request experiences.

Upon examining these operational metrics, Oracle found interesting results that helped it to better manage its customer relationships in the service request process. For example, using total time to resolve the SR, Oracle found that customers whose SRs were resolved more quickly were more satisfied than customers whose SRs took longer to resolve (see Figure 8.6). This study verified Oracle's use of this metric as a way of managing the customer relationship with respect to the SR process. Improving the SR process to reduce total time to resolution would lead to more satisfied customers.

Using initial response time to the SR, Oracle found that customers were no more satisfied or dissatisfied with their SRs whether the initial response time was fast or slow (see Figure 8.7). Despite the expectation that initial response time to the SR would greatly impact customers' satisfaction with the

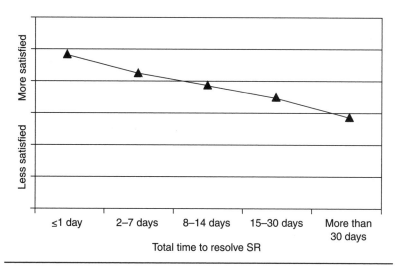

Figure 8.6 Relationship between total time to resolve SR and customer satisfaction with SR.

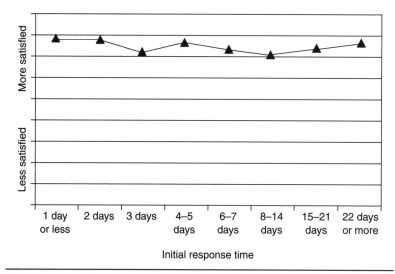

Figure 8.7 Relationship between initial response time and customer satisfaction with the SR.

SR, this study showed that it had no impact on the satisfaction of customers. Consequently, improving performance on this operational metric would have no direct impact on improving customer satisfaction with the SR.

Using number of ownership changes, Oracle found that customers whose SRs had fewer ownership changes were more satisfied than customers whose SRs had more ownership changes (see Figure 8.8). This study verified Oracle's use of this metric as a way of managing the customer relationship with respect to the SR process.

The use of applied research at Oracle has provided much insight regarding how the management of customers through the service request process can be facilitated with the use of operational metrics. The research findings show that operational metrics are predictive of customer satisfaction. Additionally, Oracle's research revealed that initial response time was unrelated to customer satisfaction, suggesting that monitoring metrics associated with that aspect of the process is unnec-

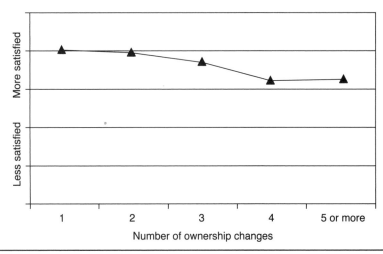

Figure 8.8   Relationship between number of ownership changes and customer satisfaction with the SR.

essary in improving customer satisfaction, and that customer-centric business process changes to the service request process are best directed at elements of the process that will impact the response time and the number of ownership changes.

LINKING CUSTOMER FEEDBACK DATA TO CONSTITUENCY ATTITUDES

Many factors drive the level of customer loyalty. As we saw in the business model in an earlier chapter, customer loyalty is impacted by employee and partner satisfaction. The satisfaction of these constituencies is crucial in the management of customer satisfaction and loyalty. Understanding which elements of employee and partner satisfaction impact customer satisfaction helps human resources allocate resources into employee programs that will not only impact employee morale but ultimately impact customer satisfaction.

Management, armed with this information, would be better able to allocate resources to help improve the employee and partner experience. The resulting increase in satisfaction of these constituencies would result in higher levels of employee retention and partner allegiance. Providing employees and partners the necessary tools and resources to improve their experience allows them to better serve the customers, thereby improving customer satisfaction and loyalty.

USING EXISTING CUSTOMER INFORMATION TO SEGMENT CUSTOMERS

Customer satisfaction and loyalty scores will vary across the customer base. Explaining why some customers are satisfied while others are dissatisfied helps companies better understand ways to improve customer loyalty. One way to identify reasons for the variability in satisfaction and loyalty scores is to

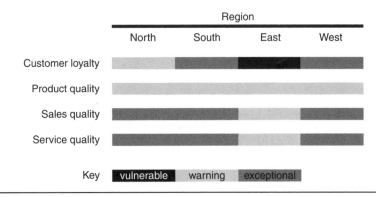

Figure 8.9   Segmentation of customer feedback results by region.

compare customers across different customer segments. Segmentation variables can include different types of customer information, such as location, products purchased, and service levels, to name a few.

Take, for example, the company that segments its customers according to region (see Figure 8.9). Within each segment, various customer feedback metrics are calculated and compared across each group. On the basis of this type of analysis, management might find that certain geographical regions show higher customer satisfaction and loyalty scores than other regions. This process can help the company identify and implement best practices across different customer groups.

EXAMPLES OF APPLIED RESEARCH

American Express Business Travel

Many businesses use a third party to assist in their business travel needs. American Express Business Travel, a global leader in business travel management, works with companies around the world to design and manage comprehensive travel programs that meet the business goals of these companies.

In existence for six years, the American Express Business Travel CFP measures the satisfaction of two major constituents: (1) the purchaser or the decision maker of travel booking services and (2) customers who make reservations. All customer feedback is collected via Web-based surveys. American Express Business Travel regularly conducts in-depth research that reflects its customer-centric position with respect to its operating principles. Top executives demonstrate the theme of customer centricity through their support of applied research. This support is expressed in the use of customer research in the decision-making process. The applied research helps the executives gain a deeper understanding of the customer and his or her needs and, consequently, drives the company toward a customer-centric culture. For example, before widespread corporate initiatives to improve business processes are adopted, executives want to know how the business process changes will impact customer satisfaction. This customer-focused value was demonstrated in one such business initiative that examined the booking process.

The booking process for travelers was a largely manual process for American Express' travel consultants. Specifically, when making travel arrangements for customers on the telephone, the travel consultants would manually enter much of the personal information for each caller. This likely increased the time to complete the reservation and, consequently, decreased customer satisfaction. To resolve this problem, American Express wanted to implement a new process in which the accounts would be transferred to a quality-check system where personal information would be added. A small-scale study was conducted to compare the manual process with the centralized quality-check finishing process. The results showed that customers who were routed to the centralized quality-check finishing system were significantly more satisfied than customers who were routed through the manual process. After management reviewed the study results, the new centralized quality-check system was implemented for all customer accounts.

Oracle

Oracle regularly conducts applied research using customer feedback data collected across the relationship, transactional, and targeted survey programs. This customer-centric research helps maximize the value of the CFP through in-depth satisfaction and loyalty research. Jeremy Whyte, director of customer feedback and reporting at Oracle, developed and continues to direct the research efforts at Oracle. He says, "Oracle continues to employ a comprehensive research program to unlock the potential of our existing customer survey data. Results provide us with superior customer insight necessary to accelerate business growth."

Areas of research interest that provide useful insight to Oracle extend across departmental lines as well as departmental levels. Applied customer research using customer feedback data impacts such areas as service, marketing, sales, product development, and human resources. Frontline employees as well as top-level executives are affected by the outcome of various research projects. Some notable areas of research include the following:

- Creating reliable, valid, and useful business metrics for executive dashboards

- Quantifying the impact of customer loyalty on business performance measures (for example, revenue growth, sales volume, defection rate)

- Identifying business areas that significantly impact customer loyalty

- Evaluating the effectiveness of company-wide programs

- Identifying the important elements of employee and partner satisfaction that will improve customer loyalty

- Determining customer satisfaction and loyalty criteria for incentive compensation programs

- Building customer-centric operational metrics to align employees

- Benchmarking best practices across the company
- Developing employee training programs that impact the customer experience
- Validating customer survey programs

The Customer Feedback & Reporting Team regularly conducts applied research to determine how specific variables impact customer satisfaction and loyalty. Thought-leadership research in the area of customer loyalty is jointly formulated with other internal organizations. This cross-organizational research strategy ensures that the research has a far-reaching impact across the entire company.

SUMMARY

Applied research helps companies gain superior customer insight through in-depth customer-centric research. This research extends well beyond the information that is gained from the typical reporting tools offered through survey vendors. Applied research can take the general form of linking operational metrics to customer feedback data. Additionally, research can take the form of linking other constituents' attitudinal data (for example, employee, partner) with customer feedback data. Companies that conduct this sort of in-depth research gain knowledge of how to better integrate customer feedback into daily processes. Table 8.1 summarizes the CFP best practices for research.

Companies can develop comprehensive research programs to help unlock the potential of their customer feedback data. They can maximize the value of their CFP by conducting in-depth satisfaction and loyalty research, ultimately gaining the superior customer insight that is necessary to accelerate business growth. Through research, companies transform themselves into customer-centric businesses.

Table 8.1   Summary of research-related CFP best practices.

Best practice	Important points
Validate customer survey process	• Ensure results from survey process are reliable, valid, and meaningful • Good measurement leads to better business decisions • One of the first research projects that needs to be conducted
Identify linkage between customer feedback and operational metrics	• Demonstrate that operational metrics are related to customer satisfaction • Use operational metrics to manage customer relationships • Operational metrics used in employee incentive programs
Regularly conduct applied customer-focused research	• Develop a comprehensive research program
Identify linkage between customer feedback and business metrics	• Illustrate that customer satisfaction and loyalty scores are statistically linked to financial metrics (e.g., profit, sales, revenue)
Identify linkage between customer feedback and other constituency's attitudes	• Identify factors of constituency attitudes that are linked to customer satisfaction/loyalty • Ensure proper management of employee and partner relationships to ensure customer loyalty
Segment customers using existing customer information in company databases	• Segment customers and compare satisfaction/loyalty among segments • Identify best practices internally among customer segments

9

Common Roadblocks to Increasing Customer Loyalty

As part of the CFP best practices study, CFP professionals were asked to identify the roadblocks to improving customer loyalty. Additionally, specific executives were interviewed in depth to understand the challenges they face in making improvements in their CFPs.

Over 100 respondents answered the open-ended question regarding their company's biggest roadblock to increasing customer loyalty. Similar items were grouped together using the five building blocks of CFPs. The roadblocks fell into the following four areas:

- Strategy/Governance (34 comments: lack of time, budget, top management not customer-centered, no solid commitment from executives)

- Process (15 comments: lack of integration with frontline tools, lack of complete view of customer, establishing a sound and simple process, maintaining program consistency)

- Reporting (13 comments: understanding what drives the satisfaction scores, knowing what they want and *when* they need to know it, lack of tools to analyze the third-party data and the ability to develop meaningful metrics, inability to develop meaningful metrics, need data to help us know how to improve)

- Method (10 comments: having enough data to analyze, data collection process is biased, incomplete root cause analysis for product performance complaints, insufficient/ inaccurate data from customer)

It appears roadblocks can be categorized using five of the six building blocks of CFPs outlined in Chapter 1: (1) strategy/ governance (cost/resources, top management), (2) reporting (lack of timely/actionable data), (3) method (survey/improvement process), and (4) process (IT/integration of customer information). The only area not mentioned as a roadblock is research. A summary of the types of roadblocks and their respective comments appear in Table 9.1.

Table 9.1 Roadblocks in CFPs to improving customer loyalty.

Category	Sample customer comments
Strategy/Governance	• CEO • Management not taking customer satisfaction seriously • Change in mentality in order to be able to focus on customer requirements • Focus on immediate revenue versus long term customer lifetime value • Cost of making changes and required process changes and impact on turn times • Resource availability to meet customer's demand • A solid commitment from executive leadership to actually focus on and take the "voice of the customer" into account. We claim to care about our customers, yet don't really understand what we should be doing to support them properly.

(Continued)

Table 9.1 Roadblocks in CFPs to improving customer loyalty. (Continued)

Business process integration	• Consistent and efficient use of technology and current systems • Integrated systems to tie all aspects of a customer together. • Consistent organizational processes for addressing customer feedback • Customer experience program and customer satisfaction feedback are new programs for the company and are still being integrated • Issue resolution to identified areas for improvement. • Minimal integration into organizational functioning; data are reviewed but then the process stops; nothing done with results other than looking at them; little connection made to how we might improve satisfaction and loyalty
Reporting	• Getting the right feedback; lack of computer program or software for analyzing customer feedback • Lack of tools to analyze the third party data and the ability to develop meaningful metrics • Know what they want, *when* we need to know it • Understanding real time customer needs • Getting timely responses and getting our own people over their defensive posture to truly change
Method	• Having enough data to analyze • Actually receiving honest feedback is our major roadblock • Getting honest opinions and genuine feedback • Incomplete root cause analysis for product performance complaints, due to insufficient/ inaccurate data from customer, and qualitative nature of responses

STRATEGY/GOVERNANCE

The most frequently mentioned roadblock was related to the cost/resources needed to run a CFP. The issues of cost and lack of resources were evident in a few ways. Respondents indicated that there is simply a lack of money in the budget to support the CFP (for example, "Budget—lack of allocating resources to comprehensive customer research," "Budgetary constraints"). Additionally, other respondents indicated that there is simply a lack of time to do the work needed to increase customer loyalty (for example, "Lack of time," "Time to do the things we know we should be doing").

Another governance-related roadblock to improving customer loyalty appears to be simply a matter of lack of top management support. When this was mentioned as a roadblock, respondents simply believed that management was more interested in financial matters (for example, "Focus on immediate revenue versus long term CLV") or simply just did not care about building a customer-centric culture (for example, "A solid commitment from executive leadership to actually focus on and take the 'voice of the customer' into account. We claim to care about our customers, yet don't really understand what we should be doing to support them properly," "Management not taking customer satisfaction seriously," and "Recognition of importance of customer feedback for contract renewal—by top levels of leadership").

These findings are in line with the earlier conclusion that governance-related activities are a key element in the success of CFPs.

BUSINESS PROCESS INTEGRATION (IT/ INTEGRATION OF CUSTOMER INFORMATION)

The next most frequently mentioned roadblock pertains to process-related issues of the CFP. The issues around process fell into two specific areas needing attention: (1) integration of customer feedback data into business systems and (2) use of the CFP in the improvement process. For example, respondents indicated that there are considerable IT limitations that hinder the effectiveness of their CFP; these include "Unavailability of a more powerful CRM tool," "Lack of integration with the front line tools," and "We don't make individual customer level customer satisfaction data available to our call center employees."

Additionally, beyond the IT limitations, there appears to be a problem with having a standard method for improving business processes, such as "Establishing sound and simple processes that work for a multitude of business units," "Clear action program," and "Issue resolution to identified areas for improvement."

REPORTING (LACK OF TIMELY/ACTIONABLE/CORRECT DATA)

Other major roadblocks to CFP success were related to the reporting process of the CFP data. Respondents indicated that the data did not provide timely/actionable/correct information that allowed for improvement of the business (for example, "Access to automated reports, for a business audience," "Getting actionable data. Instead of just knowing our performance, getting the data we need in order to learn how to improve, e.g., How fast is fast? What does it mean to be friendly? Responsive? Knowledgeable?" and "The authenticity of the data, the correct cross section of the population, etc., and the analysis of future scenarios").

Also, respondents indicated that the results of the CFP did not help them understand the customers' needs. Specifically, respondents said that roadblocks to improving customer loyalty revolved around "Understanding what drives the satisfaction/NP scores," "Understanding real-time customer needs," and "Knowing what they want, *when* we need to know it."

METHOD (SURVEY/ IMPROVEMENT PROCESS)

The next most commonly mentioned roadblocks reflect issues related to the method of how the customer feedback is collected. Some respondents indicated, for example, that there were too few responses to draw any substantive conclusions about their customer base (for example, "Low N," "Not having enough data to analyze," and "Actual feedback from about 25% of our customers").

Other respondents indicated that the customer feedback itself was not valid or was inaccurate. Specifically, comments around the validity of the survey method included, "Incomplete root cause analysis for product performance complaints, due to insufficient/inaccurate data from customer, and qualitative nature of responses" and "Actually receiving honest feedback is our major roadblock." While poor customer survey methods could be the roadblock in the path toward customer loyalty improvements, a company can verify if this really is the case. In particular, this methodological roadblock might simply be an excuse for poor survey results; employees receiving negative marks on their performance often point to deficiencies in the method by which the feedback was gathered. The excuses could be targeted at the survey questions themselves, the reporting of results, or the sample of customers who responded to the survey. To support the survey method, companies can conduct (and publish) a validation study of the survey process. Publicizing the rigor that goes into any survey program minimizes the potential for making excuses that could arise when the customer feedback does not match up with what the company expects.

SUMMARY

Companies report many types of problems that prevent them from improving customer loyalty. The results are in line with the quantitative results of the best practices study. The success of CFPs depends on multiple fronts. First, companies need the right strategy and governance model to guide the CFP and set an appropriate customer-centric tone throughout the company. Additionally, companies need to ensure that the CFP is embedded in daily business processes, from inclusion in the executive dashboard to integration with the company's existing CRM system/processes. Additionally, the ways in which customer feedback is collected and reported are important ingredients to the success of the program. Web-based customer surveys, which can be easily integrated into current business systems for tracking and reporting purposes, help companies collect customer feedback in a timely manner. Customer feedback reporting should occur at the aggregate level for system changes as well as at the individual respondent level for quick resolution for at-risk customers. While respondents did not specifically mention applied customer research as a primary roadblock to increasing customer loyalty, the quantitative analysis showed that the absence of applied customer research had a deleterious impact on the CFP.

PART IV

Customer Feedback Programs—Two Stories

10

Turning Data into Profit the Oracle Way: Using the Customer Experience to Drive Improvement and Growth

O racle Corporation is the world's largest business software company. Since its inception, Oracle has focused on innovation and results, and how it can benefit companies representing a variety of sizes around the globe to transform their businesses and achieve greater success. Oracle customers use Oracle technology, applications, and services to build information systems that help them retain the value of existing investments, stay competitive in the current economic climate, cut costs and improve security, make compliance easier, and manage complex upgrades with fewer risks. These complete, open, and integrated solutions enable customers to manage their business systems, information, and customer relationships with reliable, secure, and integrated technologies.

Customer centricity is a script that is supported from the top down, driving innovation on a daily basis. But innovation isn't enough. At the core of Oracle's approach is a focus on the best practices that allow the company to support its customers' success. Developing and implementing those best practices have led to strong growth for Oracle. Its global customer base is 320,000 and growing across all industries and company sizes. Revenues grew from $10.15 billion in 2004 to $22.4 billion in 2008, and the company's operating margin has grown from 14.4% to 35% on a GAAP basis and 43% on a non-GAAP basis[4] over the last 15 years. Oracle's IT infrastructure supports more than 85,000 internal users and 4 million external users, processes more than 1 million e-mails each day, and keeps oracle.com functioning through 200,000 daily page views.

"Oracle is one of the most proactive seekers of customer feedback in our industry," says Jeb Dasteel, Oracle's senior vice president and chief customer officer. "We've developed a coordinated set of customer-centric programs and created a company culture that is invested in nurturing customer success and long-term relationships. Our customers are truly at the heart of our vision."

It is this feedback that is used to drive product strategy and direction and is incorporated into day-to-day activities. The company focuses on giving its customers what they ask for—and on winning their loyalty in return. Oracle Applications Unlimited, Oracle Lifetime Support, Oracle Application Integration Architecture—all of these key Oracle strategies have their roots in the feedback collected and analyzed under Oracle's customer programs.

Oracle's forums and feedback programs (see Figure 10.1) look, in effect, like a pyramid. At the top are programs that involve participants from Oracle's largest enterprise customers—programs like key accounts; a CIO advisory board; and industry, product, and services strategy councils. At midtier are programs addressing a broader audience, such as focus groups and customer advisory boards. At the base and with the widest customer participation are user groups, special interest groups, and customer surveys.

[4] GAAP to non-GAAP reconciliations are available on the Oracle Investor Relations Web site at http://www.oracle.com/investor.

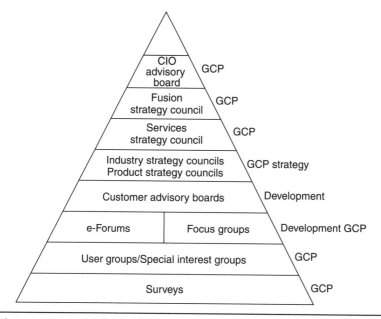

Figure 10.1 A graphical illustration of Oracle's forums and feedback programs.
Source: Web site at http://www.oracle.com/investor

"Our ultimate objective is to use customer feedback to continually improve and enhance our customers' experiences," says Dian Thompson, senior director, customer forums. "A superior ownership experience comes as a result of satisfying the most important expectations expressed by our customers across the ownership life cycle. Our customer forums and feedback programs are structured to allow us to continuously collect input across a broad spectrum of channels and to validate and communicate our customers' experiences and expectations to stakeholders throughout Oracle."

"Customer care and customer feedback intersect with customer strategy through constant dialogue," says Jeff Henley, Oracle chairman. This constant dialogue across the global customer base provides customers with a voice into how Oracle delivers its products and services. Through collaboration with customer care and services teams across all lines of businesses, Oracle identifies customer needs and uncovers the root causes of customer issues across geographies and industries. Customer-driven programs are then designed to address opportunities in a consistent manner throughout the company. This helps align Oracle's business operations and executive priorities with those of its customers and continually translate requirements into action.

This focus on the customer has resulted in measurable benefits:

- Customer satisfaction with Oracle has consistently been increasing each year over the past five years

- Customers are more likely than ever before to recommend Oracle and continue purchasing from Oracle

- Customers are receiving greater business value from their Oracle solutions

- Customer satisfaction with acquired products has been consistently increasing—most notably with PeopleSoft Enterprise, Siebel Business Applications, and JD Edwards Applications—which has led to continual increases in customer satisfaction with Oracle as a company

"The key to acquiring and cultivating long-term, highly profitable, customer relationships is understanding the evolution of the customer experience and upholding the customer lifetime value," says Cliff Godwin, senior vice president, Oracle Applications. "The Development organization leverages customer feedback received across multiple channels in a coordinated and consistent manner to pinpoint areas of concern from our customer base, implement action plans to improve customer satisfaction, and measure the success of our efforts."

This continual measurement, assessment, and refinement have led to focused investments in key areas, impacting the value that customers receive from their Oracle solutions. Customers are consistently satisfied with Oracle products meeting their business needs, and they enjoy the features, functionality, and reliability of the products. Standards-based architecture and enhanced integration capabilities across homogeneous and heterogeneous environments have been driven by customer needs to reduce total cost of ownership and optimize return on investment. Products are easier to use and easier to upgrade with each release, leading to improved efficiency and effectiveness and measurable benefits received.

Oracle's commitment to providing industry expertise and world-class products to its customers could not be stronger. Customers, partners, and analysts recognize the comprehensiveness and strength of Oracle products and services, all developed with the input of thousands of valued customers through customer advisory boards, surveys, online communities, and Oracle user groups. Every step of the way, Oracle's commitment to innovation is driven by its commitment to customer success.

BEST PRACTICE CUSTOMER PROGRAMS

Oracle's customer programs incorporate many industry-accepted best practices:

- Loyalty concepts included in strategic vision, mission, and goals
- CFPs integrated into business processes and technology
- Survey results tied to employee objectives and incentive compensation
- Loyalty metrics benchmarked against competitors and industry averages
- Survey data analyzed against financial metrics such as revenue and margins

- Linkage studies conducted between customer, partner, and employee data

- Survey results and research presented internally and externally

- Best practice studies and results presented at thought-leader events

- Structured, defined follow-up processes to resolve individual customer issues

CLOSED-LOOP FEEDBACK PROCESS

In its simplest form, Oracle uses a closed-loop process to collect and respond to customer feedback across customer segments, following three primary steps:

- Gathering, analyzing, and reporting customer feedback

- Defining, taking action on, and communicating critical themes and initiatives

- Tracking, monitoring, and trending results to quantify the effects of improvement programs

Listening and responding to customers promotes customer loyalty and forms the foundation for a solid reference program. Identifying issues at a macro level facilitates the prioritization of organization-wide business improvements, resource allocation, and the refinement of strategic action plans to ensure customer success with Oracle solutions. Similarly, at a micro level, Oracle employees are empowered to take immediate action to address individual customer concerns. Ideally, addressing customer concerns at the time of feedback ensures these at-risk customers do not defect. This sense of urgency toward unhappy customers creates a level of trust and transparency that sustains customer satisfaction and drives profitability.

GATHERING, ANALYZING, AND REPORTING CUSTOMER FEEDBACK

Customer feedback is collected across a variety of channels with the objective of providing customers with a voice into how Oracle delivers its products and services. These channels include the following:

- CIO advisory board and strategy councils

- Customer advisory boards, focus groups, user groups, special interest groups, and usability labs

- Proactive outreach programs and facilitation of feedback from one-to-one engagements

- Customer surveys, social media outlets, and other online communities

This multichannel approach provides customers with numerous avenues to voice ideas, highlight successes, and engage other customers to share common challenges and opportunities.

DEFINING, TAKING ACTION ON, AND COMMUNICATING THEMES AND INITIATIVES

While many companies collect feedback, few effectively prioritize customer issues and implement improvement programs. Oracle consolidates feedback from the preceding channels, analyzes it across different customer segments, and identifies key themes. Statistical analysis from survey programs enables prioritized actions to improve customer relationships, and root cause analysis helps identify underlying issues and business impact. This insight enables Oracle to engage all lines of business to define corrective actions that span the full customer life cycle. Results of those actions are then communicated to customers, helping ensure alignment with customer expectations while demonstrating that Oracle actually acts on the feedback received. This in turn deepens customer participation in future feedback forums and events, increases customer engagement with all Oracle organizations, and provides greater opportunities for customers to influence Oracle's product strategy and direction.

TRACKING, MONITORING, AND TRENDING RESULTS

Upon identifying key themes and communicating the Oracle response, Oracle repeats the collection of feedback. This recurring process allows Oracle to verify the effectiveness of the improvement programs as well as identify future opportunities for enhancement from those customers directly impacted.

OBTAINING INSIGHT THROUGH SURVEYS

The foundation of the voice of the customer program is the comprehensive survey program. Over 200,000 customer and partner survey responses—across executives, management, staff, and end users—are received annually. The input provided, combined with feedback from various customer forums and Oracle partners, creates an integrated program providing an enterprise-wide view of the customer experience that can be used to manage customer relationships across the life cycle.

A centralized measurement strategy is used across the company, with a primary organization led by senior vice president and chief customer officer Jeb Dasteel, who is responsible for overseeing and validating all customer and partner survey activity. This leads to increased alignment of the feedback program with company and line of business objectives while ensuring the right type of feedback is collected from the right contacts at the right time without oversurveying. To maximize both efficiency and effectiveness, a structured survey program featuring a portfolio of the following surveys is used:

- **Relationship survey:** Role-based survey designed to capture customer satisfaction consistently across products and services and identify loyalty drivers across cumulative contact experiences over the full ownership life cycle

- **Transactional survey:** Measures service quality of each organizational unit and triggers improvements to enhance operational effectiveness

- **Targeted survey:** Facilitates qualitative research, enables deep dives, and complements the relationship and transactional surveys

Surveys are complemented with the integration of business processes and Oracle solutions to provide 360-degree views of customer relationships, in addition to a comprehensive applied research program to quantify linkages between survey data and operational and financial data. This insight provides the information necessary to optimize customer loyalty to facilitate continued growth and maximize shareholder value. Figure 10.2 provides a graphical illustration of the global Oracle survey program.

It is well documented that optimizing customer loyalty has a direct and positive impact on a company's financial performance. However, customer loyalty depends on providing satisfaction not only to customers themselves—although this is critical—but also to those employees and partners who can impact, positively or negatively, the customer relationship. In an economy in which employee productivity and global alliances are essential to success, a customer loyalty strategy must embrace these three constituencies. Measuring satisfaction and performance in all three areas enables Oracle to understand which business attributes really drive customer loyalty, leading to the appropriate allocation of resources for the greatest customer retention. Effectively managing all three relationships is

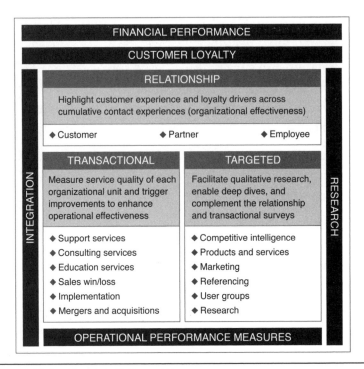

Figure 10.2 Oracle's CFP model.

the key to customer loyalty, competitive advantage, and financial stability.

Relationship Survey

From a customer-constituent perspective, Oracle uses the Global Relationship Survey to provide an enterprise-wide view of the customer by capturing specific, actionable, and relevant information around customer experiences with Oracle products and services across the full ownership life cycle. Conducted semiannually, the survey is role-based, ensuring content is targeted to a customer contact's interactions and experiences with Oracle. This approach provides a more holistic and accurate assessment of customer satisfaction across multiple levels of customer organizations at a single point in time. Armed with this information, Oracle account teams and management are empowered to take timely action to more effectively manage customers through their life cycles, optimize customer loyalty, and maximize CLV. Analysis is focused on identifying the drivers of customer loyalty across customer segments and combining those results with qualitative feedback provided through customer forums to drill into greater detail and establish root cause. This enables Oracle to prioritize focus areas and allocate resources to areas that have the greatest impact on customer satisfaction and loyalty. Results are linked to operational and financial data across account types, product lines, geographies, and industries, leading to greater insight and better business decisions that impact customer success and company growth.

Key objectives of the Global Relationship Survey reflect customer feedback best practices:

- Identify the drivers of customer loyalty across customer segments

- Ensure key loyalty issues within individual customers are addressed immediately

- Gain accurate and timely insight into the attitudes, preferences, and expectations of customers

- Notify appropriate employees to enable immediate action and resolution of customer satisfaction issues

- Provide 360-degree view of customer relationships and gain visibility into the strategies and tactics having the greatest impact on customer loyalty

- Tailor sales, marketing, and services programs to maximize loyalty

- Continually improve people, processes, products, and services

A structured, integrated, and closed-loop process is followed globally to increase consistency, efficiency, and alignment across geographies and lines of business. Business processes supporting the survey life cycle, including contact management, follow-up, and reporting, are integrated with Oracle applications and technology to streamline efforts and increase visibility for account team members across lines of business. Using the results from partner and employee relationship–based surveys, Oracle is able to track the variables across the entire ecosystem, which ultimately impacts the customer experience and the bottom line.

Transactional Surveys

Oracle uses a host of transactional surveys designed to capture customer satisfaction after a specific event or interaction has taken place. Results are used to drive improvements to enhance operational effectiveness across lines of business, leading to better customer experiences across a variety of touch points. Example transactional surveys are provided in Table 10.1.

Targeted Surveys

Targeted surveys enable Oracle to drill into a much more granular level of detail around specific topics or themes. The results of these surveys, which are conducted on an as-needed basis and sent to highly targeted audiences, expand upon feedback collected through the relationship and transactional surveys.

Oracle works with the global user group community to conduct joint targeted surveys, increase customer engagement, and share successes. "Oracle has the largest independent user groups community in the world," says Jeb Dasteel. "There are more than 420 officially organized groups with more than 200,000 members participating worldwide. Although not organized or directed by Oracle, these groups are given a great deal

Table 10.1 Transactional surveys at Oracle.

Transactional survey	Objective
Global Customer Support	Measures customer satisfaction with the support services experience after a service request has been closed.
Mergers and acquisitions	Measures satisfaction of customers of companies Oracle acquires, who are surveyed immediately after legal entity combination. Establishes a baseline, facilitates benchmarking across customer segments and acquired companies, provides an early warning system for at-risk customers, and enables future trending through standard Oracle relationship and transactional surveys.
Oracle University	Measures customer satisfaction with the quality of training provided by Oracle University instructors upon course completion.

of attention and support by the company. No matter the size, industry, product interests, or geography of a customer's company, there is a way for the customer to have a voice in what Oracle does next and a way for them to learn from other customers with like challenges and opportunities."

Transactional, and oftentimes targeted, surveys provide an assessment on internal operational performance measures that impact the customer experience. "Through our research we know that transactional results are lagging indicators of internal operational performance measures and leading indicators of customer satisfaction across the lifecycle as measured through the Global Relationship Survey," says Jeremy Whyte. "While customer loyalty is the outcome variable we are trying to optimize, loyalty is multi-dimensional. A superior ownership experience is derived from numerous, inter-related interactions and experiences across multiple touch points spanning the customer lifecycle. It is only by properly understanding these inter-relationships as measured through our relationship, transactional and targeted surveys, combined with linkages to operational and financial metrics, that enables Oracle to make the right prioritized business decisions to drive growth and enhanced financial performance while improving the customer experience."

INTEGRATION

The Global Relationship Survey and core transactional surveys are fully integrated with Oracle applications and technology. Using the best-in-class solutions provided by Oracle in the marketplace, Oracle employees can identify survey contacts, view survey responses, track and manage follow-up, and view results through Oracle Customer Relationship Management (CRM) and Business Intelligence (BI)/Analytics solutions. The attitudinal data collected through the surveys, combined with the behavioral data stored in the CRM system, provide a 360-degree view of the customer to those employees empowered to take action. Employees leverage the CRM system to efficiently manage all phases of the survey life cycles, while the program office realizes significant gains in scalability and reach. The additional integration of both survey and CRM data in the business intelligence systems enables Oracle to instantly link survey data with operational and financial data directly on the dashboards that executives use to drive the business and that frontline employees use to manage customer relationships.

RESEARCH

To gain superior customer insight necessary to accelerate business growth, Oracle regularly links customer feedback results to operational data (for example, resolution time and severity) and financial data (for example, license revenue and maintenance revenue). This allows the company to understand the relationships among organizational variables, leading to better business decisions while growing support for the CFP throughout the company. This interorganizational research strategy ensures that customer feedback has a far-reaching impact across the entire company, leading to more targeted and prioritized actions that will have the greatest impact on increasing loyalty in the shortest time. Examples of applied research conducted at Oracle were highlighted in Chapter 8.

APPLIED RESEARCH

To help translate the insight provided across the various survey programs into action, Oracle conducted a series of studies to examine the factors impacting customer loyalty across customer segments and over time periods. Based on the results of those studies, a model was created to highlight the primary components impacting customer perceptions of value and loyalty. In its simplest form there are three primary components impacting the perceived value customers receive from their Oracle solution: products, services, and relationships. Customer satisfaction with each of these components influences the perceived value, which in turn impacts their loyalty to Oracle and post-purchase behavior.

Figure 10.3 illustrates Oracle's service value model. The model is focused on external service value and modified from the service delivery model documented in *The Service Profit Chain* (Heskett, Sasser, and Schlesinger 1997).

Providing customers with a superior ownership experience is achieved through all interactions with Oracle, whether it's with the company's products, services, or people. This experience spans the entire ownership life cycle—from the time customers become aware of Oracle products and services, through

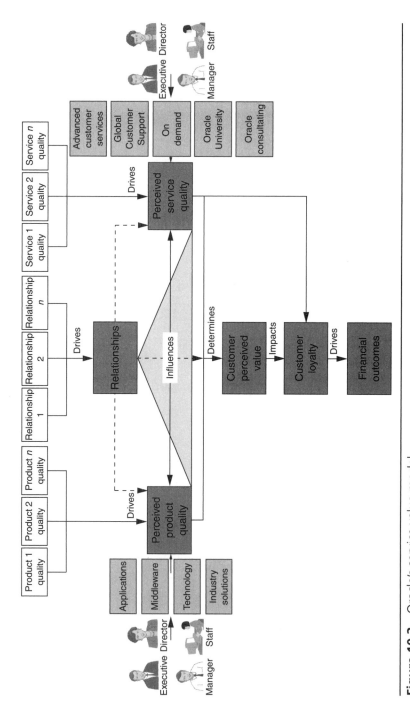

Figure 10.3 Oracle's service value model.

Source: Modified from Heskett, Sasser, and Schlesinger (1997).

the evaluation process, and the completed implementation. It continues into the longer-term relationships that follow, as customers enhance and expand their use of Oracle solutions. Following are details of each component:

- **Products:** The perception of product quality is driven by many factors and varies by job level and job role. Management and staff in the IT function refer to key measures such as products meet business needs, features and functionality, performance, scalability, reliability, upgrading, and integration. Executives generally focus on improvements in efficiency and effectiveness, flexibility to meet industry-specific needs, return on investment, and return on asset.

- **Services:** Oracle services help customers extract the most from their technology investments and span the full solution life cycle. These generally represent functional areas such as consulting, support, education, and partners. Within each of these areas is a series of core and unique measures designed to accurately understand customer experiences and attitudes while providing the ability to benchmark across organizations.

- **Relationships:** Relationships within customer organizations and across job roles and levels have proved to have a high impact on customer loyalty. Within any customer, multiple levels of employees are engaged and critical to the overall success of the implementation. While executives are the ultimate decision makers and fund solutions, the perceptions of their employees—directors, managers, staff, even partners—impact executive satisfaction and the perceived value received. As a result, the role-based information collected across the relationship, transactional, and targeted surveys is critical to properly understand expectations and the interrelationships across job roles and levels—and across surveys and time periods.

Research has validated that it is the combination of these three areas that impact the value customers receive from Oracle solutions. Contrary to longtime sales strategies used in the software industry, it is not just about product quality or support services; relationships are key and critical to nurturing customer success, referenceability, and loyalty. It is this combination of the formalized feedback strategy and a better understanding of customer value systems that led Oracle to create a unified approach to managing customer relationships, no matter how many points of contact a customer has in the company, and to bring the right expert resources to bear for customers at the right time, whether those customers are buying software, implementing it, maintaining it, or planning their technology road map. The programs are also designed to make sure that the company offers a consistent set of behaviors and responses across all customer accounts, all designed to make every customer successful—based on how the customer measures success. It's an approach that has little to do with product push and everything to do with creating and sustaining a strategic, mutually beneficial relationship.

Oracle tracks the interrelationships in the service value model across customer segments. This is especially true given that the company's growth has been driven both organically and through acquisitions. In the 48 months leading up to 2009, Oracle completed 54 acquisitions with the objective of finding innovation in the industries it thought could add value to customer environments and solve specific problems. Many of those opportunities were identified by customers and the voices they have in Oracle through the various feedback channels. Research shows that the flexibility to meet industry needs is a large driver of customer loyalty, and so Oracle continues to invest in broadening its solution set to increase operational efficiency and effectiveness for customers across a variety of industries. Several of the larger acquisitions in this time frame include PeopleSoft, JD Edwards, Siebel, Hyperion, and BEA. To a certain extent, Oracle is a company made up of many smaller companies. "As a result, it is critical that we have a comprehensive understanding of customer expectations and preferences across the customer base regardless of how the customer was acquired to ensure we can deliver the business value our customers expect, can continue expanding our product footprint and making our customers more successful, and continue growing in a highly consolidated industry," says Whyte.

The acquisition strategy has provided immense opportunities to gain greater insight into customer loyalty drivers—and value drivers—across the installed base. Research shows that customers have different value systems depending on how they became Oracle customers. For example, a legacy Oracle database or middleware customer has a completely different set of value drivers than a Siebel or JD Edwards customer. Database and middleware customers tend to be more focused on product satisfaction and functionality, while Siebel and JD Edwards customers tend to be more focused on overall relationships and customer-centric behavior. Furthermore, a customer gained from an acquisition may have a perception around existing Oracle product offerings. This enables Oracle's lines of businesses to modify sales, marketing, and services strategies in order to enhance customer success.

The service value model is applied holistically; it is not limited to a specific survey or channel for collecting feedback. As an example, data from the Global Relationship Survey and the Global Customer Support Survey were linked and a longitudinal study was conducted to quantify the impact of the support experience on the customer relationship. The results highlighted that a customer's experience, as measured through the Global Customer Support Survey, was a leading indicator of overall satisfaction across the customer life cycle, as measured through the Global Relationship Survey:

- A contact's individual support experience, as measured through the Global Customer Support Transactional Survey, directly impacted results for future Global Customer

Support surveys. When a contact had a positive experience, the contact was significantly more likely to provide higher ratings in future surveys.

- Those support experiences in turn impacted customer satisfaction, as measured through the Global Relationship Survey. Customers with more positive service request experiences were more satisfied with product quality, support services, and the value provided by Oracle solutions and had greater loyalty toward Oracle.

- The perceptions of that population, which is targeted toward management and staff, in turn directly impacted executive perceptions.

On the basis of this knowledge, resources were allocated to focus on providing consistently superior support experiences.

IMPROVING END-USER EXPERIENCE THROUGH USABILITY LABS

Research completed at Oracle has also shown that successful software implementations are dictated by the end users responsible for utilizing the software to complete daily activities. Ease of use, understanding of system capabilities, and the alignment of software and business processes all drive higher usage and approval of the software, which in turn impacts management and executive satisfaction.

To help discover and analyze how end users want and need to do their work, Oracle conducts usability studies across the world. This partnership with customers during the product design and development cycle exemplifies Oracle's belief that the customer experience matters. Every year, more than 200 customers participate in about 800 comprehensive sessions testing the usability of various applications, middleware, and database technologies. The result: improved user experience of Oracle products in a variety of spaces.

"We see our customers year round in our global usability labs," says Steven Miranda, senior vice president, applications development. "Our labs give our customers a hands-on experience with our products and enable us to collect real-world data. But more importantly, our labs provide an opportunity for us to build a relationship with our customers and convey to them how valuable their feedback is."

Technologies like Eye Tracking and Digital Recording of Usability Activities are used to collect detailed information about participant experiences using Oracle software. These usability studies enable Oracle to collect task-critical information, such as how long it takes users to complete certain tasks, how many errors typically occur during a task, how many times users request assistance in completing tasks, and the percentage of tasks that users are able to complete in a certain time frame.

The outcomes of these usability studies are communicated to the development and design teams through quick findings, presentations, and detailed reports. Development teams generate issue lists from this information and work with Oracle engineers to resolve problems and retest the improved designs until resolutions are found.

DELIVERING CUSTOMER SUCCESS THROUGH ACTION: AN EXAMPLE FROM ORACLE GLOBAL CUSTOMER SERVICES

The importance of providing superior service is well known in the enterprise software industry. Research efforts at Oracle have validated this guiding principle, and Oracle has directly engaged customers to influence future services strategy and direction. In an ongoing effort to make customer-driven enhancements, Oracle Customer Services leveraged customer feedback provided across a variety of channels to build a next-generation support portal.

To effectively achieve this, results from the Global Relationship Survey and the Global Customer Support Transactional

Survey were used to form a foundation. The Global Relationship Survey identified a need for greater breadth of services, a focus on delivering solutions, and better relationships with the support organization through increased contact and engagement. Results from the transactional survey highlighted service request handling, responsiveness, quicker resolutions, and enhanced online tools and services to make it easier to find information to either self-diagnose or assist with the resolution. With Oracle being a mixture of acquired companies, several support systems were in place before being migrated to a single system. So Oracle needed more information to find out exactly what customers wanted and what would be most effective to increase solution effectiveness and resolve service requests quicker. To achieve this, two targeted surveys were conducted with different audiences with the specific objective of drilling into more detail and identifying future requirements as stated by the customers themselves.

What customers communicated through the targeted surveys was consistent across industries and geographies:

- Proactive and predictive support to avoid system outages and disruptions

- Personalized service to detect, address, and resolve customer-specific issues quicker

- Embedded configuration management to automatically diagnose issues and enable faster, more accurate service request creation

- Greater access to online information via knowledge bases and communities to empower customers to resolve issues autonomously

- Increased search capabilities

Results from the surveys were combined with feedback received from strategy councils, customer advisory boards, user groups, and focus groups. Themes emerged and specific actions were taken to apply customer-driven enhancements. This led to the next-generation support portal, built from customer feedback and designed to enhance customer success, which included the following customer-driven enhancements:

- Embedded configuration management

- Extensive knowledge base and communities

- Extended preventive, automated support capabilities

- Personalized and proactive service

Releasing the next-generation My Oracle Support portal, built from customer requirements, had immediate tangible benefits:

- 25% of problems avoided

- 30% faster service request creation

- 40% faster resolution

- 97% of problems resolved quicker with targeted knowledge

As the Oracle service value model depicts, this should lead to improved satisfaction with individual support experiences, which in turn will yield improvements in customer satisfaction across the life cycle and increased loyalty to Oracle.

USING INSIGHT TO DRIVE ACTION

To embed the voice of the customer into the company's DNA and drive growth through customer-centric behavior, Oracle leverages guiding principles to manage its customer programs:

- Executive sponsorship

- Employee commitment

- Formalized strategy

- Defined governance model

- Demonstrated ability to evolve

- Embedded compensation structures

- Integrated business processes

- Detailed communication and education program

Executive sponsorship is critical to internalizing behavior across an organization. Oracle customer programs are run in partnership with Oracle executive management, which consists of stakeholders across lines of business and geographies. This collaboration ensures alignment of the program with company, organizational, and line of business objectives while operationalizing customer feedback into daily business practices. Executive management incorporates customer feedback into strategic action plans and allocates resources to the areas driving customer loyalty. This action addresses common causes of loyalty and disloyalty, focusing on improving systemic issues and organization-wide improvements over the long term.

At the same time, a bottom-up approach through committed employees helps internalize customer satisfaction within the company and demonstrates customer-centric behaviors across the installed base. This is achieved by getting key information into the hands of frontline employees, who can take timely action to address individual customer concerns. This in turn addresses special causes of disloyalty and focuses on changing individual issues and making customer-specific improvements in the short term.

Both macro and micro approaches impact customer loyalty, as Oracle is able to address specific customer concerns and improve the service delivery system. They also help reinforce a focus on the customer and a move toward being more customer-driven. With this support, Oracle is effective at embedding feedback into the corporate strategy, messaging, and communications.

Reinforcing the formalized strategy is a defined governance model. Executive management and line of business leaders incorporate customer feedback into strategic action plans and organizational objectives across all levels of their organizations. This helps ensure continual alignment with corporate strategy, further embedding the program across the company and using key customer metrics to guide critical business decisions.

CFPs, like corporate strategy, industry conditions, and economic outlooks, evolve over time. In order to keep customer feedback at the forefront of Oracle culture, the program continually evolves to align with company and market conditions. This evolution provides additional opportunities to further tie feedback to key company objectives across lines of business and geographies, thereby strengthening governance and increasing the value of the program—both internally and externally.

In order to solidify the transformation to customer-centric behavior, customer feedback is incorporated into compensation structures across the company. Key metrics, such as customer loyalty or results by functional or product area, are used to reinforce customer focus and drive desired behavior. This action achieves several objectives:

- Demonstrates a commitment to customer success from executive management

- Incentivizes employees to incorporate customer requirements into products and services

- Motivates employees to cultivate long-term strategic relationships with customers and focus on ongoing customer success

The integration of business processes with Oracle application functionality enables employees to view key customer information using the same applications they use on a daily basis. Role-based information provides employees across job levels with access to information in a timely manner. Account teams, customer care, support, and product marketing can share information seamlessly, thereby increasing coordination and presenting a unified image to the customer.

Business process integration further embeds customer feedback into daily business practices. Similarly, applied research studies are a quick and effective way of engaging employees by demonstrating the impact of customer satisfaction and loyalty on operational and financial metrics. Linking customer loyalty data to hard metrics further highlights the importance of listening and responding to the voice of the customer. By understanding customer requirements, expectations, and preferences, Oracle continually translates requirements and insight into action, communicates results of actions to ensure alignment with customer expectations, and aligns corporate strategy and operations with those of its customers.

SUMMARY

Oracle adheres to many of the best practices of CFPs. Executive support and communication of the program goals and the customer feedback results help Oracle embed the customer-centric culture throughout the company milieu. Oracle's use of customer feedback in executive dashboards and for setting strategic goals solidifies the importance of customers as a key business metric and keeps them customer-focused from the top. Sharing of the customer feedback results (as well as results of applied research) throughout the company helps Oracle ensure that all employees are aligned with top management's view regarding the importance of the customer in daily operations.

Additionally, applied customer-centric research helped Oracle gain superior customer insight. This research extends well beyond the information that is gained from the survey reporting tools offered through its survey vendors. Oracle's applied research takes the general form of linking customer feedback data to different types of customer variables, including operational metrics, constituents' attitudinal data (for example, employee, partner) and financial metrics. Oracle understands that this sort of in-depth research improves its knowledge of how to better integrate the customer feedback into daily business processes.

The combination of top executive support, the communication of program goals and results, and the development of a rigorously applied customer-centric research program are key ingredients to Oracle's successful CFP.

11

Development of a Customer Feedback Program: The Akamai Story

Akamai Technologies, Inc., provides market-leading managed services for powering rich media, dynamic transactions, and enterprise applications online. Akamai pioneered the content delivery market in 1998, and its services have been adopted by the world's most recognized brands across diverse industries such as retail and consumer goods, software and technology, media and entertainment, hotel and travel, financial services, and the public sector. The alternative to centralized Web infrastructure, Akamai's global network of tens of thousands of distributed servers provides the scale, reliability, insight, and performance for businesses to succeed online. One of the top 100 fastest-growing technology companies of 2007 and delivering between 10% and 20% of all Web traffic, Akamai achieved over $790 million in revenue in 2008 across its diverse product portfolio. Akamai's goal is to become a member of the elite billion dollar technology club.

As is illustrated in Figure 11.1, Akamai's success is based on three general pillars: technology, customers, and employees. Akamai views its accomplishments as the direct result of acquiring the right employees, focusing on technological innovation, and, most importantly, ensuring that the customers receive an exceptional experience in their interactions with

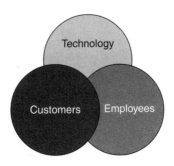

Figure 11.1 Akamai's three pillars of success.

Akamai's products and services. While each pillar represents a separate entity, the impact of Akamai's technology and employees on its success is largely dependent on the customers' perceived value of these elements. The CFP, providing a mechanism for improvements in Akamai's products and services, plays a crucial part in guiding the direction of Akamai's technology and employees.

Akamai has been conducting customer surveys since 2000. In the early years of the CFP, Akamai's customer survey was, self-admittedly, a simple exercise of data collection with no structured agenda. Customers were surveyed for their feedback, yet there was no clear organizational guidance on how to use that feedback. Having made incremental improvements over the years, Akamai's survey program began to shift from a mere data collection exercise to a comprehensive CFP that embraced the best practices needed to realize a successful program. In the first half of 2008, Akamai began examining survey results, carefully studying satisfaction trends, and building strategy around customer feedback results based on statistical analyses. Using the results of the survey, Akamai established a "customer first" initiative to expand and strengthen its CFP. In general terms, Akamai's CFP is currently designed to:

- Keep customer satisfaction a regular executive priority
- Make customer satisfaction data relevant to product marketing and engineering

- Ensure customers are asked the right questions at the right time

- Provide relevant reporting and visibility of customer feedback results

Next, we will see how Akamai addresses each area of its CFP. It is important to note that, in the process of updating its CFP, Akamai was able to incorporate many of the best practices found to be essential in ensuring high levels of satisfaction with the program as well as high levels of customer loyalty.

STRATEGY AND GOVERNANCE

"The governance of the customer feedback program is a key element to ensuring our customer-centric culture extends across all levels of the company, and is the key factor that is responsible for the success of our program," says Sanjay Singh, vice president of global services and support at Akamai. Akamai's CFP is formally supported by four elements: (1) corporate customer satisfaction metric, (2) customer experience scorecard, (3) Customer Leadership Council, and (4) Customer Champion Award. These four elements help support the CFP through executive leadership, employee motivation, and widespread use of customer feedback data. Akamai's "customer first" initiative is presented in Figure 11.2.

First, Akamai introduced a formal, standardized customer satisfaction metric, allowing it to track and measure overall customer loyalty in a consistent manner across all customers. Using three popular customer loyalty questions (for example, overall satisfaction, likelihood to continue purchasing, and likelihood to recommend), the standardized customer loyalty measurement supports Akamai's "customer first" initiative and allows it to clearly communicate progress toward its objective of ensuring a high degree of customer loyalty. Its goal is to

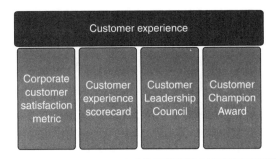

Figure 11.2   The four elements of Akamai's "customer first" initiative.

have customers so satisfied that they do not take phone calls from competitors.

The Customer Leadership Council at Akamai is a cross-functional team tasked with the responsibility of measuring and improving the customer experience. Each council member is responsible for leading improvement in his or her specific area. Improvements in each functional area—professional services, marketing, engineering, sales, finance, product management, and services—are designed to improve the customer experience.

Additionally, the Akamai Customer Champion Award, used to acknowledge employees, is presented to an employee or team that distinguishes itself through a significant accomplishment that contributes to Akamai's vision of creating long-term customers. Each Akamai employee is eligible for this award through an employee nomination process. The nominations, received from across all company divisions, are reviewed by the executive team, which requires executive discussions about the merits of each nomination. The CEO presents the Akamai Customer Champion Award to the employee who embodies the *Akamai Difference*—the slogan used by the company to identify its unique technology and attributes. The award consists of both a monetary incentive and a two-foot glass trophy. Akamai's Singh continues, "This award is a great way to instill a sense of urgency about customer issues across all levels of the company, from the CEO to the front-line employee."

Finally, Akamai circulates the customer feedback results throughout the company in a variety of ways. First, customer feedback results are included in the executive dashboard. Customer loyalty ratings are presented for each of the three loyalty questions (overall satisfaction, continue purchasing, recommend) across all respondents as well as important customer segments. For executives, results are presented in the form of percentages rather than means. Additionally, customer feedback results are a key part of the company meetings, in which customer metrics are reported to all employees. Customer feedback results are summarized and published in company and divisional quarterly reports. In addition to aggregated customer metrics, individual customer responses are also reported. Specifically, customer feedback results are sent to the account team as soon as the customers submit their survey responses.

These four basic elements work together to help Akamai effectively set, modify, and track the strategy around customer issues by focusing executives on a standardized customer metric and demonstrating their commitment to customers. Additionally, the governance of the CFP is organized around a common metric used to improve business processes and motivate employees to engage in customer-centric behaviors.

The head of the CFP reports to three executive-level employees: the vice president of global services and support, the vice president of global marketing, and the executive vice president of global sales/service/marketing.

BUSINESS PROCESS INTEGRATION

The CFP results are integrated into the daily business processes at Akamai. The raw customer feedback data are housed in Akamai's sales force CRM system, so sales employees have quick access to customer feedback results at the account level. Having customer feedback results for specific accounts facilitates account management activities for each sales employee and can be the difference between making a sale and losing additional revenue. Craig Adams, director of customer experience at Akamai, says, "Account managers, knowing the current level of satisfaction of accounts, understand their customers' pain points and, consequently, can be proactive in resolving problems before they become deal breakers." Before meeting with customers, account managers can quickly review an account's state of affairs, including attitude toward Akamai; the attitudinal information, along with sales and service information (also housed in the CRM system), provides a comprehensive picture of account health. Customer feedback data are used in conjunction with Akamai's Customer Health Dashboard (CHD). The CHD classifies accounts into three groups—red, yellow, or green—indicating the quality of their health, with respect to such things as the number of technical support issues they have and the frequency with which the customers are contacted.

Integration of the CFP is reflected in the communication of processes and goals of the program. Communication of the customer feedback goals occurs at the all-hands meeting. CFP goals are communicated throughout the entire all-hands meeting. The information delivered at these meetings reinforces the "customer first" initiative and emphasizes the importance of the customer in employees' daily activities. Also, along with the overall results, general themes are presented to the employees at the all-hands meeting.

Communication of customer feedback data is improved by delivering customer feedback results that are relevant to the recipient. At Akamai, each survey question has an executive sponsor who is accountable for the results. Also, results are communicated regionally to ensure recipients find the communication relevant to their business areas.

METHOD

Akamai employs four types of customer surveys: (1) relation-ship, (2) implementation, (3) technical support, and (4) churn. The latter three surveys collect feedback about specific inter-actions and address "moments of truth" on why prior custom-ers left Akamai. The relationship survey measures the overall health of the customer relationship by collecting feedback across a broad range of topics, each impacting the overall cus-tomer experience. The discussion focuses on the relationship survey, the major customer survey for Akamai.

Akamai employs a Web-based relationship survey that is conducted for all customers. Deployed every quarter, the customer survey is initiated via an invitation e-mail sent to selected customer contacts. To ensure customers are not over-surveyed, only 25% of customers are invited to the survey each quarter. To ensure Akamai obtains a comprehensive picture of each account, different types of customer contacts are asked for their feedback. Respondents include customers from differ-ent levels of the organization (for example, decision makers, influencers, and end users). With this sort of distinction among customer segments, Akamai will be able to better understand different respondent types, which will allow it to manage cus-tomer relationships in ways that best suit the needs of the spe-cific customer.

The customer survey includes quantitative as well as quali-tative questions. The quantitative questions allow each respon-dent to indicate his or her opinion about Akamai on a rating scale from 0 to 10. Qualitative questions allow each respondent to either clarify responses to the rating questions in his or her own words or answer open-ended questions.

The satisfaction Akamai's customers experience is not the result of just one aspect of a single product, service, or depart-ment; it is a combination of their experiences that touches the entire company across the customer life cycle, from market-ing and sales to service. Ensuring long-term customer loyalty requires constantly measuring, evaluating, and improving the customer experience across all areas where customers touch Akamai. Additional rated questions in the survey allow Aka-mai to assess the customer experience across different customer touch points. The customer survey includes questions regarding the sales experience, the implementation experience, how cus-tomers work with EdgeControl Portal, and technical support.

Customer Experience Questions

Akamai's customer survey contains 42 questions that measure different areas of customer experience and customer loyalty. Areas impacting the customer experience, such as product, sales, support, ease of use, and reporting tools, are included in the survey. It needs to be noted that Akamai focuses on tailoring questions around how the customer interacts with Akamai rather than identifying departments in the survey ques-tions. This customer-centric approach, in addition to prevent-ing gamesmanship by stakeholders impacted by the responses, helps Akamai look more broadly at the customer experience and make improvements. Specifically, customer survey ques-tions fall into eight areas, shown in Table 11.1.

Three business areas covered in the survey are universally applicable across all customer segments: overall, marketing, and product/services. Questions in these three business areas are asked of all respondents. Some other business areas, how-ever, are applicable only to select customer groups based on their experience with Akamai as well as their job role. There-fore, only respondents with relevant experience (as determined by two qualifying survey questions) are asked questions regard-ing the following:

- Sales
- Account management

Table 11.1 Business areas in the Akamai customer survey, sample questions, and the number of items in each area.

Business area	Sample questions	Number of items
Overall	Overall satisfaction with Akamai; How likely would you be to recommend Akamai Technologies' products and services in the future?	5
Marketing	Please rate the frequency of Akamai's customer communications; Is it clear who to contact within Akamai for any particular issues or questions you might have?	3
Product/ Services	Quality of Akamai products & services; Degree to which Akamai's products & services meet my needs	3
Sales	Sales team's knowledge of my business; Sales team's responsiveness to my inquiries	6
Account management	Account management's knowledge of my business; Account management's ability to engage appropriate Akamai resources to meet my needs	6
Professional/ Integration services	Consultant's courtesy/professionalism; Consultant's technical knowledge & effectiveness in meeting your needs; Usefulness of online configuration tools & documentation	7
Customer care	Customer care team's ability to resolve technical issues; Customer care's service quality compared to other support organizations with whom you work	6
EdgeControl Portal	Degree to which EdgeControl Portal tools meet my business needs; Ease of navigating the EdgeControl Management portal; Ability to find documentation on the EdgeControl Management Center portal	6

- Professional/Integration services
- Customer care
- EdgeControl Portal

Customer Loyalty Questions

Akamai employs three standard customer loyalty questions, each rated on a 0–10 scale, for measuring advocacy loyalty:

- Overall satisfaction
- Likelihood to recommend
- Likelihood to continue purchasing

Akamai reports scores for all three customer loyalty indices. It understands that each individual loyalty question used in isolation is less reliable than all three loyalty questions used simultaneously. One question might indicate that a customer is loyal, while the other questions might indicate the customer is at risk. Using all three customer loyalty questions helps Akamai ensure that the measurement and management of advocacy loyalty provides reliable results, which will, ultimately, lead to better business decisions.

Reliability and Validity of the Survey Process

Akamai regularly uses customer feedback results in business decision making, from overarching organizational process changes to specific changes for a given customer. Akamai's Craig Adams says, "The effectiveness of the customer feedback results in decision making is only as good as the reliability and validity of those results. Decisions based on poor quality data will result in the mismanagement of customers that will negatively impact the customer experience." Akamai's survey process delivers trustworthy results that are in-line with other organizational metrics.

Along with its customer feedback metrics, other quality measures such as bookings, retention rates, and revenue are used to assess the well-being of Akamai's business. One way that Akamai assesses the validity of its survey process is to show that these different metrics are predicted by customer feedback. Accounts that report low customer loyalty scores will, in the end, be the same accounts that have lower revenue numbers and will likely stop purchasing services from Akamai, compared to accounts with high customer loyalty scores. These results verify the effectiveness of the CFP. Because the customer feedback results help predict future customer purchase behavior, Akamai can feel confident that the customer feedback results provide a reliable and valid source of information by which it can manage customer relationships.

REPORTING

Akamai's reporting structure revolves around the business goals of the company. Without disclosing specific numerical goals, Akamai's overall annual business goal is to grow its business, measured by three specific means: (1) acquiring a specific number of new customers, (2) realizing accelerated revenue growth, and (3) significantly decreasing churn rates. These three specific business goals help guide how the customer feedback data are analyzed, summarized, and distributed throughout the company.

Reporting of customer feedback results embodies the two general approaches: macro and micro. For the macro approach, standardized reports summarize the survey results in aggregate form to help guide decision making at the executive level. For the micro approach, individual customer responses are disseminated to responsible organizations to help resolve a specific customer's problems.

Macro Approach

Customer feedback results are aggregated with the use of basic statistics. For quantitative questions, frequencies and means are regularly used to summarize the survey results. For rated questions, top box percentages (percentage of respondents who answered 9 or 10 on a 0–10 scale) and bottom box percentages (percentage of respondents who answered 0 or 1 on a 0–10 scale) are reported to indicate the percentage of customers who are extremely satisfied and dissatisfied, respectively, with their customer experience. Additionally, for each question, the arithmetic average, along with the sample size used to calculate the average, is computed to help understand the customer experience for the typical customer.

Akamai regularly uses statistical analysis methods to determine if observed differences in customer survey ratings across different customer groups (or across time periods) are meaningful or merely due to chance. Using the average ratings, Akamai examines trends in satisfaction over time and determines if customer satisfaction and loyalty vary over different customer segments (for example, tiers, regions, and support contracts).

Akamai reports trends in satisfaction and loyalty over time. These trend charts help Akamai's divisional managers keep track of their division's performance and help them understand the impact of organizational programs designed to impact change. At Akamai's executive level, these trend charts help executive management keep track of its organizational goals. Akamai examines specific items across quarterly survey periods and can study differences over time as new product releases are issued.

Akamai uses segmentation analysis to understand differences across key customer groups. For example, separating its customers into six tiers, Akamai examines the differences in customer satisfaction and loyalty to ensure the extra resources dedicated to the top-tier customers lead to high customer satisfaction and loyalty results for these important customers.

Akamai applies a variety of statistical analysis methods on its customer feedback data, such as *t*-tests, ANOVA, and correlational analysis. When studying trends over time and differences across customer segments, Akamai employs an ANOVA to ensure the observed differences over time or across groups are real and are not due to chance. To understand why customers are loyal or disloyal, Akamai correlates satisfaction ratings with measures of customer loyalty.

Micro Approach

Customer feedback results are also used at the respondent level to help manage specific customers who report problems. A negative response to a predetermined question or questions by a respondent initiates an e-mail to the Akamai sales representative who is responsible for the customer. Facilitated by the functionality of the Web-based survey system, this automatic trigger e-mail notifies the responsible party of the specific respondent's answers to the survey. The trigger e-mail contains pertinent contact information so the responsible party can easily contact the respondent to better understand the issue and help solve it.

Reports

Customer feedback results are shared throughout the entire company in a systematic format after every quarterly survey period. The survey results—the information that makes up the content of the reports—are presented at the corporate all-hands meeting. The reporting of customer feedback results at these employee meetings ensures all employees are aware of important corporate initiatives around the company, embedding a culture of customer centricity throughout the company.

Several standardized reports of aggregated results are prepared for wide distribution in hard-copy form. Reports to executive management contain a high-level summary of major trends and differences across customer segments. These executive reports are created in PowerPoint format and include simple graphical presentation (for example, trend charts, averages, percentages) as well as textual interpretation of the graphs, helping facilitate communication of the results for easy consumption.

Other reports to line staff are manuscripts and are delivered to managers responsible for sales, support, and products. Akamai's Craig Adams says, "Our 'State of the Customer Report' is tailored to our specific industries and helps Akamai broaden our customer initiative by reaching every single employee throughout the company."

While the reports provide a standardized method for sharing major themes found in the customer feedback data, employees also have access to each customer survey. Toward that end, the raw customer feedback data are accessible by any employee. The raw data (in the form of an Excel file) are used for executive meetings and briefings for new sales employees.

RESEARCH

Customer research at Akamai, while in the infancy stage, is continuing to grow as the CFP matures. Akamai currently conducts some applied research using customer feedback data. In its reporting process, customer segmentation analysis is augmented using statistical analysis such as ANOVA to ensure the differences across customer segments are real and meaningful. The statistical analyses used on the customer feedback data help Akamai to be more rigorous in understanding the variation seen in the data. Adams continues, "Statistical analyses help us to properly interpret our customer feedback results so that we know when differences among customer segments are meaningful. This sort of research helps our executives make correct business decisions."

In validating its survey process, Akamai linked customer feedback data to objective business metrics and found that customer satisfaction was predictive of important financial metrics. Sanjay Singh sees a host of future research opportunities at Akamai: "With our customer feedback data now housed in our CRM system, we will be able to understand operational factors that impact customer satisfaction as well as understand the financial metrics that are impacted by customer satisfaction."

SUMMARY

Akamai adopts many of the best practices behind successful CFPs. Its strategy of business growth through focusing on enhancing the customer experience is supported by the CFP. Additionally, Akamai's governance model guides all aspects of the program by the use of the following four elements: a common metric to gauge progress toward the strategic objective, customer experience scorecard, Customer Leadership Council, and a company-wide Customer Champion Award.

The CFP is integrated into business processes via the CRM sales force automation system. Program goals are communicated throughout the company in regular all-hands meetings. The use of Web-based surveys helps Akamai integrate the CFP into its business processes. The Web survey allows for easy import of feedback data into Akamai's CRM system and automates the customer resolution process with automated e-mail triggers to employees responsible for solving customer issues.

Customer feedback results are shared with all levels of the organization, from top management to frontline employees. Results are shared through company meetings and standard reports. Customer research, in conjunction with rigorous statistical methods, has begun at Akamai. The development of its research program started with validation of the customer feedback process and identification of variables that are statistically linked with customer satisfaction and loyalty.

PART V

Appendices

Appendix A
Determining Customer Requirements

We usually describe a product or service in terms of several dimensions or characteristics. For example, after receiving a service, we might describe the service provider as fast, always available when needed, and unpleasant. These descriptions represent three different aspects of the service: *responsiveness, availability,* and *professionalism,* respectively. These are a subset of all possible dimensions by which the service can be described. The composite of all possible dimensions describes the entire product or service.

We can regard customer requirements as those characteristics of the product or service that represent important dimensions. They are the dimensions on which customers base their opinions about the product or service. I will use the term *quality dimensions* to describe these important dimensions. Also, I will interchange the terms *customer requirements* and *quality dimensions* throughout the book.

The purpose of determining customer requirements is to establish a comprehensive list of all the important quality dimensions that describe the service or product. It is important to understand the quality dimensions in order to know how customers define the quality of your service or product. Only by understanding the quality dimensions will you be able to develop measures to assess them.

Although there may be some standard quality dimensions that generalize across many products or services, some dimensions will apply only to specific types of products or services. Quality dimensions applicable to many service organizations include availability, responsiveness, convenience, and timeliness (Kennedy and Young 1989). These quality dimensions seem applicable to many service industries such as banking, hotels, and hospitals. This list of quality dimensions, however, is not comprehensive for each of these industries. The hospital industry might include additional quality dimensions such as quality of food and quality of care. Similarly, other industries may possess quality dimensions that uniquely define their services and products.

It is important that each company identify all relevant quality dimensions in order to ensure understanding of the definition of quality for its products or services. Analyzing the services or products will provide a comprehensive picture of these dimensions.

This appendix will present two methods designed to identify important quality dimensions of products or services. The first method is the *quality dimension development approach*. This approach calls for the provider to establish the quality dimensions of its service or product. The second method is the *critical incident approach* (Flanagan 1954); it involves customers in determining the quality dimensions.

QUALITY DIMENSION DEVELOPMENT

This method involves the people who provide the service or product. This might be individuals within a quality circle addressing a particular problem or individuals working independently to better understand their customers' requirements. In either case, these people are closely involved with the business process and should be in a good position to understand the purpose and function of the services or products they provide. Essentially, this process involves two steps: first identifying the dimensions and then defining these dimensions with specific examples.

Identification of Quality Dimensions

The first step involves identifying the dimensions that define the quality of the service or product. This list of dimensions can be generated in various ways, using different sources of information. One way is to investigate literature (such as scientific, professional, and trade journals) that discusses specific industries. These publications might provide dimensions of the service or product.

As an example of information found in scientific journals, researchers (Parasuraman, Zeithaml, and Berry 1985) have concluded that service quality can be described on the basis of 10 dimensions. Attempts to measure these 10 dimensions, however, reveal that customers can only distinguish between five dimensions (Parasuraman, Zeithaml, and Berry 1988). This suggests that the original 10 dimensions overlap each other considerably. The five dimensions of service quality are *tangibles, reliability, responsiveness, assurance,* and *empathy*. Definitions of these dimensions are available in a publication on service quality by Zeithaml, Parasuraman, and Berry (1990).

Some trade journals include articles that pertain to a particular industry. For example, various quality dimensions of staff support areas were presented by Kennedy and Young (1989). Five dimensions of staff support and their definitions appear in Figure A.1. These quality dimensions were identified as important characteristics of staff support areas.

These examples demonstrate the value of journals, either scientific or trade, as resources for establishing lists of quality dimensions. By reading journals, you can gain insight from knowledgeable people who have extensive experience in a particular field.

Another way to establish a list of quality dimensions is to study the service or product. This study should include people involved in the business process, people who are in a good position to understand the purpose or function of their jobs in relation to meeting customer expectations. This examination of the service or product should lead to identification of numerous quality dimensions.

Some dimensions might include those found in Figure A.1, or the dimensions might be specific to a particular industry or organization. An initial list of quality dimensions will be identified by general terms such as *timely* or *professional*, each term representing a particular customer require-ment. These terms are to be used as guides toward understanding the dimensions of the service or product.

It is important to define these terms so that someone reading the definition will understand precisely what is meant. To clarify the definitions of the quality dimensions further, write specific examples for each defini-tion. This process follows.

Establishing Specific Examples of Quality Dimensions

The process of clarifying quality dimensions is one of generating specific examples. Each example defines a particular dimension, and each dimen-sion may include multiple examples. These examples take the form of

---

1. *Availability of support:* the degree to which the customer can contact the provider

2. *Responsiveness of support:* the degree to which the provider reacts promptly to the customer

3. *Timeliness of support:* the degree to which the job is accomplished within the customer's stated time frame and/or within the negotiated time frame

4. *Completeness of support:* the degree to which the total job is finished

5. *Pleasantness of support:* the degree to which the provider uses suitable professional behavior and manners while working with the customer

---

Figure A.1   Some quality dimensions for staff support areas and their definitions.

specific declarative statements, each describing a specific instance of the quality dimension it represents. Each statement could be a specific task or behavior performed by a person within the process or it could describe a specific example illustrating the dimension. The former statement type should include an action verb describing a specific behavior of the service provider or product. The latter statement should include a specific adjective reflecting the content of the dimensions. Example statements that contain both specific behavior and specific adjectives are included in Figure A.2. These statements were generated by the author using definitions presented by Kennedy and Young (1989).

These statements should reflect instances of performance by the staff or of product that customers can assess. It is important that your list include all possible examples for a particular dimension. This list of examples reflects the content of the dimensions; if the list is deficient, a complete understanding of each dimension will also be deficient. You should try to include at least four or five statements for each dimension. After generating the list of statements, you may take the additional step of combining any that seem redundant or repetitive. Some of the statements may overlap considerably and may not warrant separate dimensions.

The two steps in this process (generating dimensions and developing specific examples), although presented as independent of each other, are sometimes performed simultaneously. In some situations you may first generate specific examples that, in turn, lead to the generation of customer requirements. In either case, it is important that quality dimensions be defined by specific examples. Ultimately, the quality dimension development process will result in a list of customer requirements or quality dimensions, each defined by specific statements. The following software industry example illustrates the process and outcome of the quality dimension development process.

Software Industry

Murine (1988) discusses the measurement of software quality and lists 13 software quality factors. These factors are user oriented and can be evaluated by the customer. I have extracted the dimensions and their definitions directly from the article and have written statements to provide specific examples of each. The dimension, a brief definition, and the specific statements are presented in Figure A.3. These specific statements are only a small portion of the possible statements that could have been generated. Other questionnaire developers, examining the same quality dimensions, could generate additional statements similar in content to the ones presented here.

Availability of support
1. I could get help from the staff when I needed.
2. The staff was always available to help.
3. I could contact the staff at any time I needed.
4. The staff was there when needed.
5. I could arrange convenient meeting times with the staff.

Responsiveness of support
1. They were quick to respond when I asked for help.
2. They immediately helped me when I needed help.
3. I waited a short period of time to get help after I asked for it.

Timeliness of support
1. They completed the job when expected.
2. They met my deadline(s).
3. They finished their responsibilities within the stated time frame.
4. The project was completed on time.

Completeness of support
1. They ensured that every aspect of the job was completed.
2. They completed everything they said they would do.
3. They were there to provide help from the beginning to the end of the project.

Professionalism of support
1. The staff members conducted themselves in a professional manner.
2. The staff listened to me.
3. The staff was courteous.
4. The staff cared about what I had to say.

Overall satisfaction with support
1. The quality of the way the staff treated me was high.
2. The way the staff treated me met my needs.
3. The way the staff treated me met my expectations.
4. I am happy with the way the staff treated me.
5. I am satisfied with the way the staff treated me.

Overall satisfaction with product
1. The quality of the final job they provided was high.
2. The job met my expectations.
3. I am satisfied with the job the staff provided.

Figure A.2   Declarative statements describing the quality dimensions of staff support areas.

I. Correctness: the degree to which the software meets customers' specifications
   1. I am able to complete my job with this software.
   2. The software meets my specifications in getting my job done.

II. Reliability: the extent to which programs perform intended functions with precision
   3. I am able to perform functions with precision.
   4. The software allows me to perform functions accurately.

III. Usability: effort required to understand output from programs
   5. I was able to learn about the output from programs in a short amount of time.
   6. The output of the programs is easy to understand.

IV. Maintainability: effort required to find and correct an error in operational programs
   7. Locating an error in the operational program is easy.
   8. Fixing an error in the operational program is easy.

V. Testability: effort required to test programs to ensure they perform intended function
   9. The testing of the program required a short amount of time.
   10. Testing the program to ensure it performed functions was easy.

VI. Portability: effort required to transfer programs between hardware configurations and/or software environments
   11. Transferring the program between different hardware configurations is easy.
   12. I am able to transfer programs between different software environments with little problem.

VII. Interoperability: effort required to couple one system to another
   13. Coupling one system to another is easy.
   14. The software allows for simple coupling between systems.

VIII. Intra-operability: effort required to communicate between software components
   15. Communicating between software components is simple.
   16. I am able to communicate between software components easily.

IX. Flexibility: effort required to modify operational programs
   17. I am able to modify the operational program with little effort.
   18. Changing the operational program is easy.

Overall satisfaction:
   19. I am very happy with the software.
   20. The software meets my expectations.

Figure A.3 Quality dimensions, their definitions, and statements for the software industry.

Summary

Quality dimension development is a process of identifying customer requirements through various sources. One source is industry-specific literature. People within the company are another potential source. You might ask them to examine the business process and determine the key quality dimensions of the service or product they provide. In addition to determining these dimensions, you should generate specific examples illustrating exactly what is meant by each dimension. This process will lead to the development of a list of customer requirements, each defined by several specific statements.

CRITICAL INCIDENT APPROACH

The critical incident technique (Flanagan 1954) is another approach to determining customer requirements. It has been used in establishing performance dimensions for performance appraisal systems (Latham, Fay, and Saari 1979; Latham and Wexley 1977). This method is applicable in developing customer satisfaction questionnaires and equally valuable in business process analysis in which companies attempt to define and understand customer requirements. The present method can greatly facilitate this process of definition and understanding.

The critical incident approach focuses on obtaining information from customers about the services and products they receive. *Customers* is a generic term referring to anybody who receives a service or product from some other person or group of people. It is clear that various customer satisfaction questionnaires can be developed for different types of customers and that customers can be people who are external to an organization or people from a different department within the same organization. In either case, the critical incident approach can identify customer requirements.

The strength of the critical incident approach lies in its utilization of customers in defining customer requirements. Customers are in a good position to help you understand these requirements because they are the recipients of your services or products. Relying solely on organization or department standards in determining customer requirements might lead to a poor list that does not include factors important to customers. Also, such a list may reflect imagined customer requirements that should not be included. The critical incident approach identifies specific performance examples that illustrate organizational performance related to the services or products they provide.

Critical Incidents

A critical incident is an example of organizational performance from the customers' perspective. That is, critical incidents are those aspects of organizational performance in which customers come in direct contact with your product or service. These incidents usually define staff performance (in service organizations) and product quality (in manufacturing organizations).

A critical incident is a specific example of the service or product that describes either positive or negative performance. A positive example describes a characteristic of the service or product that the customer would like to see every time he or she receives that service or product. A negative example describes a characteristic of the service or product that would make the customer question the quality of the company.

A well-written critical incident example defining customer requirements has two characteristics: (1) it is specific and (2) it describes the service provider in *behavioral terms* or describes the service or product with *specific adjectives*. The incident description should be written so that it is unambiguous, able to be interpreted the same way by different readers. These characteristics should be explained to those responsible for describing the critical incidents.

A critical incident is *specific* if it highlights a single behavior or characteristic of the service or a single characteristic of the product. The critical incident is not specific if it describes several aspects of performance. For example, a nonspecific critical incident description might say:

> I went to the bank to cash a check and waited in line for a long time. While I was waiting, I noticed that the teller was quickly servicing her customers.

This critical incident is not specific because it describes more than a single behavior or characteristic of service. The reader would not know whether to focus on the fact that the customer waited a long time or that the teller was quick in the service she provided. Improve this example by rewriting it to describe two separate characteristics:

1. I waited in line for a long time.

2. The teller was quickly servicing her customers.

A well-written description of a critical incident should focus on *behaviors* of the service provider and should use specific *adjectives* that describe the service or product. Saying "the teller was not able to help me" does not specify what the teller did and why the teller was unable to help. Improve this example by focusing on specific behaviors and including specific adjectives:

1. The teller carefully listened to my request.

2. I received immediate service for my transaction.

The first description focuses on the behavior of the teller while the second uses a specific adjective to describe the service.

GENERATING CRITICAL INCIDENTS

This procedure involves two steps. In the first, customers are interviewed to obtain specific information about the service or product. In the second, this information is categorized into groups, each group reflecting a quality dimension. A detailed discussion of both steps follows.

Interview

There are two approaches for identifying critical incidents: group interviewing and individual interviewing. The major difference is that either groups or individuals are the focus of the identification process. A minor difference is that individual interviews can be conducted either in person or over the telephone. In either group or individual interviewing, the method of identifying critical incidents is the same, and the following procedure is equally applicable.

For the first step, it is essential that you obtain input from people who have received the service or product. These people must be actual customers who have had several interactions with the service provider or the product, since they will be providing specific examples of service or product quality.

The recommended number of interviews ranges from 10 to 20. This high number of interviewees is recommended so that deficient information from one will be offset by sufficient information from another. Thus, information obtained from the interviews will more likely completely cover the spectrum of customer requirements. In group interviews, critical incidents described by one person may stimulate mention of incidents by other group members.

The interviewer should ask each participant to describe five to 10 positive instances and five to 10 negative instances of that service or product. These positive and negative instances constitute the critical incidents that define good and poor service or product quality.

Recall that the interviewee should avoid using general terms to describe critical incidents. If the interviewee uses general phrases such as "the service was nice" or "the product was good," the interviewer should determine what the merchant actually did, in behavioral terms, that made him or her "nice" or which aspects of the product made it "good."

For example, a customer may describe a critical incident in more than one way: "The merchant was quick to respond when I arrived" and "The merchant was good." The latter description does not specify why the merchant was good. The former provides specific information: the merchant was quick in responding to the customer. By pressing the interviewees to supply specific examples of performance or specific adjectives describing the service or product, the interviewer obtains critical information that more efficiently defines customer requirements. Such specific descriptions of critical incidents will facilitate the development of the customer satisfaction questionnaire.

Categorization of Critical Incidents

After interviewing 10 people, you may have a list of 200 critical incidents. This list is likely to include some incidents that are similar to others and these should be grouped together. The key to categorizing similar critical incidents is to focus on a specific adjective or verb they share. After forming the clusters, write a phrase for each cluster that reflects the content of its incidents. This phrase is called a *satisfaction item*. One guideline for writing satisfaction items is that they should contain a specific descriptive term of the service or product or a verb that describes an actual event involving the service or product. For example, the following critical incidents, experienced by three different people, would fall under one satisfaction item:

1. I waited too long before I was helped.

2. I was in a big hurry but had to wait in line for a very long time.

3. I waited in line for a very short time.

A satisfaction item that would encompass these three similar incidents could be

I waited a short period of time before I was helped.

As indicated by this example, both positive and negative critical incidents can be included under one satisfaction item. The three critical incidents just listed, even though they reflect positive and negative aspects of service, are all reflected by the verb *wait*. Therefore, the satisfaction item was written to include the word *wait*.

Writing satisfaction items may take some practice. The most important thing to remember is that satisfaction items, like critical incidents, should be specific in describing the service or product. Quite often, the satisfaction item might even be one of the critical incidents.

Once all of the critical incidents are categorized into their respective satisfaction items, repeat the categorization process using the satisfaction items. That is, group similar satisfaction items in order to identify a specific customer requirement or quality dimension. Label these customer requirements with phrases or a single word describing the content of the satisfaction items. These summary labels reflect specific quality dimensions. Unlike satisfaction items, these labels need not be specific. The only requirement is that the label should reflect the content of the satisfaction items. Using the previous example, we may generate a second satisfaction item that results in these two satisfaction items.

1. I waited a short period of time before I was helped.

2. Service started promptly when I arrived.

Both of these satisfaction items would be included under one customer requirement category labeled *Responsiveness of service.*

Having finished all the groupings, you will see a hierarchical relationship representing three levels of specificity falling on a specific-general continuum. The critical incidents fall on the specific end of the continuum, the customer requirements fall on the general end of the continuum, and the satisfaction items fall somewhere in between.

Although the outlined process leads from critical incidents to satisfaction items that lead, in turn, to customer requirements, this is not the only order in which the critical incidents approach can flow. It may be easier to first categorize the critical incidents directly into the customer requirement categories. Next, within each customer requirement category, categorize critical incidents into various satisfaction items. Thus, both methods result in a hierarchical relationship between critical incidents, satisfaction items, and customer requirements. This hierarchical relationship is illustrated in Figure A.4. Customer requirements are defined by satisfaction items that are, in turn, defined by critical incidents.

Three forms are presented in Appendices A and B that will help you conduct interviews to determine the critical incidents. These forms are designed to facilitate each step in the critical incidents approach. The first form (Appendix A) will help you divide positive and negative aspects of the service and will make it easier to list all the critical incidents in a simple format. After conducting the interviews and recording the information, you can cut apart the form and allocate the critical incidents into separate satisfaction items. The second form (Appendix B) will allow you to place critical incidents into clusters and write satisfaction items as headings for each cluster. After writing all the satisfaction items, you can place similar satisfaction items in one customer requirement category. The third form (also Appendix B) allows you to list satisfaction items that fall under a particular customer requirement.

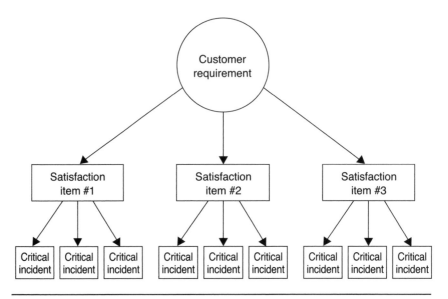

Figure A.4   Hierarchical relationship among critical incidents, satisfaction items, and customer requirements.

QUALITY OF THE CATEGORIZATION PROCESS

The allocation process (from incident to satisfaction item and from satisfaction item to customer requirement category) is critical to understanding quality dimensions. Since the resulting customer requirements are derived from the initial solicitation and description of critical incidents, it is important to guarantee the quality of this allocation process.

Quality can be assured by having two people involved in the allocation process. These people are referred to as *judges* since their role involves judging the similarity of critical incidents and satisfaction items. The first judge will follow the previously described process, grouping incidents into satisfaction items and then grouping satisfaction items into customer requirement categories. The second judge looks at the customer requirement categories established by the first judge and allocates the critical incidents directly into them, bypassing the satisfaction items.

Inter-judge Agreement

The quality of the allocation process is indicated by the extent of agreement between the two judges. This "inter-judge agreement" is the percentage of incidents both judges place in the same customer requirement category. Inter-judge agreement is calculated by dividing the number of incidents both judges place in a customer requirement category by the total number of redundant and distinct incidents the judges place in the category. The index can range from 0 to 1.0. As this index approaches 1.0, it indicates that the judges are in high agreement. When the index approaches 0, it indicates that the judges are in low agreement. An index of approximately .8 should be used as a cutoff to determine whether the customer requirement was acceptable. This criterion has been suggested elsewhere (Latham, et al. 1979).

Let's look at an example to illustrate this index. Suppose the first judge grouped 100 critical incidents into 20 satisfaction items. Next, assume that this judge allocated two satisfaction items (a total of seven incidents) into one particular customer requirement category. Specifically, the first judge included incidents 1, 4, 6, 7, 9, 13, and 40 in the customer requirement category *availability*. Next, the second judge allocated all 100 critical incidents directly into the customer requirement categories that were established by the first judge, skipping the allocation of incidents into satisfaction items. Suppose the second judge included incidents 1, 2, 4, 6, 7, 9, 13, and 40 in the *availability* customer requirement category. The inter-judge agreement for this particular category would be .88 (7/8). The inter-judge agreement index would also be calculated for the remaining customer requirement categories.

If the criterion of .8 is not obtained, one or both judges may have made an error in the categorization process. A judge may have accidentally included or omitted a critical incident because he or she did not read the incident or category correctly. Thus, a brief check of the critical incidents could correct this problem. Also, a low inter-judge index could occur when a small number of incidents make up one customer requirement. If one judge omitted a single incident from a total possible set of four incidents, the resulting inter-judge agreement would be .75 (3/4). Although this value is below the recommended cutoff of .8, it seems to be an acceptable value given the small number of incidents that comprise the customer requirement category.

If a low inter-judge agreement index is apparent, the judges should discuss their disagreement and come to a consensus as to the appropriate incidents that comprise a particular customer requirement category. If they cannot agree, a third judge could be included to categorize the incidents. This third judge could highlight the differences between the first two judges, which may lead to consensus.

COMPREHENSIVENESS OF THE CUSTOMER REQUIREMENTS

Customer requirements obtained from the interviews should define comprehensively the quality of the service or product. If one important customer requirement category is overlooked during the initial interviewing process, the resulting customer satisfaction questionnaire would be deficient in measuring all customer requirements. In other words, you would be unable to assess your customers' perception of an important element of your service or product. Subsequently, you might not be able to improve overall customer satisfaction because you do not know why your customers are satisfied or dissatisfied.

You may also establish the quality of the content of critical incidents (Latham, et al. 1979). Do this by removing a random group of approximately 10 percent of the critical incidents from the initial list *before* they are categorized into satisfaction items and customer requirement categories. After the entire allocation process is completed with 90 percent of the critical incidents (determining customer requirements category), examine the remaining 10 percent to see whether they can be placed in the customer requirements categories.

If the 10 percent clearly can be placed into the customer requirement categories, then the categories are probably a comprehensive list of all possible customer requirement categories for that organization or group. If one or more of the 10 percent cannot be placed into any customer requirement category, then the list is probably deficient in defining all possible customer requirement categories. This problem can be handled by interviewing more customers to obtain more critical incidents. The recommended number of additional interviews, however, will depend on the extent of the deficiency; the more deficient, the more interviews are needed. As a general rule, you should conduct five additional interviews for every critical incident that could not be allocated in the initial list of customer requirements. Once you have conducted these additional interviews, reallocate all critical incidents into satisfaction items, then into customer requirement categories.

The next part of this chapter illustrates the use of the critical incidents technique to determine customer requirements in the service and manufacturing sectors. The service sector is represented by the banking industry, and the manufacturing sector is represented by the automobile industry. In addition, because customers can be internal to an organization, there is an illustration of the critical incidents approach as applied to a department that provides statistical support to other departments in the organization.

BANKING INDUSTRY

The first step in this process included interviews with 10 people who have had interactions with the bank's service. Critical incidents are confined to those related to customer interactions with personnel in the banking facility.

Responses from the 10 interviewees resulted in a total of 146 critical incidents. Some of these incidents appear in Figure A.5. In addition, the figure includes the 10 satisfaction items (preceded by Roman numerals) that

Responsiveness of Service
I.   I waited a short period of time before I was helped.
    1. I waited too long before I was helped.
    2. Lines were too long.
    3. I waited in line for a very long time.
II. The service started immediately when I arrived.
    4. I went into the bank and the teller responded immediately to me.
    5. I received immediate service for my transaction.
    6. I could not get the teller's attention even though I was the only one in line.

Speed of Transaction
III. The teller handled transactions in a short period of time.
    7. The teller handled transactions fast.
    8. The handling of the transaction was quick after I told him or her what I wanted.
IV. The teller took a long time to complete my transaction.
    9. The entire transaction took too long.
    10. I waited a long time once I got to the window.

Availability of Service
V.   The financial consultant was available to schedule me for an appointment at a good time.
    11. I was able to set up an appointment with a financial consultant at a good time.
    12. The appointment time with the financial planner was when I wanted it.
VI. My appointment with the financial consultant was at a convenient time.
    13. The financial planner was available at a convenient time.
    14. My appointment was at an inconvenient time.

Professionalism
VII. The teller talked to me in a pleasant way.
    15. The teller took the time to talk to me to get all my requests completed.
    16. The teller was rude to me (specifically, he or she was short with me).
    17. The teller yelled at me when I could not open the depository canister.
VIII. The teller was very personable.
    18. The teller gave a personal compliment on my appearance.
    19. The teller had a friendly smile.
    20. The teller was not personal (did not say hello or goodbye).
IX. The teller carefully listened to me when I was requesting a transaction.
    21. The teller carefully listened to my request.
    22. The teller took the time to listen to me when I requested a lot of things.

Figure A.5 Critical incidents, satisfaction items, and customer requirements related to the banking industry.   *(Continued)*

(Continued)

X. The teller knew how to handle the transactions.
23. The teller knew how to handle a special transaction I requested.
24. The teller had to ask for help from another teller for a special transaction I asked for.
25. The teller looked confused when I asked for a special transaction.
Overall Satisfaction with Service
XI. The quality of the way the teller treated me was high.
XII. The way the teller treated me met my expectations.
XIII. I am satisfied with the way the teller treated me.

Figure A.5 Critical incidents, satisfaction items, and customer requirements related to the banking industry.

represent their respective critical incidents. Furthermore, satisfaction items are grouped into four customer requirement categories.

There is also a category labeled *Overall Satisfaction with Service*. The satisfaction items for this category are less specific than the items in different customer requirement categories and are not based on any critical incidents. This category represents overall service quality; it is not focused on any particular quality dimension. The value of these items will become clear in Chapters 3 and 6.

It is important to note that customer requirements reflect only aspects of the banking industry that are related to personal interaction. Not included are incidents related to other aspects of the banking industry, such as phone transaction banking, automatic teller machines, and account statements.

AUTOMOBILE INDUSTRY

The next illustration of the critical incidents technique applies to the automobile industry. Critical incidents were confined to aspects of the automobile's interior and its "drivability." Aspects of car driving quality were gathered in customer interviews. The categorization process resulted in three customer requirements. The critical incidents, satisfaction items, and customer requirements appear in Figure A.6.

Another way to conceptualize the groupings of these satisfaction items is to place them all into one customer requirement category called *perception of driving quality*. This customer requirement could be paralleled by another aspect of car quality such as *reliability of car*. This customer requirement might be measured by more objective indices such as the number of repairs, amount of money spent on repairs, or number of breakdowns. Using this conceptualization could result in two customer requirements: (1) the customers' perception of driving quality and (2) the car's reliability.

Interior Quality
I.   The seating position was very comfortable.
  1. The seats are comfortable.
  2. The seats were very uncomfortable.
  3. There is ample leg room.
II. The visibility through the window was good.
  4. There were many blind spots from the driver's seat.
III. The inside of the car was noisy.
  5. There is loud interior noise.
  6. The interior noise interfered with the sound of the stereo.
  7. Air whistles through the window.
  8. There was little noise while I was driving.

Instrumentation
IV. The instrumentation panel was simple to understand.
  9. The instrumentation panel is difficult to read.
  10. The dials for the accessories were too complex to understand.
  11. The dials for the controls were easy to understand.
V.   The instrumentation panel was clearly visible from the driving seat.
  12. I could clearly see all the instruments and gauges.
  13. I had a clear view of the instrumentation.
  14. Instruments are within good reaching distance.

"Drivability"
VI. The car stopped smoothly when I applied the brakes.
  15. The car did not brake well. (It would vibrate when I was braking.)
  16. The car vibrated when I applied the brakes.
  17. The car stopped smoothly when I applied the brakes.
VII. The car vibrated at high speeds.
  18. The car vibrated at high speeds.
  19. The car rides smoothly, even at high speeds.
VIII. The car handled corners well.
  20. The car handles corners well.
  21. I could negotiate corners very well.
  22. The car would consistently skid around tight corners.

Overall Satisfaction with Automobile
IX. I enjoyed driving the car.
X.   I liked the overall driving experience of the car.
XI. The drive was excellent.

Figure A.6   Critical incidents, satisfaction items, and customer requirements related to the driving quality of automobiles.

STATISTICAL SUPPORT

The next illustration of the critical incidents technique applies to a statistical department that provides support to other departments within the organization. A total of nine customers who have had previous contact with the staff in this department were interviewed. The categorization process resulted in five customer requirements. A partial list of the critical incidents, satisfaction items, and customer requirements is included in Figure 2.7.

Statistical Support

I. The staff person explained the statistical tests in understandable words.
   1. There was good explanation of the statistical tests.
   2. I received good explanation of the statistical analyses.
II. The statistical analyses were thorough.
   3. There was good analysis of data.
   4. Statistical help was minimal.
   5. The data analysis was incomplete.
III. The staff understood my software requirements.
   6. The software problem was never resolved.
   7. The staff understood the kinds of software I needed.

Enthusiasm

IV. The staff person was always willing to help.
   8. The person was always willing to help.
   9. The person would always help when I asked.
V. The staff person went out of his or her way to help.
   10. The person did not do the tasks.
   11. The person refused to do the project.
   12. The person did not do the project I asked him or her to do.

Final Written Report

VI. The written report was sufficiently detailed.
   13. The writeup of the project was not detailed.
   14. The written report was not complete.
   15. The document needed to be more comprehensive.
VII. The written report contained what I needed.
   16. Everything I asked for was in the final report.
   17. The report contained everything I asked for.

Responsiveness

VIII. The staff person completed the job quickly.
   18. Projects are completed quickly.
   19. The project started very late.
   20. I received fast turnaround time on my project.

Figure A.7 Critical incidents, satisfaction items, and customer requirements related to the quality of a statistical support department. *(Continued)*

(Continued)

Project Management

IX. The staff person finished the project in the stated time frame.
   21. The staff person did not meet the specified deadlines.
   22. The staff person did not have the job completed for a meeting.
   23. The project was turned in late.

X. The staff person planned the entire project through its completion.
   24. The planning of the project was complete.
   25. The project was well organized.

XI. The staff person understood how much time the project required.
   26. The person did not understand my requirements.
   27. The person understood the magnitude of the project.

Overall Satisfaction with Support

XII. I am satisfied with the service I received.
XIII. The quality of the service met my expectations.

Figure A.7 Critical incidents, satisfaction items, and customer requirements related to the quality of a statistical support department.

SUMMARY

This chapter demonstrated two techniques for determining customer requirements, those aspects of your service or product that define its quality. The first technique, the quality dimension development process, involves people closely linked to the service or product, those people who best understand the needs of the customer and the function and purpose of the service or product. They are responsible for determining and defining quality dimensions and citing specific examples of each dimension.

The second technique, the critical incident technique, involves obtaining information from customers about actual incidents they consider to define good and bad aspects of the product or service. These incidents define the satisfaction items, and the satisfaction items, in turn, define the customer requirements. Some examples demonstrated the effectiveness of the critical incidents approach in establishing customer requirements for both non-manufacturing and manufacturing organizations and internal customer support groups.

Figure A.8 presents the basic steps to follow for each method when establishing your customer requirements. This figure includes some important points at each step to facilitate the process.

Quality Dimension Development

Steps	Important Points
1. Create list of quality dimensions.	• Read professional and trade journals to obtain list of quality dimensions. • Generate list from personal experience.
2. Write definition of each dimension.	• Definition can be in general terms.
3. Develop specific examples for each quality dimension.	• Examples should use specific adjectives reflecting the service or product. • Examples should include specific behaviors of the provider. • Examples should use declarative statements.

Critical Incidents Approach

Steps	Important Points
1. Generate critical incidents.	• Interview customers. • Critical incidents should be specific examples of good or poor service or product quality. • Each critical incident reflects only one example.
2. Categorize critical incidents into clusters.	• Categorization is based on similarity in content of the incidents.
3. Write satisfaction items for each critical incident cluster.	• Each satisfaction item should be a declarative statement. • Satisfaction items should be specific.
4. Categorize satisfaction items into clusters, each cluster representing a customer requirement.	• Categorization should be based on similarity of satisfaction items. • Customer requirement must reflect the content of satisfaction items.

Figure A.8   Procedures for establishing customer requirements.   *(Continued)*

(Continued)

5. Determine the quality of the categorization process.	• Two judges should do categorization steps. • Calculate inter-judge agreement.
6. Determine the comprehensiveness of customer requirements.	• Remove 10 percent of the critical incidents before establishing customer requirements. • Determine whether the 10 percent can be placed into the customer requirements.

Figure A.8   Procedures for establishing customer requirements.

The next chapter will discuss measurement issues related to questionnaire development and use. These measurement principles should be considered when evaluating any type of questionnaire designed to measure people's opinions, perceptions, and attitudes.

Appendix B
Customer Satisfaction Questionnaire Construction
Item Generation, Response Format, and Item Selection

This appendix will give you some practical guidelines to follow when developing customer satisfaction questionnaires. In addition to reiterating the significance of customer requirements and satisfaction items, I will include new information on the characteristics of good items, scaling procedures, and item selection. Finally, I will present a process for questionnaire construction integrating this information.

Customer satisfaction questionnaires are constructed in four phases: (1) determining questions (items) to be used in the questionnaire, (2) selecting the response format, (3) writing the introduction to the questionnaire, and (4) determining the content of the final questionnaire (selecting items from the initial set of satisfaction items that will compose your measure).

DETERMINING QUESTIONS OR ITEMS

Let's start with an example of an organization that would like to develop a customer satisfaction questionnaire. Suppose that the organization, in an attempt to gauge how well it services its customers, includes these requests in its questionnaire:

1. Please rate the availability of the service.

2. Please rate the responsiveness of the staff.

3. Please rate the professionalism of the staff.

These three requests were obviously designed to measure three customer requirements: availability of service, responsiveness of service, and professionalism of service.

Although these customer requirements may be meaningful and valid service characteristics, there are problems with the requests. There is ambiguity in the vocabulary; *availability* and *responsiveness* might be interpreted differently by different people. Responses to these questions will reflect this ambiguity. To illustrate how different people may have differing definitions for the same word, I asked 10 people to tell me the meaning of *some* using a number. Their answers ranged from *three* to *seven*.

Similarly, if you ask your customers to indicate how satisfied they are with the availability of service they received, they may have different definitions of the word *availability* and thus be thinking of different things when they respond. Subsequently, it would be difficult to interpret customer responses. To avoid this problem, a customer satisfaction questionnaire should use more specific statements that leave less room for varying interpretations. The following statements could more clearly describe *availability:*

1. The merchant was available to schedule me at a good time.

2. I could get an appointment with the merchant at a time I desired.

3. My appointment was at a convenient time.

Availability is now defined more precisely in terms of scheduling and appointment time. Thus, responses to these items are more definitive than responses to the previous items. In addition, all three of these items still reflect the customer requirement of availability of service.

When we use more specific statements, the questionnaire provides specific feedback concerning organizational and staff performance. For example, a questionnaire using the word *availability* may discover that customers are not satisfied with the availability of service. Knowing that the customers are not satisfied, however, does little to help the organization pinpoint how to accomplish improvements. If the organization used more specific items (as in the second example), it would know precisely how to increase customers' level of satisfaction with the customer requirement of availability of service.

In summary, when developing questionnaires to assess customer satisfaction with a given product or service, we must ensure that our questions are not ambiguous. Using specific statements in questionnaires will enhance the information gained, because responses mean the same thing for all customers (no differing definitions) and responses will provide more specific feedback on ways to improve the service or product.

Satisfaction Items Revisited

Because we want the questions in our questionnaire to be specific, the next step would be to determine which questions or statements to include. Recall, from Appendix A, that the critical incident technique includes the creation of satisfaction items. These can be used as items in the questionnaire. Satisfaction items related to the banking industry from Figure A.1 are presented in Figure B.1.

---

1. I waited a short period of time before I was helped.

2. The service started promptly when I arrived.

3. The teller handled transactions in a short period of time.

4. The teller took a long time to complete my transaction.

5. The financial consultant was available to schedule me at a good time.

6. My appointment with the financial consultant was at a convenient time.

7. The teller talked to me in a pleasant way.

8. The teller was very personable.

9. The teller carefully listened to me when I was requesting a transaction.

10. The teller knew how to handle the transactions.

11. The quality of the way the teller treated me was high.

12. The way the teller treated me met my expectations.

13. I am satisfied with the way the merchant treated me.

Figure B.1   Satisfaction items from Figure A.1.

Satisfaction items can also provide indirect help by aiding the generation of new items for the questionnaire. This process entails rewriting the satisfaction items to reflect a neutral statement (neither positive nor negative) rather than a declarative statement. These items, however, are still specific in their content. These items (using the banking industry) appear in Figure B.2.

The items, either satisfaction items or items generated from them, are specific enough to be of value for feedback purposes. Instead of indicating only that customers are satisfied or dissatisfied with the level of professionalism of the service, these items can specify exactly *why* customers are satisfied or dissatisfied (items 7 through 10). After studying the specific feedback these satisfaction items offer, we can then calculate a general index of the professionalism customer requirement by combining the responses of items 7 through 10. We can also calculate indices for other quality dimensions or customer requirements using specific satisfaction items: responsiveness (items 1 and 2), speed of transaction (items 3 and 4), availability (items 5 and 6), and overall satisfaction with service (items 11 through 13). We can then determine the reliability of these summary scores using the reliability estimate formulae in Chapter 3.

1. Period of time waited before I was helped
2. Promptness of service when I arrived
3. Length of time of the transaction
4. Time to complete my transaction
5. Availability of financial consultant to schedule me for an appointment
6. Convenience of my appointment with the financial consultant
7. Way in which the teller talked to me
8. Way in which the teller conducted the transaction
9. Way in which the teller listened to me when I was requesting a transaction
10. Knowledge of teller in handling the transactions
11. The quality of the way the teller treated me
12. Overall quality of the visit
13. The way I was treated

Figure B.2   New items generated from original satisfaction items.

The quality dimension development process also resulted in statements that could be included in the questionnaire. Recall that these statements also describe specific instances of the service or product that defined their respective quality dimensions. These statements are similar to the satisfaction items that result from the critical incident approach. Consequently, these statements can also be used directly in the customer satisfaction questionnaire.

CHARACTERISTICS OF GOOD ITEMS

It is important that items in the questionnaire possess certain characteristics, and writing them can be difficult. They should appear relevant to what you are trying to measure, assessing customer requirements established earlier in the process. Items that do not appear to measure anything relevant to the service or product might confuse respondents, especially if the instructions indicate that the questionnaire is designed to assess the quality of the service or product.

Items should also be concise. Items that are too long can make the questionnaire too long and difficult to read. Discard superfluous words. The following is an example of a long item:

The service person seemed to act in a very personable manner to me when I asked for service.

This concise version reflects the same content:

The service person was very personable.

Items should be unambiguous. The respondent should be able to understand precisely what the items are asking. Any ambiguity in the items can lead to equivocal responses. Try to avoid items that are vague and imprecise, such as this example:

The transaction with the service provider was good.

This item does not reflect precisely why the service was good. Some respondents might interpret the item as assessing the promptness of the transaction, while others might think it assesses the service provider's professionalism. To avoid this confusion, we can write two items:

The transaction took a short period of time.
The service provider talked to me in a pleasant way.

Each of these items reflects an unambiguous thought, each representing one customer requirement.

A good item will contain only one thought. That is, the item should ask only a single question. If an item asks more than one question, the respondent may be frustrated trying to respond affirmatively to one part of the question and negatively to the other part. A positive response to this type of item would indicate that the respondent agrees to both parts of the item. A negative response might indicate either that the respondent disagrees with one part of the item or that the respondent disagrees with both parts of the item. This is an example of a poor item:

The provider listened to me and took a short time to handle the transaction.

This item contains two parts, one dealing with how the provider listened to the customer and the other with how much time was needed to handle the transaction. This item can be divided into two separate items:

The provider listened to me.
The provider took a short time to handle the transaction.

The fifth characteristic of a good item is that it should not contain a double negative. This is an example of an item with a double negative:

The clerk was never not there when he or she was needed.

This is a better way to write this item:

The clerk was there when he or she was needed.

In summary, a good item should appear relevant, should be concise and unambiguous, should contain only one thought, and should not contain double negatives. Items with these characteristics offer respondents clear and simple questions for response. They contribute to a questionnaire that is easy to read and easy to complete.

Although the items are an important part of the questionnaire, the response format of the items can also influence the quality of the responses obtained. The following section discusses response formats.

RESPONSE FORMATS

The second step in scale construction is to select a response format for the questionnaire that determines how customers will respond to the items. The choice of response format is an extremely important step in the development process since it determines how the data from the questionnaire can be used.

There are several possible response formats or scaling methods for questionnaires. These scaling methods include Thurstone's method of equal-appearing intervals (Thurstone 1929), Guttman's scalogram approach (Guttman 1950), and the Likert scaling method (Likert 1932), to name a few. Questionnaire development using either the Thurstone or Guttman approach is more laborious than the Likert method. In addition, scales developed using the Likert method yield higher reliability coefficients with fewer items than scales developed using the Thurstone method (Edwards and Kenney 1946). Therefore, for the sake of simplicity and utility, I will not present the Thurstone or Guttman approaches. I will limit this discussion of response formats to two approaches: the checklist format and the Likert-type format. Several books discuss the other types of scaling procedures that are not presented here (Dawes 1972; Fishbein 1967; and Reckase 1990).

Checklist Format

The quality of a service or product can be quantified by the number of positive things said about it. The more positive things said about a service (or the fewer negative things said about it), the better the service. For each item in the questionnaire, customers will be allowed to respond either "yes" or "no." Customers are asked to respond "yes" if the satisfaction item reflects the service or product they received and "no" if the item does not reflect the service or product they received. An example of a checklist format appears in Figure B.3. The checklist format should be used only when the satisfaction items are being used as the items in the questionnaire. The benefit of the checklist method is the ease with which customers can respond to the items. Customers can easily indicate whether or not the item describes the service they received.

Likert-Type Format

The quality of the service or product can also be indexed by the strength of response toward each satisfaction item. The Likert-type format is designed to allow customers to respond in varying degrees to each item that describes the service or product. For example, although two customers may say that a particular item describes the service, one customer may want to indicate that the item describes the service to a greater extent than does the other customer.   ·

To allow customers to respond in varying degrees to each item, a Likert-type response format can be used. R. A. Likert (1932) developed a scaling procedure in which the scale represents a bipolar continuum. The low end

---

Please indicate whether or not each statement describes the service you received. Check "Yes" if the statement describes the service or "No" if the statement does not describe the service.

	Yes	No
1. I could get an appointment with the merchant at a time I desired.	_____	_____
2. The merchant was available to schedule me at a good time.	_____	_____
3. My appointment was at a convenient time for me.	_____	_____
4. The merchant was quick to respond when I arrived for my appointment.	_____	_____
5. The merchant immediately helped me when I entered the premises.	_____	_____
6. My appointment started promptly at the scheduled time.	_____	_____

Figure B.3   Example questionnaire using a checklist response format.

represents a negative response while the high end represents a positive response. Some Likert-type formats, each representing a bipolar continuum, appear in Figure B.4.

We can use these response formats for a particular type of item. The first response format in Figure B.4 (the agree-disagree continuum) is used with satisfaction items. Recall that satisfaction items are declarative items that reflect specific good or bad aspects of the service or product. The response scale, therefore, should reflect whether the satisfaction item describes the service. Customers respond to each item in terms of how well that particular item describes the service they received. The quality of the service is then indexed by the extent to which the items describe the service received. An example of a questionnaire using this rating format appears in Figure B.5.

The second and third response formats in Figure B.4 (dissatisfied-satisfied or poor-good continua) can be used for items like those found in Figure B.2. Although these items still reflect specific aspects of the service, they are somewhat neutral. The response scale, therefore, should reflect the degree to which the items (aspects of service) are satisfying (or good) versus dissatisfying (or poor). The quality of the service is indexed by the degree to which people say they are satisfied with the service or the degree to which the service is rated as good. Examples of questionnaires using these rating formats appear in Figures B.6 and B.7.

Advantage of Likert-Type Format

The advantage of using the Likert-type format rather than the checklist format is reflected in the variability of scores that result from the scale. With the quality dimension represented in our questionnaire, we allow customers

Strongly Disagree	Disagree	Neither Agree nor Disagree	Agree	Strongly Agree
1	2	3	4	5
Very Dissatisfied	Dissatisfied	Neither Satisfied nor Dissatisfied	Satisfied	Very Satisfied
1	2	3	4	5
Very Poor	Poor	Neither Poor nor Good	Good	Very Good
1	2	3	4	5

Figure B.4 Examples of Likert-type response formats.

Please indicate the extent to which you agree or disagree with the following statements about the service you received from [company name]. Circle the appropriate number using the scale below.

1—I Strongly Disagree with this statement (SD).
2—I Disagree with this statement (D).
3—I Neither agree nor disagree with this statement (N).
4—I Agree with this statement (A).
5—I Strongly Agree with this statement (SA).

	SD	D	N	A	SA
1. I could get an appointment with the merchant at a time I desired.	1	2	3	4	5
2. The merchant was available to schedule me at a good time.	1	2	3	4	5
3. My appointment was at a convenient time for me.	1	2	3	4	5
4. The merchant was quick to respond when I arrived for my appointment.	1	2	3	4	5
5. The merchant immediately helped me when I entered the premises.	1	2	3	4	5
6. My appointment started promptly at the scheduled time.	1	2	3	4	5

Figure B.5   Questionnaire using a Likert-type response format.

to express the degree of their opinion in the service or product they received rather than restricting them to a "yes" or "no" answer. From a statistical perspective, scales with two response options have less reliability than scales with five response options (Lissitz and Green 1975). In addition, reliability seems to level off after five scale points, suggesting minimal incremental utility using more than five scale points.

In addition, using the Likert-type format will still allow you to determine the percentage of positive and negative responses for a given item. You may do this by combining the responses on the ends of the scale (for example, combining Strongly Disagree with Disagree and combining Strongly Agree with Agree). A response of 1 or 2 is now considered to be a response of 1, a response of 3 is considered to be a response of 2, and a response of 4 or 5 is now considered to be response of 3. We have transformed our five-point scale into a three-point scale. A score of 1 represents a negative response, while a score of 3 represents a positive response. This transformation, therefore, creates somewhat of a checklist format.

Please indicate the extent to which you are satisfied or dissatisfied with the following aspects of the service you received from [company name]. Circle the appropriate number using the scale below

    1—I am Very Dissatisfied with this aspect (VD).
    2—I am Dissatisfied with this aspect (D).
    3—I am Neither satisfied nor dissatisfied with this aspect (N).
    4—I am Satisfied with this aspect (S).
    5—I am Very Satisfied with this aspect (VS).

	VD	D	N	S	VS
1. Appointment time with the merchant	1	2	3	4	5
2. Availability of merchant to schedule me at a good time	1	2	3	4	5
3. Convenience of my appointment	1	2	3	4	5
4. Responsiveness of the merchant when I arrived for my appointment	1	2	3	4	5
5. Promptness of the start time of my appointment	1	2	3	4	5

Figure B.6   Questionnaire using a Likert-type response format of the satisfaction continuum.

INTRODUCTIONS TO CUSTOMER SATISFACTION QUESTIONNAIRES

The next step is to write the introduction to the questionnaire. The introduction should be brief. It should explain the purpose of the questionnaire and provide instructions for completing the questionnaire.

Also, you might explain how the data will be used. Keep this in simple terms that are easily understood. Usually the questionnaire is designed to assess the customers' level of satisfaction. In some circumstances, however, a questionnaire may be designed for a special research project. To the extent that customer knowledge of the purpose of the project does not influence their responses, you might explain the purpose in the instructions. Inclusion of the purpose could increase customer perceptions that their responses are highly valued, thus making them more likely to complete the questionnaire.

The introduction should tell responders how to complete the items and should explain the scale to be used. These instructions must be consistent with the type of response format in the questionnaire. When you use the agree-disagree continuum as the response format, the instructions should

Please rate the extent to which the aspect of the service from [company name] was good or bad. Circle the appropriate number using the scale below.

    1—Aspect of service was Very Poor (VP).
    2—Aspect of service was Poor (P).
    3—Aspect of service was Neither poor nor good (N).
    4—Aspect of service was Good (G).
    5—Aspect of service was Very Good (VG).

	VP	P	N	G	VG
1. Appointment time with the merchant	1	2	3	4	5
2. Availability of merchant to schedule me at a good time	1	2	3	4	5
3. Convenience of my appointment	1	2	3	4	5
4. Responsiveness of the merchant when I arrived for my appointment	1	2	3	4	5
5. Promptness of the start time of my appointment	1	2	3	4	5

Figure B.7   Questionnaire using a Likert-type response format.

ask respondents to indicate the extent to which they agree or disagree with the statements in the questionnaire. When you use the satisfaction continuum as the response format, the instructions should ask respondents to indicate the extent to which they are satisfied.

I have been asked why some of the items in the questionnaires seem redundant. Because some customers become irritated when they feel they are answering the same question over and over again, you may want to include the reason for the similarity of some items. Explain that the questionnaire was designed to include multiple items in order to obtain a more accurate assessment of your customers' opinion. This may not be necessary if the items in the questionnaire are not highly similar. You could pilot test the questionnaire to see whether respondents comment about the apparent redundancy of items.

Here is an example of an introduction for a questionnaire using the agree-disagree continuum:

To help us better serve you, we would like to know your opinion of the quality of service you recently received at [name of company or department]. Please indicate the extent to which you agree or disagree with the following statements about the service you received from the staff. Circle the appropriate number using the scale below. Some statements are similar to others; this will ensure that we accurately determine your opinion concerning our service.

1—I Strongly Disagree with this statement (SD).
2—I Disagree with this statement (D).
3—I Neither agree nor disagree with this statement (N).
4—I Agree with this statement (A).
5—I Strongly Agree with this statement (SA).

This introduction includes the purpose of the questionnaire and instructions for completing the questions. Also, the introduction explains the purpose of using multiple items that are similar.

ITEM SELECTION

Step four in the construction process involves selecting the items to be used in the final questionnaire. Item selection might be warranted if the critical incidents technique resulted in a large number of satisfaction items. For example, if the critical incidents technique resulted in four quality dimensions each containing 10 items, it might not be practical to use all of the items because it could be difficult to get customers to complete a 40-item questionnaire. In this situation, we might want to select the best items from the original set in order to create a smaller, yet equally effective, customer satisfaction questionnaire. If the ratio of satisfaction items to quality dimensions is small (2:1 or less), we may not need to conduct any item selection procedure. Excluding items from an already small set could result in a customer satisfaction questionnaire with low reliability.

I will present two methods that will help you select the best satisfaction items to include in the customer satisfaction questionnaire. The first method is based on human judgment, the second on mathematical indices.

Judgmental Item Selection

One way to select items is to use your best judgment. For your final customer satisfaction questionnaire, try to include items that best represent customers' requirements. The most critical element of this process is to examine the similarity of items within a given quality dimension or customer requirement. Because the goal is to select items that best represent a particular dimension (customer satisfaction or various dimensions of customer requirements), these items should be somewhat similar to each other. If the items obtained from the critical incidents technique are all good, however, selecting the best items might be difficult.

One way to select the best satisfaction items—those that clearly reflect the quality dimension—is to have two people independently select a specified number of items from the total list. Those chosen by both people will be retained. If there is low agreement, it is possible that all satisfaction items are equally good indicators of the underlying quality dimension; if people cannot easily make a distinction between the items, the low agreement may be due to chance factors.

If there is no agreement in selected items, if all the satisfaction items are judged to be equally good indicators of the quality dimensions, then another method must be tried. In the random selection process, any randomly selected set of satisfaction items from the original list will be a representative sample of items from the entire list. A version of random selection is to select either every odd or every even numbered satisfaction item from the full list.

Mathematical Item Selection

Another method of selecting items is to administer all items generated from the critical incidents approach to some actual customers. After these customers complete the questionnaire, conduct item analysis on the data. Item analysis is a catch-all phrase that includes such processes as correlational analysis and factor analysis. You may conduct these statistical techniques to select the best items (those that have equal means and are highly interrelated). These statistical procedures require the help of an expert in questionnaire development. The following section of this chapter illustrates one approach that can be used in item selection.

Statistical procedures such as these will allow you to select which items to retain for your final measure of customer satisfaction. Although this approach is more complex than judgmental item selection, you achieve the invaluable payback of knowing your final questionnaire is statistically reliable; items retained as a result of the item analysis will be, by design, mathematically sound. The general goal in the selection of items is to retain those that differentiate between customers who are dissatisfied and those who are satisfied and drop those items that do not. That is, the items should be able to discriminate between varying levels of customer satisfaction. Items on which highly satisfied and highly dissatisfied customers score the same are not very useful. Item analysis will allow us to identify those items that can discriminate between varying levels of satisfaction.

Item-total correlations. Item-total correlations are correlations between an item and the overall dimension score to which that item belongs (not including the one item being correlated). For example, if we had three items, each measuring the same quality dimension, we would calculate three item-total correlations: (1) item 1 correlated with the composite of items 2 and 3, (2) item 2 correlated with the composite of items 1 and 3, and (3) item 3 correlated with the composite of items 1 and 2. This type of correlation will tell you the extent to which each item is linked to the overall dimension score with which it should be highly linked. The criterion for a cutoff for a correlation coefficient varies depending on the purpose of the measure being developed. When developing a general type of measure, you would use less stringent criteria compared to a measure designed to assess a more specific attitude (Likert 1932). An important requirement is that the overall score of the measure be reliable.

As an example, we might have five items we want to combine into an overall score of professionalism. We must ensure that combining the five items makes sense. If all the items are designed to measure the same dimension (perception of professionalism), then all items for that dimension should be positively related to each other; we would expect to see high item-total correlations. Let's say we used the questionnaire on 100 customers and calculated five item-total correlation coefficients, one for each item. The results of a hypothetical item-total correlation analysis appear in Figure B.8. We see that item 3 is not highly correlated with a composite of the remaining four items; it might be dropped from the questionnaire. The remaining items show relatively high item-total correlations with the composite score of the remaining items. The results suggest that it would make sense to combine items 1, 2, 4, and 5 to obtain an overall score of professionalism.

The low correlation between item 3 and the remaining items could be due to several things. One possibility of why an item demonstrates a low correlation with its subscale might be that it is poorly written. For example, it might include more than a single thought, causing some respondents to want to respond favorably to one part of the item and unfavorably to the other part. It might be necessary to rewrite the item to reflect only one thought or divide it into two separate items.

Overall score **(minus item being correlated)**	
Item 1	$r = .67$
Item 2	$r = .55$
Item 3	$r = .23$
Item 4	$r = .59$
Item 5	$r = .77$

Figure B.8 Hypothetical results of item-total correlations of items designed to measure perception of professionalism.

Another possibility is that a particular item measures some other customer requirement than what was originally thought. For the previous example, we could calculate a correlation between item 3 and the other customer requirements. If item 3 does show a high correlation with another customer requirement, perhaps it should not be dropped from the questionnaire but, instead, included in the summary score for that particular customer requirement to which it is highly linked.

Another possibility is that the item represents a different customer requirement than those included in the questionnaire. An item may not correlate highly with any of the customer requirements. It could be that we failed to establish an important customer requirement in our clustering of critical incidents. This correlational approach could address such errors of omission. When this situation arises, perhaps we could write more items to reflect the content of that particular item. Subsequently, we could re-administer the revised questionnaire (with the new items) to conduct additional item analysis. If the new items are representative of that lone item, then that lone item should now correlate highly with the new items, thus forming a new customer requirement scale.

Group differences. Another mathematical item selection strategy employs the comparison of two groups of respondents (Likert 1932). This procedure is also conducted after respondents have completed the questionnaire. Within each subscale (for example, availability or timeliness), we select two groups of people, each group representing the extreme of the attitude measured by a particular scale. Usually, the top and bottom 10 percent are selected, based on their overall score for the particular subscale. Next, for each group, we calculate means for each item. Then we calculate a difference score for each item, subtracting the mean of the lower extreme group from the mean of the higher extreme group.

For each item we obtain a difference score. This difference score reflects how much a particular item was able to discriminate between the two groups on an attitude the item was designed to measure. The higher the difference score, the higher the discrimination. If an item does not differentiate between the two groups, then we would obtain a difference score of 0. These items are dropped from the questionnaire. For items that are positively phrased (higher score means higher level of the attitude), we select items that have a large positive difference score. For those items that are negatively phrased (higher score means lower level of the attitude), we select items that have a large negative difference score.

The indices used in the item-total correlation procedure (item-total correlation) and the group differences procedure (difference score) have been shown to be highly correlated (Likert 1932). This suggests that both procedures will result in similar outcomes with respect to the inclusion of items in the final form of the questionnaire.

Factor analysis. Another statistical technique of item selection, often used in conjunction with item-total correlations, is factor analysis. This technique (see Appendix K) will demonstrate which items are more highly related to the underlying dimension they are designed to measure.

Factor analysis is a highly specialized form of analysis. It is beyond the scope of this book to provide you with exact procedures for the selection of items. However, here are some general guidelines. It is essential that items within each scale load on a single factor if the items are to be used in a composite score. When an item loads highly on a different factor than the one for which it was intended, this suggests that the item might best be combined with items with which it is highly related. When an item does not load highly on any factor, this suggests that the item does not discriminate between high and low groups on the attitudes that are measured with the items in the current questionnaire.

An advantage of using factor analysis is the identification of underlying constructs (customer requirements) being measured by the items in the questionnaire. Also, factor analysis allows us to determine which customer requirement each item is measuring. A disadvantage of factor analysis is that it requires a large number of questionnaire respondents if the results are to be reliable. The number of respondents should be five to 10 times the number of items in the questionnaire. For example, if the questionnaire contains 20 items, the factor analysis should be conducted using the responses of 100 to 200 people.

Factor analysis has been used in applied research. For example, Parasuraman, Zeithaml, and Berry (1988) used factor analysis in developing a service quality questionnaire. The goal of the research was to develop a reliable scale that assesses various components of service quality. The authors present the results of the exploratory factor analysis of responses to 97 items.

On the basis of the factor analysis, the authors selected items that were good indicators of underlying dimensions. They also presented the results of the factor analysis, which included the number of factors as well as the factor pattern matrix (after rotation). This article presents an excellent example of the use of factor analysis in developing customer satisfaction questionnaires.

Mathematical item selection is usually used in the initial stages of questionnaire development. Even if you use the judgmental item selection process, you may conduct item analysis on the retained items (after customers have completed them) to determine whether the items chosen constitute a reliable scale. Figure B.9 presents the chronological use of item analysis in the selection of items when using either the mathematical item selection or the judgmental item selection process.

Judgmental Item Selection	Mathematical Item Selection
1. Select small set of items using judgmental criteria or random selection.	1. Place all satisfaction items in the questionnaire.
2. Place this set of satisfaction items in the questionnaire.	2. Use questionnaire on customers.
3. Use questionnaire on customers.	3. Conduct item analysis to determine which items to retain for final questionnaire (need sufficient sample size of approximately five people per item if factor analysis will be used).
4. Conduct item analysis to determine if these items measure quality dimensions.	4. Examine outcome of item analysis and select good items for final version of questionnaire.
5. Examine outcome of item analysis to retain good items.	5. Use final version of the questionnaire.
6. Results may indicate entire questionnaire revision (if items do not measure the underlying dimensions).	

Figure B.9   The use of item analysis in judgmental item selection and mathematical item selection.

SUMMARY OF ITEM SELECTION

Items in the customer satisfaction questionnaire should be relevant, concise, and unambiguous. They should also be written clearly to avoid double negatives and to reflect only a single thought. A well-written introduction describes the purpose of the questionnaire and provides instructions for completing it.

This chapter presented two response formats that can be used in questionnaires. A checklist format allows customers to indicate whether a particular item represents the service or product. A Likert-type format allows customers to further distinguish their responses beyond what is allowed by the checklist format. The choice between these two types of format depends on the type of data desired from the questionnaire.

Also, this chapter outlined two procedures used when selecting items for the customer satisfaction questionnaire. The judgmental procedure can be useful when the initial items are all good items. If you are using the mathematical approach, consult somebody conversant in these mathematical procedures when you attempt to select items. Mathematical item selection is designed to select items that are statistically sound.

Figure B.10 outlines the general steps to follow in questionnaire development. Each step is accompanied by various methods that are used for that step and by other important issues for consideration. This figure is designed to summarize and highlight the important points in the chapter and can be used as a checklist when developing the questionnaire.

WEB-BASED CUSTOMER SURVEYS

Web-based surveys are popular for collecting customer feedback data. According to a recent survey (Hayes, 2008), 68 percent of customer feedback professionals indicated that their company uses web-based surveys to collect customer feedback data. This web-based platform for collecting these data was as popular as or more popular than other traditional methods, including telephone (66 percent), paper-pencil (47 percent), and interviews (47 percent).

In Web-based surveys, respondents are typically invited via email containing a hyperlink that takes them directly to the survey. An example of an email introduction and survey appears in Figure B.11.

Survey invitations have an embedded hyperlink that directs respondents to the hosted survey. Some companies use surveys that provide a unique hyperlink to each respondent, the hyperlink identifying the respondent. In these cases, existing customer data (for example, product owned, service warranty levels, region, and age) can be matched to each respondent's survey responses for later segmentation. The existing customer data can be used to personalize the email invitation and can help to deliver the appropriate customer survey to the right people (for example, customers in the sales cycle receive the sales survey; customers in the service cycle receive the service survey). Additionally, the existing data helps reduce the number of survey questions asked of the respondent.

The hyperlink sends the respondents to a survey in which they canBprovide feedback about the company. (See Figure B.12 for an example of a web-based survey.)

Steps	Important Issues
1. Generate items for questionnaire.	• Select items from satisfaction item list. • Write items based on satisfaction items.
2. Ensure items are written appropriately.	• Items should appear relevant to what you are trying to measure. • Items should be concise. • Items should be unambiguous. • Items should contain only one thought (items ask only one question). • Items should not contain double negatives.
3. Select response format for items.	• Checklist format. • Likert-type format.
4. Write introduction to questionnaire.	• State the purpose of the questionnaire. • State instructions on how to complete the questionnaire.
5. Select representative sample of items.	• Items within each quality dimension should be similar in content.
a. Using judgmental item selection	• Use multiple judges to select the items.
b. Using mathematical item selection	• Use item-total correlations or group differences approach in selecting items. • Could also use factor analysis.
6. Evaluate the retained items.	• Calculate reliability of the scales within questionnaire using split-half method or Cronbach's estimate.

Figure B.10   Guidelines in the development of questionnaires.

We are conducting a survey to help us understand your opinions about our products and services. To that end, we have developed a survey enabling you to provide specific feedback on how you feel about our company. Your feedback will help us make improvements to ensure we deliver the best products and services to you.

Survey Company is conducting this survey for Business Over Broadway; we invite you to connect to the survey site and complete your response. To access the survey, please click on the URL below. The survey will take approximately 10 minutes to complete. It will remain open until <CLOSE DATE>.

http://www.surveyhyperlinkgoeshere.com

Individual responses to this survey will remain strictly confidential. Results will be reported in aggregate form only.

Thank you for your time and feedback.

Sincerely,

Bob E. Hayes, Ph.D.
President, Business Over Broadway
bob@businessoverbroadway.com
www.businessoverbroadway.com

Figure B.11   Sample email invitation to Web-based survey.

Benefits of Web-Based Surveys

There are a few benefits of collecting customer feedback using Web-based surveys, compared to other traditional methods. First, Web-based surveys are relatively inexpensive to conduct. Unlike paper-pencil methods, there are no costs associated with printing, stuffing envelopes, postage, or data entry. Additionally, no interviewer is needed with Web-based surveys.

Response rates for Web-based surveys are typically higher than for other methods because they are easier to complete and respondents can respond at their own convenience.

Dillman (2000) has listed other advantages of web surveys, which are related to faster response rate, ease of sending reminders to participants, and ease of data processing because survey responses can be downloaded to a spreadsheet, data analysis package, or database without the need for manual data entry.

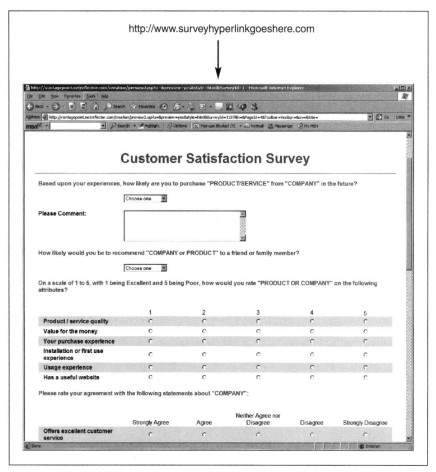

Figure B.12   Hyperlink takes respondent directly to the web-based survey.

Survey presentation and completion are greatly facilitated with the use of Web-based surveys compared to other survey methods. Specifically, survey questions can be sorted randomly or in any other desired order. Dynamic error checking (that is, verifying that responses are appropriate or valid) is also an advantage of Web-based surveys. Additionally, skip patterns for survey questions are facilitated with Web-based surveys where a response to a given question dictates future survey questions which are asked. (For example, respondents are asked whether they received technical support. If yes, they are asked additional questions about technical support. If no, they are not asked these additional questions.). Web surveys allow for the inclusion of pop-up instructions for selected questions as well as multiple methods for answering questions (for example, check-box, drop-down boxes, and so on).

Principles for Designing Web-based Surveys

Dillman et al. (1998) outlines several principles to consider when designing Web surveys:

1. Introduce the questionnaire with a welcome screen that is motivational, that emphasizes the ease of responding, and that instructs respondents on the action needed for proceeding to the next page.

2. Begin with a question that is fully visible on the first screen of the questionnaire, one that will be easily comprehended and answered by all respondents.

3. Present each question in a conventional format similar to that normally used on paper questionnaires.

4. Limit line length to decrease the likelihood of a long line of prose extending across the screen of the respondent's browser.

5. Provide specific instructions on how to take each necessary computer action for responding to questionnaires.

6. Provide computer operation instructions as part of each question for which action is to be taken, not in a separate section prior to the beginning of the questionnaire.

7. Do not require respondents to provide an answer to every question before being allowed to proceed to subsequent questions.

8. Construct questionnaires that scroll from question to question unless sequence is a major concern, a large number of questions must be skipped, or a mixed-mode survey is being done for which telephone interview and web results will be combined.

9. When the number of answer choices exceeds the number that can be displayed on one screen, consider double-banking; be sure to include appropriate navigational instructions.

10. Use graphical symbols or words that convey a sense of where the respondent is in completing the survey.

Tips for Conducting Web-Based Surveys

1. Shorten the timing between notice and reminders and the total duration of the response period. Most of the time, 8-10 working days or less is sufficient.

2. Shorten the length of invitation and reminder messages.

3. Keep the questionnaires short.

4. Simplify the questions even more so than in paper surveys.

5. Think of the survey as an outline version of a conversation. Build in a natural flow, with appropriate transitions between one thought and the next.

6. Pilot test each survey with a variety of people using different browsers.

7. Avoid undeliverable e-mail invitations by developing accurate potential respondent e-mail lists.

8. Extract narrative text responses from data before importing into the numerical data analysis program SPSS. Extraneous commas and other characters will require "cleaning" the data.

CUSTOMER LOYALTY MEASUREMENT

The concept of customer loyalty is as broad as the fields to which it is applied. Marketing departments create customer loyalty programs to ensure that customers purchase more frequently and exclusively at their company. Companies add new features to increase the "stickiness" of their Web sites so customers stay longer, increasing the opportunity that customers will make a transaction. While these areas of customer loyalty are beyond the scope (or intent) of this discussion, this section will focus on the measurement of customer loyalty as it applies to customer survey research. Please see the bibliography for useful books on these topics.

Customer Loyalty and Financial Performance

Customer loyalty has been shown to be a leading indicator of business performance metrics. Researchers have demonstrated a link between customer loyalty and financial success and growth. For example, Reichheld et al. (1990) demonstrated that decreasing customer defections by 5 percent increases profits from 25 percent to 85 percent across a variety of industries. While they focused on defection rates, there are several objective measures of customer loyalty that show a relationship with financial performance:

- Number of referrals
- Word of mouth/word of mouse
- Purchase again
- Purchase additional products
- Increase purchase size
- Customer retention/defection rates

Based on the objective measures of customer loyalty, we can see how company financial growth can occur through the increase in customer loyalty. Through the referral process, companies can grow through the acquisition of new customers. The idea is that the customer acquisition process relies on existing customers to promote and recommend the company to their friends; these friends, in turn, become customers. Another way to strengthen the financial growth of a company is to affect the purchasing behavior (that is, increase the number of purchases or stimulate the purchase of additional products or services) of existing customers. Finally, company growth is dependent on its ability to not lose existing customers at a rate faster than they are acquired. For example, customer defection rate is an important metric in the wireless service industry, where customer defections not uncommon.

MEASUREMENT OF CUSTOMER LOYALTY

Customer loyalty, when measured through surveys, is typically assessed through the use of standard questions or items, mirroring the objective measures listed above. For each item, customers are asked to rate their level of affinity for, endorsement of, and approval of a company. The items usually ask for a rating that reflects the likelihood that the customer will exhibit future positive behaviors toward a company. Commonly used customer loyalty survey questions include the following items:

- Overall satisfaction
- Likelihood to choose again
- Likelihood to recommend
- Likelihood to continue purchasing the same products and services
- Likelihood to purchase additional products and services
- Likelihood to increase frequency of purchasing
- Likelihood to switch to a different provider

The first question is rated on a scale (for example, 0 = Extremely dissatisfied to 10 = Extremely satisfied). The remaining questions allow respondents to indicate their likelihood of behaving in different ways toward the company (for example, 0 = Not at all likely to 10 = Extremely likely). Higher ratings reflect higher levels of customer loyalty.

Customer loyalty questions should appear at the start of the survey, before business attribute questions are presented. Presenting loyalty questions at the start of the survey ensures that responses to those loyalty questions reflect the respondents' general perceptions regarding their relationship with the company. When loyalty questions follow other business attribute questions, respondents' rating of the loyalty questions is affected.

Standardized Loyalty Questions

The loyalty questions mentioned previously have been used in many research studies across a variety of industries; results have shown that these loyalty questions are reliable, valid, and useful measures of customer loyalty (see Chapter 6 for detailed research behind these questions).

Additionally, these loyalty questions are both theoretically and empirically linked to financial growth of companies across a variety of consumer groups. Responses to these loyalty questions help organizations understand their expected growth.

The loyalty questions presented have merit. However, my intent is not to discourage you from developing your own loyalty questions for your particular organizational needs. Nevertheless, your time might be better spent developing specific business attribute questions for your particular needs rather than developing loyalty questions.

CUSTOMER SURVEYS AND CUSTOMER LOYALTY

While many objective measures of customer loyalty exist (for example, defection rate, number of referrals), customer surveys remain a frequently used way to assess customer loyalty. There are valid reasons for the popularity of customer surveys in customer experience management. First, customer surveys allow companies to quickly and easily gauge levels of customer loyalty. Companies may not have easy access to objective customer loyalty data; they may simply not gather such data. Second, results from customer surveys can be easily used to change organizational business process. Customer surveys commonly include questions about customer loyalty as well as the customer experience relative to product, service, and support. Used jointly, both business attribute items and loyalty indices (driver analysis, segmentation analysis) can be used to identify reasons why customers are loyal or disloyal. Finally, objective measures of customer loyalty (for example, defection rates and repurchase rates) provide a backward look into customer loyalty levels. Customer surveys allow companies to examine customer loyalty in real time. Surveys ask about expected levels of loyalty-related behavior and let companies "look into the future" regarding customer loyalty.

Customer Relationship Management and Customer Experience Management

While there has been a change in business nomenclature around the application of customer surveys, from "customer relationship management" to "customer experience management," the analytical techniques used to understand the survey data (for example, segmentation analysis and driver analysis) remain exactly the same. The ultimate goal of customer loyalty survey analyses, no matter what business nomenclature you use, is to identify the reasons why customers are loyal or disloyal. You might think of customer loyalty as the ultimate criterion in customer relationship and experience management.

The use of customer loyalty survey data to help manage customer relationships has benefited from technological innovation over the past decade. Web-based surveys provide an easy vehicle for customers to provide feedback. For example, in B2B uses of customer loyalty surveys, individual customer concerns are addressed by means of automated prompts (typically in the form of emails) to account team members who are responsible for quickly resolving specific issues. Additionally, organization-wide customer loyalty issues are identified through automated analyses (for example, driver analysis) that highlight common causes of customer loyalty and disloyalty. Furthermore, customer survey results are accessible 24x7 by all employees through Web-based reporting tools. Finally, companies even link customer survey data to their CRM systems in order to enhance day-to-day account management with both attitudinal data and operational data. It is clear that efforts in the field of customer loyalty have simplified the process of data collection, analysis, reporting, and integration with existing business systems.

Chapter 7 will discuss in more detail how customer surveys can be used in customer relationship and experience strategies to improve customer loyalty.

Appendix C
Measurement Scales

Measurement scales are the means by which we assign a number to an object or entity. The number on the scale represents some characteristics of that object or entity. Stevens (1951) divided measurement scales into four types: nominal, ordinal, interval, and ratio. The degree to which these scales differ is reflected in the degree to which arithmetic operations make sense with the values of the entity represented by the numbers on the scale. The discussion of each scale will clarify this.

NOMINAL SCALE

A nominal scale categorizes objects. These objects are mutually exclusive, and the numbers on the nominal scale reflect only that the objects are different from one another. For example, we might use a nominal scale to categorize customers on the basis of their marital status.

Single people are assigned a 1.
Married people are assigned a 2.
Divorced people are assigned a 3.

We may also use a nominal scale to label a set of stores.

Bob's Barn is assigned a 1.
Tom's Tent is assigned a 2.
Stephen's Store is assigned a 3.
Marissa's Mall is assigned a 4.

Let's look at arithmetic operations using the scale values for customers' marital status. Some operations that would *not* make sense are addition and subtraction. For example, a Stephen's Store (3) minus a Tom's Tent (2) would not equal a Bob's Barn (1). The only arithmetic operations that can be used on a nominal scale are the equality and inequality operations. For example, within our present store categorization system, a Stephen's Store (3) is the same as another Stephen's Store (3). Also $1 \neq 2$ indicates that a Bob's Barn is not the same as a Tom's Tent.

Because the values on the nominal scale represent categories, they can also be identified by different symbols, such as letters of the alphabet. For example, a Bob's Barn might be labeled an "A," a Tom's Tent as "B," a Stephen's Store as "C," and a Marissa's Mall as "D."

ORDINAL SCALE

An ordinal scale uses numbers to order objects with respect to some characteristic. For example, we can place customers in order according to their satisfaction level. If person A is more satisfied than person B, and person B is more satisfied than person C, then person A is more satisfied than person C. Using an ordinal scale, we may assign a number to each of these people and rank them from least satisfied (person C) to most satisfied (person A). The numbers corresponding to this satisfaction ordinal scale could be:

> Person C is a 1.
> Person B is a 2.
> Person A is a 3.

Let's look at some arithmetic operations applied to ordinal scales. Equality/inequality operations can be applied to ordinal scales. For example, in an equality/inequality operation, we can say that person C (1) is not equal to person A (3). We can also use the operations of less than (<) and greater than (>) on ordinal scales. Statements such as $3 > 2$ and $1 < 3$ make sense, indicating that person A is more satisfied than person B and person C is less satisfied than person A, respectively.

Another example of ordinal scales is reflected in the ranking of companies on some variable. For example, in studying a wide variety of companies, a research firm may assess the satisfaction level of its customers. In a final report, the research firm ranks the companies from highest to lowest in terms of its customers' overall satisfaction level. Suppose the study included five companies. The company with the highest average score on the customer satisfaction questionnaire would be ranked 5; the company with the second highest score would be ranked 4; and so forth:

> Company A is a 5.
> Company B is a 4.
> Company C is a 3.
> Company D is a 2.
> Company E is a 1.

Although ordinal scales allow us to order objects, they do not allow us to determine the distance between the objects with respect to the characteristic being measured. For the example of ranking customers in terms of satisfaction, we know the order of the people but do not know how much more satisfied one person is relative to another. Also, ranking the companies does not tell us how much more satisfied company A's customers are compared to customers of other companies. This inability to determine differences between objects relates to the ordinal scale's lack of a unit of measurement.

INTERVAL SCALE

An interval scale orders things so that differences between scale values are equal, because the interval scale has a unit of measurement. One example is the Fahrenheit scale.

We can use more arithmetic operations with interval scale values. In addition to the equality/inequality and ordering operations, we can perform subtraction. For example, the difference between 50°F and 40°F equals the difference between 120°F and 110°F.

Attitude questionnaires are assumed to possess the features of an interval scale. If this assumption is true, we can perform useful arithmetic operations with the data from such questionnaires, which will aid in the interpretation of the data.

RATIO SCALE

A ratio scale is similar to the interval scale in that it possesses a unit of measurement. The ratio scale has one additional feature: a meaningful zero point. An example of a ratio scale is the measurement of length. All arithmetic operations are meaningful for the ratio scale. This includes equality/inequality, ordering, subtraction, addition, and division. Table C.1 summarizes the characteristics of measurement scales.

Table C.1   Types of measurement scales and the functional uses of each.

		Functional uses			
		Establish equality/ inequality	Establish rank ordering	Establish equal differences between scale points	Establish zero point
	Nominal	yes	no	no	no
Scale	Ordinal	yes	yes	no	no
types	Interval	yes	yes	yes	no
	Ratio	yes	yes	yes	yes

MEASUREMENT SCALES
IN CUSTOMER SATISFACTION

Some of the measurement scales can be used in customer satisfaction questionnaires to categorize customers (nominal scale) and differentiate customers along some continuum (interval scale). Development of questionnaires to assess customers' perceptions and attitudes is based on the notion that the scales possess features found in the interval scale. In addition, we imply the use of a scale when we rank companies on the basis of their quality (ordinal scale). The ranking of companies is best accompanied by evidence that the ranking reflects meaningful, statistically significant differences between companies (see Appendix F).

Example

A hospital wanted to determine the quality of its physicians and front office staff. The survey was to be used to track this information over time and to compare the various office locations across the western region, where the company has its offices. The survey is presented in Figure C.1.

We can divide the various questions into the types of measurement scales. Nominal scales are illustrated by the following questions: location of exam, name of patient, gender of patient, and name of physician. There is some debate as to the classification of rating scales for surveys. While some might classify rating scales as ordinal measures, we make the assumption that rating scales possess features of interval measures. Ratio scales are illustrated by the following questions: time with doctor and wait time (time you saw your doctor minus the time of your appointment).

The goal at Doc in a Box is to ensure you get the best service possible. Please take the time to answer the following questions. Your opinions are important to us. We will use this information to help us learn how to meet your needs in the best way we possibly can. To mail, please fold at the lines on the back of this sheet and seal with tape and drop in any mailbox. Thank you.

Date of exam:————————— Location of exam:—————————

Name of patient: ——————————————————————————

Physician's name: —————————————————————————

For each of the following questions, please indicate whether the phrase describes your experience at Doc in the Box. Please use the rating scale below. Circle your response for each question.

Y = Yes, describes my experience   N = No, does not describe my experience   ? = Not sure

Physician Quality

	Yes	No	Not Sure
1. Introduced himself/herself to me.	Y	N	?
2. Asked me how I was injured/became ill.	Y	N	?
3. Listened to me.	Y	N	?
4. Treated me with respect.	Y	N	?
5. Was professional in doing the examination.	Y	N	?
6. Spent enough time with me (not rushed).	Y	N	?

7. Please rate your overall experience of the exam, using the following scale (circle your response).

Terrible	Poor	Fair	Good	Excellent
1	2	3	4	5

Office Quality

	Yes	No	Not Sure
1. Appointment was at a convenient time.	Y	N	?
2. Waiting area was clean.	Y	N	?
3. Waiting room was comfortable.	Y	N	?
4. Examination room was clean.	Y	N	?
5. Office staff treated me with respect.	Y	N	?
6. I received a call from Doc in the Box reminding me of my appointment.	Y	N	?
7. Office staff answered my questions.	Y	N	?
8. Office staff was professional.	Y	N	?

9. Time of your appointment ———— A.M. P.M. Time you saw your doctor: ———— A.M. P.M.

Thank you for your time and for completing this survey. Please place in a mailbox. There is room for comments on the reverse side of this form.

Figure C.1   Patient satisfaction questionnaire.

Appendix D

Frequencies, Percentages, Probabilities, Histograms, and Distributions

Data can be overwhelming. Often we are confronted with large data sets consisting of hundreds of scores. We need a way of summarizing the data to make some sense of it. This appendix will discuss one way of summarizing large data sets with the use of frequencies and histograms.

FREQUENCIES

Table D.1 lists scores from a hypothetical study examining the level of customer satisfaction of a given company. The data set contains 48 scores, each representing one person's average score on the customer satisfaction questionnaire. Upon examination, we see that scores vary somewhat, ranging from a low of 1.4 to a high of 4.6. To gain a better understanding of the data, we need to summarize the scores in a simple format.

One way of summarizing data is to calculate the frequency of occurrence of a specific value, or how often that given value occurs in our data set. To calculate frequencies, we first rank the scores from lowest to highest (see Table D.2). After the ranking, we determine the frequency of occurrence of each value. We see that the value of 1.4 occurred only once. Therefore, 1.4 has a frequency of one. Likewise, the value of 2.5 has a frequency of four.

Although calculating frequencies for each specific value will help summarize the information, the amount of information can still be overwhelming. For example, with characteristics measured in small increments, we may obtain many values, each occurring with little frequency. Calculating the frequency of each value might not be enough to simplify the data. Therefore, when calculating frequencies, we usually group values with similar scores into a particular class. Then we calculate frequencies for these class values.

Table D.1 Hypothetical data set.

2.3	4.3	3.3	1.5
2.5	2.7	3.4	3.2
4.1	3.8	3.7	2.9
3.0	2.7	2.5	3.4
4.6	2.3	2.1	2.3
3.7	3.6	1.4	3.2
1.5	1.6	1.7	3.6
4.0	4.1	3.4	2.1
3.3	3.1	3.5	4.4
2.5	2.8	3.9	2.0
1.7	2.5	2.9	3.8
4.2	2.1	3.9	2.4

Table D.2 Data from Table D.1 ranked from smallest to largest.

1.4	2.3	3.1	3.7
1.5	2.4	3.2	3.8
1.5	2.5	3.2	3.8
1.6	2.5	3.3	3.9
1.7	2.5	3.3	3.9
1.7	2.5	3.4	4.0
2.0	2.7	3.4	4.1
2.1	2.7	3.4	4.1
2.1	2.8	3.5	4.2
2.1	2.9	3.6	4.3
2.3	2.9	3.6	4.4
2.3	3.0	3.7	4.6

CLASS INTERVALS

A class interval represents a range in which a set of values is included. Creating class intervals is a process of dividing the scores into specified equal intervals. Each class interval is defined by a lower bound and an upper bound. The lower bound represents the lowest possible score that can be included in the interval; the upper bound represents the highest possible score. Using the data set in Table D.2, we can create a class interval with the width of 0.4 to represent the scores. Starting with a lower bound of 1.0, the first class interval would include scores ranging from a low of 1.0 to a high of 1.4. The second class interval would include scores ranging from 1.5 to 1.9. The last class interval would include scores ranging from 4.5 to 4.9. Table D.3 presents these class intervals and the frequency of values that occur in the class.

We use arbitrary numbers to select class intervals and determine the width of each interval. It has been shown that, if continuous data are divided into intervals, you lose less information about the data by creating more intervals. A reasonable number of intervals is seven (Shaw, Huffman, and Haviland 1987), although more intervals would result in less information loss.

PERCENTAGES

Another way of looking at the frequency of values is through the use of percentages. A percentage reflects the proportion of scores of a particular value. The percentage for a particular value is calculated by dividing the frequency of a given value by the total number of scores in the data set. For

Table D.3   Frequencies for the class variable.

Class interval	Frequency	Percentage
1.0 to 1.4	1	2.1%
1.5 to 1.9	5	10.4%
2.0 to 2.4	8	16.7%
2.5 to 2.9	9	18.8%
3.0 to 3.4	9	18.8%
3.5 to 3.9	9	18.8%
4.0 to 4.4	6	12.5%
4.5 to 4.9	1	2.1%
Total	48	100.0%

our data, we see that the percentage of people with scores of 2.5 to 2.9 is 18.8 percent (9/48), and the percentage of people with scores ranging from 4.0 to 4.9 is 14.6 percent (7/48). The total of the percentages for a given question should be 100 percent (given rounding errors).

The percentage is sometimes preferred to the frequency since it incorporates the total number of scores into its calculation. A frequency of 50 may not tell us all we want to know about the data. A frequency of 50 in one sample of scores may indicate a large percentage (for example, when sample size is 60), while in another sample a frequency of 50 may indicate a minute percentage (for example, when sample size is 1,000,000). Thus, before interpreting the magnitude of the frequency, we should be aware of the total sample size.

CONSTRUCTING FREQUENCY DISTRIBUTIONS OF THE INTERVALS

We can graphically represent the frequencies of the class intervals. The graph is formally called a *histogram*. The histogram aids in summarizing the data beyond the lone use of frequencies since it captures many pieces of information in a single picture. The histogram not only indicates the frequency of each value, but also roughly indicates the range of the data (lowest to highest value) and the shape of the distribution.

The histogram has two axes. The horizontal axis (sometimes referred to as the *X axis* or *abscissa*) represents the variable or class interval. The vertical axis (sometimes referred to as the *Y axis* or *ordinate*) represents the frequency for a variable or class interval.

The horizontal axis is scaled by the midpoint of each class interval. Therefore, for the data in Table D.3, the horizontal axis would be scaled by eight values, each value representing the midpoint of it's class interval. The midpoints are 1.2, 1.7, 2.2, 2.7, 3.2, 3.7, 4.2, and 4.7. The histogram appears in Figure D.1.

Frequency tables and histograms are both useful tools for summarizing data. The frequency table reflects the frequency of occurrence of specific values or the frequency of values for a specific class interval. The histogram is a graphic illustration of the frequency table.

We can calculate frequencies for variables that are on any scale of measurement (nominal, ordinal, interval, and ratio). For example, a questionnaire could include various questions pertaining to satisfaction levels as well as questions asking for demographic information. The demographic portion could include questions pertaining to sex and age.

If the questionnaire was distributed to 150 people, we could subsequently calculate the frequency or proportion of males versus females and also determine the frequency or proportion of a given age group.

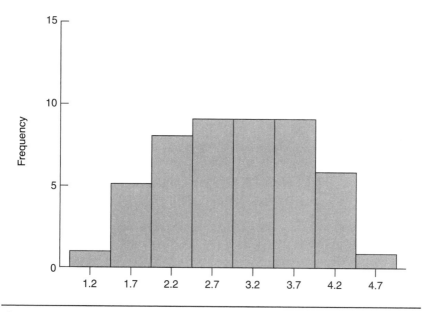

Figure D.1   Histogram of the class intervals in Table D.3.

The frequencies for the sex variable (nominal) and age variable (ratio) are listed in Table D.4. The frequencies indicate that the sample consists of more males than females. In terms of percentages, we see that males represent 58 percent (87/150) of respondents and females represent 42 percent of respondents. Also, this sample consists of a large group of people aged 36 to 45 years.

Table D.4   Frequencies and percentages for the variables of sex and age.

Sex	Frequency	%	Age	Frequency	%
M	87	58.0	0–15	0	0.0
F	63	42.0	16–25	3	2.0
			26–35	44	29.3
			36–45	64	42.7
			46–55	25	16.7
			56–older	44	9.3
Total	150	100.0%	Total	150	100.0%

DISTRIBUTIONS

The histogram in Figure D.1 can also be called a *distribution of scores*. Although there are many forms of distributions, such as a bimodal (two-humped) distribution and a unimodal (one-humped) distribution, I will present a special type called a *normal distribution*. The normal distribution is a symmetric, bell-shaped distribution. Many of the things we measure in our environment can be described by a symmetric, bell-shaped distribution. For example, if the heights of many people were plotted, the shape of the histogram would form a normal distribution.

DETERMINING PROBABILITIES FROM DISTRIBUTIONS

Given a distribution, we can calculate probabilities of various events. For example, we may have measured the height of 1000 people. The data of height forms a normal distribution described by some mean and variance (see distribution of $n = 1$ in Figure F.1). Now let's say we were to select one person at random from this sample. What is the probability that the height of that person is greater than 65"?

We determine the probability by dividing the number of people who are taller than 65" by the total number of people in the sample. We can also determine the probability by calculating the area under the curve to the right of 65". We can describe this area as a percentage of people who are taller than 65". We can then transform this percentage into a probability by dividing the value by 100.

As we increase the height of our criterion to 70", we see that the probability of selecting a person greater than that criterion decreases, since the area under the curve to the right of the criterion decreases.

Example

The percentage of respondents for each of the questions is presented in Table D.5.

As we can see in Table D.5, the distribution of scores is fairly evenly spread across the three quarters of the year. Additionally, the surveys are from all of the offices in the western region. Most of the surveys represent our San Jose, Yakima, Tacoma, and Spokane offices. San Diego and Sonoma have the least number of surveys in our sample. Furthermore, a little more than half of the surveys (53.4 percent) are from offices located in the state of Washington. Looking at the percentage of responses for our survey questions, many of the customers indicate a "Yes" to the questions. The percent of "Yes" responses range from a low of 53.4 percent to a high of 99.1 percent.

Table D.5 Frequencies and percentages for the patient satisfaction questionnaire.

Quarter of survey	Frequency	Percentage
1st quarter	462	34.4
2nd quarter	466	34.7
3rd quarter	414	30.8

Month of survey	Frequency	Percentage
January	153	11.4
February	149	11.1
March	160	11.9
April	155	11.5
May	169	12.6
June	142	10.6
July	133	9.9
August	138	10.3
September	143	10.7

Office location	Frequency	Percentage
Yakima	180	13.4
Seattle	176	13.1
San Francisco	150	11.2
Tacoma	180	13.4
San Jose	181	13.5
Sacramento	155	11.5
Spokane	180	13.4
San Diego	58	4.3
Sonoma	82	6.1

Office location	Frequency	Percentage
Washington	716	53.4
California	626	46.6

Physician Quality

	Yes	No	Not Sure
1. Introduced himself/herself to me.	1297 (97.4%)	23 (1.7%)	12 (0.9%)
2. Asked me how I was injured/became ill.	1268 (95.3%)	52 (3.9%)	11 (0.8%)
3. Listened to me.	1186 (90.5%)	60 (4.6%)	64 (4.9%)
4. Treated me with respect.	1256 (94.5%)	33 (2.5%)	40 (3.0%)
5. Was professional in doing the examination.	1261 (95.2%)	33 (2.5%)	31 (2.3%)
6. Spent enough time with me (not rushed).	1078 (83.2%)	118 (9.1%)	100 (7.7%)

7. Please rate your overall experience of the exam, using the following scale (circle your response.)

Terrible	Poor	Fair	Good	Excellent
21 (1.6%)	41 (3.2%)	178 (13.9%)	608 (47.4%)	435 (33.9)

(Continued)

(Continued)

Table D.5 Frequencies and percentages for the patient satisfaction questionnaire.

Office Quality

	Yes	No	Not Sure
1. Appointment was at a convenient time.	1156 (87.9%)	143 (10.9%)	16 (1.2%)
2. Waiting area was clean.	1319 (99.1%)	10 (0.8%)	2 (0.1%)
3. Waiting room was comfortable.	1288 (96.9%)	27 (2.0%)	14 (1.1%)
4. Examination room was clean.	1312 (98.7%)	10 (0.8%)	7 (0.8%)
5. Office staff treated me with respect.	1302 (98.1%)	18 (1.4%)	7 (0.5%)
6. I received a call from Doc in the Box reminding me of my appointment.	703 (53.4%)	554 (42.1%)	60 (4.6%)
7. Office staff answered my questions.	1205 (94.8%)	33 (2.6%)	33 (2.6%)
8. Office staff was professional.	1291 (97.9%)	16 (1.2%)	12 (0.9%)

Figure D.2 shows a histogram of the responses for the overall rating. As is indicated, most of the respondents indicate a "Good" or "Excellent" response.

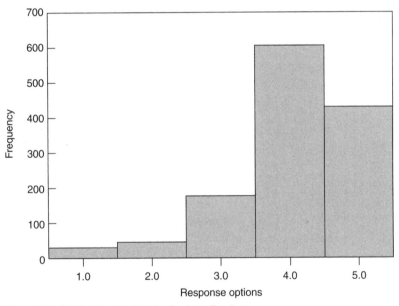

Note: 1 = Terrible, 2 = Poor, 3 = Fair, 4 = Good, 5 = Excellent

Figure D.2 Histogram of the overall rating of the exam.

SUMMARY

This appendix introduced various ways of describing and presenting data. Frequencies and percentages convey the occurrence of values in the data set. Histograms are a useful way of presenting data. They convey the frequency of values as well as the range of the data set. Histograms can also be thought of as distributions. The probability of a given event occurring can also be determined using the distribution.

Appendix E
Descriptive Statistics

The use of frequencies and histograms is one way of summarizing data (see Appendix D). Another way to summarize large data sets is with the use of summary indices, which describe the shape of the histogram. Two types of summary indices help us understand the data: central tendency and variability.

CENTRAL TENDENCY

One way of summarizing data is to determine the center or middle point of scores. Measures of central tendency allow us to determine roughly the center of the scores in the data set. For example, we may measure the satisfaction level of 10 customers. The data are presented in Table E.1. The scores vary considerably. We can capture a lot of information about these scores by determining the middle point. By doing so, we get an estimate of where the scores fall. Three statistics that describe the central tendency are the mean, median, and mode.

Table E.1   Hypothetical data set.

Customer	X
1	4
2	1
3	3
4	2
5	4
6	1
7	5
8	4
9	3
10	2

MEAN

The mean is the arithmetic average of all scores in the data set. It is calculated by adding all the scores in the data set and dividing by the total number of observations in the data set. The formula is

$$\bar{x} = \frac{\Sigma x_i}{n}$$

where n = the number of observations in the data set and Σx_i is the sum of all scores in the data set.

Using the formula, we can calculate the mean of the data in Table E.1.

$$\bar{x} = \frac{4 + 1 + 3 + 2 + 4 + 1 + 5 + 4 + 3 + 2}{10} = 2.9$$

MEDIAN

Another measure of central tendency is the median. The median is the middlemost score after the data have been rank ordered from either highest to lowest or lowest to highest. In other words, half of the scores have values larger than the median and half have values smaller than the median. If the data set has an odd number of scores, the median is the $(n + 1/2)$th largest score in the data set. If the data set has an even number of scores, the median is the average of two numbers, the $(n/2)$th largest score and the $(n/2 + 1)$th largest score. Table E.2 provides the rank order of data from Table E.1. Since the number of scores in the data set is even, the median is calculated as the average of the two middlemost scores. The median value in the data set is 3.

MODE

The third measure of central tendency is the mode. The mode is the score that occurs most often in the data set. In Table E.2, there are two 1s, two 2s, two 3s, three 4s, and one 5. Therefore, the mode of this data set is 4, since it is the most frequently occurring score. It is possible that a data set could have more than one mode. This occurs when two or more values in the data set have the highest frequency and the same frequency.

VARIABILITY

While measures of central tendency indicate the middle of the distribution, we also would like to know about the spread of data. The spread of data is indexed by measures of variability. Measures of variability indicate the extent to which scores are tightly packed together versus spread out. The measures of variability presented here are the variance and the standard deviation. Both measures indicate the spread of data around the mean.

Table E.2   Rank order of data from Table E.1.

Score	Customer	X	
1	7	5	
2	1	4	
3	5	4	
4	8	4	
5	3	3	◄─── (n/2)th score
6	9	3	◄─── (n/2 + 1)th score
7	4	2	
8	10	2	◄─── The median is (3 + 3)/2 = 3
9	2	1	
10	6	1	

VARIANCE

Table E.3 contains four columns of numbers. The first column is x, the score; the second column contains a deviation score from the mean $(x - \bar{x})$; the third column contains the squared deviation score; and the last column is the squared value of each score.

One measure of variability is the variance. Variance, s^2, is the sum of the squared deviations about the mean *(SS)* divided by the number of scores in the data set less one. The formula for the variance is

$$s^2 = \frac{\Sigma(x_1 - \bar{x})^2}{n - 1} = \frac{SS}{n - 1}$$

The numerator is the sum of the squared deviations about the mean *(SS)* and the denominator is called the *degrees of freedom*. In general, the degrees of freedom for a particular statistic is the number of observations in the data set minus the number of estimated parameters used in the equation. The total number of observations used in the calculation is the sample size *(n)*, and the number of estimated parameters used in the equation is one (the sample mean). It should be noted that some people, in calculating the variance, divide the *SS* by n instead of $n - 1$. Usually, n is used when the variance is used to describe the present data set, while $n - 1$ is used to make inferences about the population variance from which the sample is drawn. A more complete discussion about the difference is available in various introductory statistics books. Using the previous equation, the variance of the data is calculated.

Table E.3 Deviation scores and squared deviation scores for hypothetical data.

x	$x - \bar{x}$	$(x - \bar{x})^2$	x^2
1	−2	4	1
2	−1	1	4
3	0	0	9
4	1	1	16
5	2	4	25
Totals 15	0	10	55

$$s^2 = \frac{4 + 1 + 0 + 1 + 4}{10} = 2.5$$

The formula for the sum of squared deviations *(SS)* can be simplified to facilitate hand computation of the variance. The formula for the sum of squares is

$$SS = \Sigma x_i^2 - \frac{(\Sigma x_i)^2}{n}$$

Using the data, the *SS* is calculated to be

$$SS = 55 - \frac{225}{5} = 10$$

The numerator for the formula of the variance is the squared deviation of each score from the mean. As the scores are widely spread out from the mean, the numerator increases. Therefore a large variance indicates that the scores are widely spread out, and a small variance indicates that the scores are tightly packed around the mean.

STANDARD DEVIATION

Another measure of variability is the standard deviation. The standard deviation is simply the square root of the variance; it is denoted by s. The standard deviation for the data in Table E.3 is calculated to be $s = 1.58$. The larger the standard deviation, the larger the spread in the data.

If the data are normally distributed, the standard deviation can be used to estimate the percentage of scores that fall within a specified range. By definition, 68 percent of the scores fall within a range of which the limits are (mean − 1s) and (mean + 1s), and 95 percent of the scores fall within a range whose limits are (mean − 2*s*) and (mean + 2*s*). If the standard deviation is small, a high percentage of the data falls closely around the mean. For our data, approximately 68 percent of the data falls within a range from 1.4 to 4.4.

Example

Before descriptive statistics were calculated, summary scores for physician quality and office quality were calculated by averaging the items within the respective scales. The descriptive statistics for the patient satisfaction questionnaire are presented in Table E.4.

As we can see from Table E.4, the descriptive statistics indicate that customers seem to be satisfied with the overall experience of the exam. Additionally, they seem to indicate that they are satisfied with the physician quality and overall quality of the exam. This information is not surprising to us given the information regarding the frequency of responses. Although this method of presenting the data (mean, median, and mode), compared to frequencies and percentages, summarizes the data even more, we conclude the same thing. This method of reporting the descriptive statistics is easier compared to reporting the frequencies if we just want to get a general idea of what the satisfaction data tell us. The wait time indicates that the patients typically had to wait about 15 minutes before seeing the physician. Once in to see the physician, the typical patient spent about 44 minutes with the physician.

Table E.4 Descriptive statistics of items in the patient satisfaction questionnaire.

Variable	Mean	Median	Mode	SD
Physician quality	2.81	3.00	3.00	.44
Overall experience of exam	4.09	4.00	4.00	.86
Office quality	2.74	2.75	3.00	.32
Time spent with physician (minutes)	43.53	40.00	30.00	28.93
Wait time (minutes)	16.24	15.00	0.00	23.90

SUMMARY

This section included measures of central tendency and measures of variability. Both types of measures summarize information contained in a sample of scores. The central tendency measures determine the score in the data set around which all other scores cluster. Measures of variability determine the extent of spread of the data.

Appendix F

Statistics, Parameters, and Sampling Distributions

A subset of observations can be randomly selected from a larger set of observations. The larger set of observations is called the *population*; the smaller set is called the *sample*. We are usually concerned with making conclusions about the population. Since the population can be extremely large, we often examine a sample to make conclusions about the larger population. For example, we may want to know the level of satisfaction of all our customers. Due to limited resources, we may only be able to measure the satisfaction level of a small set of customers. The population consists of all the customers; the sample consists of the small set of customers we measure.

We may examine the mean and the variance of a sample to make inferences about the mean and variance of the population. Numbers calculated from a sample of data are referred to as *statistics*. Therefore, the mean, variance, and standard deviation of the sample are statistics. Numbers calculated using the entire population are called *parameters*. Statistics are denoted with the following symbols: the mean is $\bar{x}$, the variance is s^2, and the standard deviation is s. Parameters are usually denoted with Greek symbols. The population mean is μ, the variance is σ^2, and the standard deviation is σ. Because the population parameters may not be easily obtained (due to limited resources), we have to estimate the parameters. We use the statistics as estimators of the parameters.

SAMPLING ERROR

Suppose we have a population of 1000 people and want to make conclusions about their mean height. We may have only the resources to measure 50 of these people. We use the mean from the sample to estimate the mean of the population.

For the sake of argument, suppose we knew the mean height of the population to be $\mu = 60''$ with a $\sigma^2 = 50''$. Based on our sample of 50 randomly selected people, we calculate the mean of their height. Suppose we found the mean height of the sample to be $\bar{x}_1 = 62''$. Now, let's place this sample back into the population of 1000 people and take another sample of 50 randomly selected people. Suppose we found the mean of this sample to equal $\bar{x}_2 = 55''$. We notice that there is some difference between the means of the first and second sample of people, both differing from the true population mean.

The difference of the sample means from population mean is referred to as sampling error. This error is expected to occur and is considered to be random. For the first sample, we happened to select, by chance, people who are slightly taller than the population mean. In the second sample, we selected, again by chance, people who are slightly shorter than the population mean.

STANDARD ERROR OF THE MEAN

In the preceding example, we witnessed the effect of sampling error; in one sample the mean ($\bar{x}_1$) = 62″ and in the second sample the mean ($\bar{x}_2$) = 55″. If we did not know the population mean (which is usually the situation), we could not determine the exact amount of error associated with any one given sample. We can, however, determine the degree of error we might expect using a given sample size. We could do so by repeatedly taking a sample of 50 randomly selected people from the population, with replacement, and calculating the mean for each sample. Each mean would be an estimate of the population mean.

If we collected 100 means, we could then plot them to form a histogram or distribution. This distribution is described by a mean and a standard deviation. This distribution of sample means is called a *sampling distribution.* The mean of this sampling distribution would be our best estimate of the population mean. The standard deviation of the sampling distribution is called the *standard error of the mean* (sem). The sem describes the degree of error we would expect in our sample mean. If the population standard deviation is known, we can calculate the sem. The standard error of the mean can be calculated easily using the following formula.

$$\text{Standard error of the mean} = \frac{\sigma}{\sqrt{n}}$$

where n is sample size and σ is the population standard deviation. If we do not know the population standard deviation, we can calculate the sem using the sample standard deviation as an estimate of the population standard deviation.

The sampling distributions for two different sample sizes are presented in Figure F.1. The population mean (μ) is 60″ and the population variance

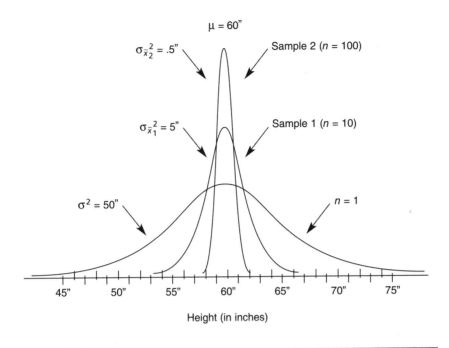

Figure F.1 Sampling distributions for sample sizes of $n = 100$ and $n = 10$ with a population mean of 60 and population variance of 50.

(σ^2) is 50″. The size of sample 1 is 10 and the size of sample 2 is 100. Using the equation above, the standard error of the mean is 2.24″ for sample 1 and .71″ for sample 2. As seen in Figure F.1, the degree of sampling error is small when the sample size is large. This figure illustrates the effect of sample size on our confidence in the sample estimate.

When the sample size is 100, we see that any one of our sample means will likely fall close to the population mean (95 percent of the sample means will fall within the range of 58.58″ to 61.42″). When the sample size is 10, our sample means will deviate more from the population mean than do our sample means when using a sample size of 100 (95 percent of the sample means will fall within the range of 53.68″ to 66.32″). In fact, when the sample size equals the population size, the standard error of the mean is 0. That is, when sample size equals population size, the sample mean will always equal the population mean.

Figure F.2 illustrates the relationship between sampling error and sample size. As sample size increases, sampling error decreases. When sample size equals one, the standard error of the mean is, by definition, the standard deviation of the observation. When sample size equals the size of

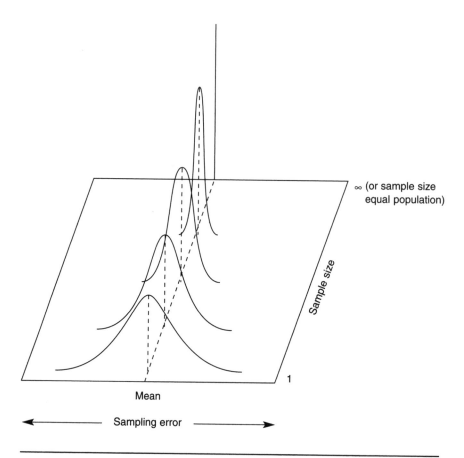

Figure F.2 The relationship between sample size and sampling error: as sample size increases, sampling error decreases.

the population, there is no error in the estimate of the population mean. Thus, the standard error of the mean is 0 when sample size equals the size of the population.

Example

The sampling error for some of the variables in the Patient Satisfaction Questionnaire are presented in Table F.1.

As we can see from the table, the sampling error is quite small, suggesting that there is not much error associated with our estimates of the population parameters. Given that we have a fairly large sample size, we can be fairly confident that our results will not vary if we were to conduct the same study using another sample of the same size. That is, if we were

Table F.1   Sampling error of the variables in the patient satisfaction survey.

Variable	Mean	SD	n (sample size)	Sampling error
Physician quality	2.81	.44	1335	.01
Overall experience of exam	4.09	.86	1283	.02
Office quality	2.74	.32	1337	.01
Time spent with physician (minutes)	43.53	28.93	1093	.88
Wait time (minutes)	16.24	23.90	827	.83

to take another 1500 or so surveys from our population of customers, our results would be very similar to the results we have here. For example, we would expect our mean for the physician quality score to vary only .01 (on the scale we are using) from sample to sample.

SUMMARY

Statistics are numbers derived from a sample of numbers. Parameters are numbers derived from a population. A sampling distribution is a distribution of a given statistic. Sampling error describes the degree of error associated with a given statistic for a specified sample size. As sample size increases, sampling error decreases. The concept of sampling error can be applied to many statistics (mean, *t*-value), and the concept of sampling error will be applied throughout the remaining appendices.

Appendix G

Decision Making and Hypothesis Testing

ecisions are made every day in the business world. On a small scale, we decide whether or not to leave early for a meeting being held on the other side of town. On a larger scale, companies select one supplier instead of another. We implicitly make decisions about some aspect of the world. In the former scenario, we might decide to leave early if the roads are icy and we need extra time to get to the meeting. In the second scenario, a company might select one supplier instead of another because one supplier makes parts of higher quality.

When we make decisions, we hope they are correct. A decision is correct if it is congruent with the state of the world. For example, a decision to leave early for the meeting is correct if the roads are icy and incorrect if the roads are not icy. In addition, a decision not to leave early for the meeting is correct if the roads are not icy and incorrect if the roads are icy.

REALITY AND DECISIONS

One morning, you are deciding whether or not to take your umbrella to work. To help you make this decision, you rely on some evidence (data). This evidence consists of several weather forecasts from various sources, each providing you with some data on the weather for the day. You must decide, based on this data, whether or not to take your umbrella with you.

You can make one of two choices based on your evaluation of the data. If you decide the data indicate it will rain today, you will take your umbrella. If you decide the data indicate it will not rain today, you will leave your umbrella at home.

There are four possible outcomes for this scenario. We can diagram these, crossing the two states of the world with the two possible decisions. The two states of the world constitute reality—the way the world truly is. The two decisions are based on the evaluation of the evidence (data), leading us to decide whether or not an umbrella is warranted. The diagram depicting the four possible outcomes is presented in Figure G.1 and illustrates the two correct decisions and the two types of error. For the sake of discussion, the errors are labeled *Type I* and *Type II*.

THE PROCESS OF DECISION MAKING

We can look at decision making as a process consisting of two important elements: the evidence and the criterion. The evidence is the data we evaluate in making our decision. In our previous umbrella-toting example, we may have gathered data from many local weather reports, the *Farmer's Almanac*, and other sources. The criterion reflects the amount of evidence or data we need to decide whether to carry an umbrella. Therefore, differences in our criterion will influence the likelihood of making a Type I versus a Type II error. We could have a stringent criterion, which means we need a lot of evidence to convince ourselves to carry an umbrella (for example, we will carry an umbrella only when all of the forecasts predict rain). With this stringent criterion, we will rarely end up carrying an umbrella on a day without rain (not likely to make a Type I error), but will likely end up not carrying an umbrella on a rainy day (likely to make a Type II error). On the other hand, we could have a lenient criterion, which means we need little evidence to convince us to carry an umbrella (for example, we will carry an umbrella if at least one forecast predicts rain). With this criterion, we would likely carry an umbrella on a day with no rain (likely to make a Type I error), but we will rarely end up without an umbrella on a rainy day (not likely to make a Type II error).

DECISION MAKING IN HYPOTHESIS TESTING

In business, we would like to know the real state of the world. To understand the true state of the world, we collect data. The data constitute the evidence we need to make conclusions about the world. Based on this

		State of the world	
		No rain	Rain
Your decision	Carry umbrella	Error (Type I)	Correct decision
	Do not carry umbrella	Correct decision	Error (Type II)

Figure G.1 Four possible outcomes, crossing the two states of the world with the two decisions.

evidence, we decide which state of the world is true.

Let's look at an example to illustrate the role of decision making in hypothesis testing. We may own two stores and have limited financial resources. We would like to give resources to the store that needs the most help (has the lowest level of customer satisfaction). We develop a customer satisfaction questionnaire and administer it to the stores' customers. Questionnaire scores constitute the data we need to make conclusions about the state of the world.

We can formally state our question: Do the two groups of customers have different levels of satisfaction? In hypothesis testing, we set up the world as consisting of two mutually exclusive hypotheses: the null hypothesis and the alternative hypothesis. The null hypothesis (HO) states:

> *There is no difference in satisfaction levels between the customers of the two stores.*

The alternative hypothesis (HA) states:

> *There is a difference in the satisfaction levels between the customers of the two stores.*

In the world, only one of these hypotheses is true. In our study, we will collect evidence to help us decide which is correct. In our hypothesis testing situation, we have a possibility of four outcomes. We have two possible states of the world crossed with two possible decisions. Each state of the world is represented by one of our hypotheses (there is no difference versus there is a difference). We also have two decisions we can make (deciding there is a difference between the two stores or that there is not a difference between the two stores). These decisions are unique to hypothesis testing. Formally, we state our decisions as either rejecting the null hypothesis (or accepting the alternative hypothesis that there is a difference between the two stores) or not rejecting the null hypothesis (not accepting the alternative).

We can construct a decision outcome matrix for this situation. This is presented in Figure G.2. The four cells, similar to the four cells in our umbrella-toting situation, can be characterized by probabilities, or likelihoods of occurrence. The probability of rejecting the null when the null is, in fact, true (upper left corner) is labeled α. The probability of not rejecting the null when the null is true is $1 - \alpha$. In addition, the probability of failing to reject the null when the alternative is true is labeled β. The probability of rejecting the null when the alternative is true is $1 - \beta$.

		State of the world	
		Null hypothesis true	Alternative hypothesis true
Your decision	**Reject null hypothesis**	Type I error (α)	Correct decision $(1 - \beta)$
	Do not reject null hypothesis	Correct decision $(1 - \alpha)$	Type II Error (β)

Figure G.2 The four possible outcomes in a hypothesis testing situation, crossing the two states of the world with the two decisions.

SOME EVIDENCE

We need to collect data to provide us with evidence of the true state of the world. Let's use our example concerning the level of satisfaction of customers from our two stores. We collect data from two samples, each representing one store. Higher scores on the questionnaire reflect higher levels of satisfaction. The data are presented in Table G.1.

Before examining the data, let's discuss the kind of evidence that would indicate whether or not we should reject the null. If the null is correct, then the two groups of scores should be roughly the same. If the alternative is true, then the two groups of scores should be different; one set should contain higher scores than the other.

We need a way of summarizing the data to allow us to decide which hypothesis is true. In this situation, we could look at the overall average of each group. The average score for Store 1 is $\bar{x}_1 = 3.5$, and the average for Store 2 is $\bar{x}_2 = 3.1$. The difference between these two scores is 0.4. We could use this difference score as the summary score. This summary score reflects the degree of difference between the two groups and is, essentially, the evidence.

DETERMINATION OF THE CRITERION

Summary scores are used to represent the state of the world, supporting either the null hypothesis or the alternative hypothesis. We need a criterion to judge whether the summary score reflects that the null hypothesis is true or that the alternative hypothesis is true. In hypothesis testing, we usually set the criterion to reflect that the alpha level (probability of rejecting the

Table G.1 Hypothetical data of satisfaction scores for two stores.

Store 1	Store 2
4	3
5	4
2	3
4	4
5	2
4	2
3	3
4	5
2	2
2	3

null when it is true) equal .05. That is, given that the null is true, we want to set a criterion with which we will incorrectly reject the null hypothesis, at the most, five times out of 100.

For our study, we found that the summary score (the difference between the two groups), is 0.4. Recall that, in Appendix F, the effect of sampling error would result in differences between two samples of scores even if the samples were selected from the same underlying population. Therefore, the difference of 0.4 revealed in our study might not indicate any real difference at all. The difference between the two samples could be due to sampling error.

For our example, the criterion we choose should reflect a difference between two samples that would occur by chance only five times out of 100 if the null were true. This criterion is established through formal methods discussed in the next three appendices.

Example

We could state some hypotheses for our study using our patient satisfaction data. Some explicit hypotheses are presented in Figure G.3.

There are many more hypotheses that can be generated using our current patient satisfaction questionnaire. We could examine the difference across the various offices using the other variables in the survey such as the office quality score, wait time, and time spent with the physician. Additionally, we could generate hypotheses examining the difference across the different months or quarters using these same variables.

Null hypothesis (H_{O1}): There is no difference in patient satisfaction levels for physician quality among the different offices.

Alternative hypothesis (H_{A1}): There is a difference in the patient satisfaction levels for physician quality among the different offices.

Null hypothesis (H_{O2}): There is no difference in the patient satisfaction levels for physician quality among the different months.

Alternative hypothesis (H_{A2}): There is a difference in the patient satisfaction levels for physician quality among the different months.

Null hypothesis (H_{O3}): There is no difference in the patient satisfaction levels for overall rating of the exam among the different offices.

Alternative Hypothesis (H_{A3}): There is a difference in the patient satisfaction levels for overall rating of the exam among the different offices.

Null hypothesis (H_{O4}): There is no difference in the patient satisfaction levels for overall rating of the exam among the different months.

Alternative hypothesis (H_{A4}): There is a difference in the patient satisfaction levels for overall rating of the exam among the different months.

Null hypothesis (H_{O5}): There is no difference in the patient satisfaction levels for overall rating of the exam between the two states.

Alternative hypothesis (H_{A5}): There is a difference in the patient satisfaction levels for overall rating of the exam between the two states.

Figure G.3   Hypotheses for the patient satisfaction questionnaire.

SUMMARY

Hypothesis testing involves determining the extent to which the differences between our samples is not likely due to sampling error. When the difference is likely due to sampling error, we do not reject the null hypothesis; the two samples are likely from the same population. When the difference is not likely due to sampling error (difference is large), then we reject the null hypothesis in favor of the alternative hypothesis.

The steps to hypothesis testing are presented in Figure G.4. The first step is to generate a null and an alternative hypothesis. The second step is to collect data to provide evidence of the state of the world (supporting the null or alternative hypothesis). The third step is determining a summary

1. Generate null and alternative hypothesis.
   • Null: there is no difference
   • Alternative: there is a difference
2. Collect data to provide evidence of the state of the world.
3. Using the data, determine the summary score that summarizes the difference between the groups.
4. Determine criterion to which to compare your summary score.
5. Decide to reject the null or not reject the null.

Figure G.4   Steps in hypothesis testing.

score using data that reflect the difference between the groups. The fourth step is determining the criterion, reflecting the point at which the summary score is likely to occur five times out of 100 if the null hypothesis is true. Fifth, if the summary score exceeds the criterion, we reject the null hypothesis and accept the alternate hypothesis.

Appendix H
T-Tests

We may want to compare two groups of people on some variable. Two companies in the retail business have a friendly competition. Bob of Bob's Barn claims that his customers are highly satisfied, while Tom, owner of Tom's Tent, claims he has more satisfied customers. Both owners would like to obtain empirical information to determine which company has the highest level of customer satisfaction.

An independent research firm was contacted to see whether it could settle the score. The research firm developed a customer satisfaction questionnaire to assess overall customer satisfaction. Higher scores on the questionnaire reflect higher satisfaction. This questionnaire was administered to two sets of customers. One set had received service from Bob's Barn and the other had received service from Tom's Tent. The research firm obtained 20 customers from each company to complete the questionnaire. The data appear in Table H.1.

The mean for the group from Bob's Barn is 2.85, and the mean for the group from Tom's Tent is 3.45. If we inspect only these mean values, we might conclude that customers from Tom's Tent are more satisfied with service than customers from Bob's Barn.

Recall that, when two small sets of data are compared, their means will almost always be different from each other, even when the two data sets come from the same population. This difference is due to sampling error (see Appendix F). This error arises because the observed mean is only an estimate of the population mean, which has inherent error because it is based on only a sample of data. Therefore, merely seeing if there is a difference between the two groups is not enough to say that the two data sets arise from two different populations.

The *t*-test provides a method by which we can more rigorously compare two data sets. Conducting a *t*-test informs us whether the degree of difference between the two data sets could be due to factors other than sampling error. If the results indicate that the difference between the groups is not

Table H.1   Hypothetical data for two companies.

Bob's Barn		Tom's Tent	
1	3	2	3
2	4	4	3
3	3	5	4
2	2	3	5
4	1	3	3
3	3	4	2
3	4	2	1
3	2	5	3
4	4	4	4
4	2	5	4

Total =	57.00	69.00
n =	20	20
$\bar{x}$ =	2.85	3.45
SS =	18.55	24.95

likely due to sampling error, we believe that the two data sets probably do not come from the same population.

CALCULATION

The formulae for the calculation of the t-test vary, depending on whether the sample sizes for each group are equal. The following general equation can be applied to situations in which the sample sizes are either equal or not equal. The calculation of the t-test is

$$t(N-2) = \frac{\bar{x}_1 - \bar{x}_2}{\sqrt{\left(\frac{SS_1 + SS_2}{n_1 + n_2 - 2}\right)\left(\frac{1}{n_1} + \frac{1}{n_2}\right)}}$$

where $\bar{x}_1$ and $\bar{x}_2$ are the means for each group, SS_1 and SS_2 are the sum of squares for each group, n_1 and n_2 are the sample sizes for each group, and N is the sum of n_1 and n_2.

Also, $(N-2)$, associated with the t statistic, is the degrees of freedom. Recall that the degrees of freedom is the total number of observations (N) minus the number of estimated parameters. Using the data in Table H.1, the observed t value is calculated to be

$$t(38) = \frac{3.45 - 2.85}{.338} = 1.77$$

If we assume that the null hypothesis is true (there is no difference between the two groups), we would expect the t statistic to equal 0.0 (since $\bar{x}_1 - \bar{x}_2 = 0$). The t statistic, like the sample mean, can also be described by a sampling distribution with associated sampling error. That is, even though the null might be true, we would not expect to obtain a t statistic of zero every time we randomly sample two samples from the same population. Given that the null hypothesis is true, the mean of the t distribution is symmetric around zero. If we were to randomly sample t values from this distribution, we would likely see a majority of t values clustering around 0. We would not likely see extreme t values. Recall that 95 percent of the data falls within two standard deviations above or below zero. If the t value we obtain from our study is more than 2s away from the mean, we know this finding is highly unlikely; therefore, we think the two sample means do not come from the same population.

When the t values are extreme, we think the two samples come from different populations (reject the null hypothesis and accept the alternative hypothesis). We say the two sample means are *statistically significantly* different from each other. In significance testing, we set a critical value that our observed t value should exceed if we are to say the means are significantly different from each other. This critical t value is determined to be the t value above which the probability of obtaining a t value, by chance, is .05.

The spread of the t distribution is determined by the sample size used in the calculation of the t statistic. The spread of the t distribution is wider when sample size is small and becomes narrower as the sample size increases. A given t distribution (with associated degrees of freedom) describes the frequency with which we would see varying t values if we repeatedly performed independent t-tests with a given sample of subjects (20 in each group). For our example we would be interested in the probability of obtaining t values using a t distribution with 38 degrees of freedom.

The observed t value we obtain in our study is 1.77. We compare this t value to a critical t value. A t table containing critical t values is located in Appendix H. We select our critical t value to be 2.04 (.05 level with 30 degrees of freedom and a two-tailed test). Although our actual degrees of freedom is 38, we select 30 to provide a conservative test of significance. This critical t value represents the point above which our chance of obtaining an obtained t value is less than 5 percent if the null hypothesis were true. Our observed t value is below this critical t value. Thus, we conclude that the difference between our observed means (2.85 and 3.45) is likely due to sampling error, or that both sets of customers come from one underlying population; the customers from Bob's Barn and Tom's Tent are equally satisfied.

FACTORS AFFECTING SIGNIFICANCE TESTING

Power is the probability of finding a significant difference with our samples when there truly is a difference between the two populations. We always strive to have a high degree of power when we conduct significance testing. One way of increasing power is by increasing the sample size on which the *t*-test is conducted. Another is to use scales with high reliability. In our example, perhaps customers from Tom's Tent were more satisfied but our test lacked sufficient power to detect this difference.

Example

A *t*-test can be conducted to test hypothesis 5 (see Appendix G). Specifically this hypothesis tests to see if there is a difference between the two states (Washington and California) in the customers' overall rating of the exam. The summary information for this *t*-test is presented in Table H.2.

From the *t*-test, we compare the obtained *t* value with our critical value. Because we did not have a directional hypothesis, we will compare this obtained *t* value with the critical value for a two-tailed test. To be conservative, we use a critical *t* value associated with a smaller degree of freedom. The critical value for *t* given 180 degrees of freedom is 1.96. We see that the absolute value of the obtained *t* statistic does not exceed the critical value. Therefore, we conclude that there was no statistically significant difference between the two states with respect to the overall rating of the exam. That is, the observed differences we see between the states is due to chance factors (sampling error).

Table H.3 contains the critical values for the *t* statistic. The table is used to compare the absolute value of the obtained *t* statistic (from the study) with the critical value of the *t* statistics for a given critical value. If the absolute value of the observed *t* statistic exceeds the critical value, we reject the null (there are no differences between the groups) and conclude that the difference between the two groups is probably not due to chance.

Table H.2   Summary information for the *t*-test examining state differences for overall ratings of the exam.

	Washington	California
Mean	4.07	4.11
SD	0.89	0.84
SE of the mean	0.03	0.03
n	678	605

$$t(1281) = -.72, p > .05$$

Note: SD = standard deviation; SE = standard error; *n* = sample size.

Table H.3 Critical values of the *t* statistics.

Degrees of freedom	One-tailed significance level *p*		Two-tailed significance level *p*	
	.05	.01	.05	.01
3	2.35	4.54	3.18	5.84
4	2.13	3.75	2.78	4.60
5	2.02	3.36	2.57	4.03
6	1.94	3.14	2.45	3.71
7	1.89	3.00	2.36	3.50
8	1.86	2.90	2.31	3.36
9	1.83	2.82	2.26	3.25
10	1.81	2.76	2.23	3.17
11	1.80	2.72	2.20	3.11
12	1.78	2.68	2.18	3.05
13	1.77	2.65	2.16	3.01
14	1.76	2.62	2.14	2.98
15	1.75	2.60	2.13	2.95
16	1.75	2.58	2.12	2.92
17	1.74	2.57	2.11	2.90
18	1.73	2.55	2.10	2.88
19	1.73	2.54	2.09	2.86
20	1.72	2.53	2.09	2.85
21	1.72	2.52	2.08	2.83
22	1.72	2.51	2.07	2.82
23	1.71	2.50	2.07	2.81
24	1.71	2.49	2.06	2.80
25	1.71	2.49	2.06	2.79
26	1.71	2.48	2.06	2.78
27	1.70	2.47	2.05	2.77
28	1.70	2.47	2.05	2.76
29	1.70	2.46	2.05	2.76
30	1.70	2.46	2.04	2.75
40	1.68	2.42	2.02	2.70
50	1.68	2.40	2.01	2.68
60	1.67	2.39	2.00	2.66
70	1.67	2.38	1.99	2.65
80	1.66	2.37	1.99	2.64
90	1.66	2.37	1.99	2.63
100	1.66	2.36	1.98	2.63
120	1.66	2.36	1.98	2.62
140	1.66	2.35	1.98	2.61
160	1.65	2.35	1.97	2.61
180	1.65	2.35	1.97	2.60
>10000	1.65	2.33	1.96	2.58

SUMMARY

The *t*-test can determine if the difference between two samples is meaningful. We calculate the observed *t* value using our data and compare it to a critical *t* value. This critical *t* value is the cutoff point above which the probability of obtaining a *t* value is .05. If our observed *t* is greater than this critical *t* value, then we say the difference between the two means is not likely due to sampling error. That is, the data likely come from two different populations. On the other hand, if the observed *t* value falls below the critical *t* value, we say the observed difference between the two means is likely due to sampling error. That is, the data from the two groups likely come from the same population and the observed difference is the result of chance. The power of detecting true differences can be increased by increasing the sample size on which the *t*-test is conducted and also by using measures with high reliability.

Appendix I
Analysis of Variance

Analysis of variance (ANOVA) is used to compare groups. When conducting an ANOVA, we can compare more than two groups simultaneously. As the name of the analysis implies, ANOVA is a method of analyzing components of variance.

Let's look at an example. Suppose we have four independent sets of data. The data are presented in Table I.1. We will calculate the variance of the observations with two methods. The first method is to calculate the variability within each group. Four separate variances, one for each group, can be calculated. These four separate variances are each an estimate of the same variance. Therefore, we can get an overall variance measure by averaging these four variances. This average variance is the pooled variance estimate (s^2_p). This approach results in a variance estimate of .625.

The second method is to calculate the variance of the means (s^2_x). The variance of the means, however, is dependent on the sample size (see Appendix F). As sample size increases, the variance of the means decreases. Thus, to correct for sample size, we multiply the variance of the means by the sample size for each group ($n = 10$). This estimate now reflects the variability of the group means corrected for sample size (ns^2_x). This approach results in a variance estimate of 7.49.

If there is no true difference between the group means, then the two variance measures should be roughly the same. We see, however, that the variability using the group means approach is 7.49, and the variance using the within-group approach is .625. The magnitude of the former variance indicates that there is considerable variability between groups, more so than variability within groups. In ANOVA, we are comparing these variance components. If the variance calculated using the means is larger than the variance calculated using individual scores within groups, this might indicate that there is a significant difference between the groups.

Table I.1   Hypothetical data of four groups.

	Set 1	Set 2	Set 3	Set 4
	2	4	2	3
	1	5	3	2
	2	5	1	3
	1	4	4	2
	2	4	3	4
	2	4	3	3
	2	5	4	4
	3	3	3	2
	3	4	3	3
	2	3	2	4
Mean =	2.0	4.1	2.8	3.0
n =	10	10	10	10

$$SS_1 = 3.996 \quad SS_2 = 4.896 \quad SS_3 = 7.596 \quad SS_4 = 6.003$$

$$s^2_1 = .444 \quad s^2_2 = .544 \quad s^2_3 = .844 \quad s^2_4 = .667$$

$$s^2_p = (s^2_1 + s^2_2 + s^2_3 + s^2_4)/4 = .625$$

$$SS_B = 20.03 + 41.02 + 28.02 + 30.02 - (20 + 41 + 28 + 30)2/4 = 6.741$$

$$s^2_{\bar{x}} = SS_B/3 = .749$$

CALCULATIONS

The standard method for presenting the results of the ANOVA is the tabular format. The ANOVA table appears in Table I.2. The first row of the ANOVA table contains information about the variance of the groups. The second row contains information concerning the variance of the subjects within each group. The third row of the table represents total variance. Each of the rows contains specific information about the variability of its respective components.

The first column identifies the sources of variation. The differences between groups is denoted by Between *(B)*. The variation due to subjects within each group is denoted by Within *(W)*. The total variation is denoted by Total. The second column in the ANOVA table represents the sum of squared deviations *(SS)*. The SS_B and the SS_W should sum to SS_{TOT}. The third column represents the degrees of freedom for each *SS*. The degrees of freedom *(df)* for SS_B are the number of groups minus one. The *df* for SS_W are the total sample size minus the number of groups. The *df* for SS_{TOT} are the

Table I.2   Analysis of variance (ANOVA) table.

Source	Sum of squares	Degrees of freedom (df)	Mean square	$F(df_B, df_W)$
Between	SS_B	$k - 1$	$SS_B/(k - 1)$	MSB
Within	SS_W	$N - K$	$SS_W/(N - k)$	MSW
Total	SS_{TOT}	$N - 1$		

Note: N = total sample size, k = number of groups, df = degrees of freedom.

total sample size minus one. The df_B and the df_W should sum to df_{TOT}. The fourth column, mean square, represents the measure of variation of a particular source. The mean squares are calculated by dividing the sum of squares by the df. The last column represents the ratio of the MS_B to the MS_W and is referred to as the *F ratio*.

TESTING

The F value is a ratio of the variance of the means corrected for by sample size to variance within the groups. A large F value indicates that the between-group variance is larger than the within-group variance. Like the t statistic, the F value can also be described by a distribution, the F distribution. The F distribution has two different degrees of freedom, one associated with the estimate of the variance of the means $(k - 1)$ and the other associated with the variance within groups $(N - k)$. The exact shape of the distribution is determined by the df_B and df_W.

The concept of testing in ANOVA is the same as the testing using the t-test. We compare the observed F value from our study to a critical F value. This critical F value is a cutoff point, above which the probability of obtaining an F value is only .05 if the null hypothesis is true. Therefore, an observed F value above the critical value, because it is such an unlikely event, would lead us to believe that the different groups in our study do not come from the same population.

The ANOVA table for the data in Table I.1 is presented in Table I.3. We see that the resulting F value is large. The critical F value with 3 and 36 degrees of freedom is approximately equal to 2.9. Our observed F value equals 11.99, which is larger than the critical F. Thus, we conclude that all four groups do not come from the same underlying population; at least one group comes from a different population than the rest.

Table I.3   ANOVA table for the data in Table I.1.

Source	Sum of squares	Degrees of freedom	Mean square	F(3, 36)
Group	22.475	3	7.492	11.987
Within	22.5	36	.625	$p = .0001$
Total	44.975	39		

Note: p = the probability of our observed *F* value occurring by chance.

POST-HOC COMPARISONS

When we compare three or more groups and find a significant effect using the ANOVA method, we can conclude only that the group means are significantly different from each other. Unlike the *t*-test, in which only two groups are compared, the ANOVA method can be inconclusive. For example, if we find the *t*-test to be statistically significant, we examine the means of the two groups to see which group is higher. In the ANOVA with three or more groups, a significant *F*-test tells us only that the groups do not come from the same population. In other words, significant effect indicates that there is at least one statistically significant difference between two of the groups in our study. Some of the groups may not be significantly different from each other, while others might be significantly different.

To determine where the underlying differences lie, we must do further testing, referred to as *post-hoc testing*. There are various methods of post-hoc testing. All are somewhat related to the *t*-test method in which individual groups are compared to determine whether they are significantly different from each other. Readers are referred to the bibliography to learn more about these techniques.

Example

An ANOVA can be conducted to test the other hypotheses stated in Appendix G. The ANOVA table is presented in Table I.4. In the table, the summary *F*-test is presented. If the result is significant, more information regarding analysis is presented. Specifically, the descriptive statistics of the customer satisfaction measure are presented for each level of the independent variable, including the mean, standard deviation, standard error of the mean, and the 95 percent confidence interval. Additionally, the result of the post-hoc comparisons (Tukey-HSD test) is presented to show you where the differences are located.

Table I.4   ANOVA table for the hypotheses in Appendix G.   *(Continued)*

Null Hypothesis 1: No difference in physician quality across offices

Source	df	Sum of squares	Mean squares	F ratio	F prob.
Between groups	8	6.1902	.7738	4.1106	.0001
Within groups	1326	249.6067	.1882		
Total	1334	255.7969			

Group	Count	Mean	Standard deviation	Standard error	95% confidence interval for mean
Yakima	178	2.8577	.3060	.0229	2.8124 to 2.9029
Seattle	173	2.7371	.5685	.0432	2.6518 to 2.8224
San Francisco	150	2.8224	.5023	.0410	2.7414 to 2.9035
Tacoma	179	2.8467	.3420	.0256	2.7963 to 2.8972
San Jose	181	2.8726	.3172	.0236	2.8260 to 2.9191
Sacramento	155	2.7989	.4004	.0322	2.7354 to 2.8625
Spokane	180	2.7988	.4421	.0330	2.7338 to 2.8638
San Diego	58	2.9233	.2619	.0344	2.8544 to 2.9922
Sonoma	81	2.6140	.6830	.0759	2.4630 to 2.7650
Total	1335	2.8119	.4379	.0120	2.7884 to 2.8355

(*) Indicates significant differences, which are shown in the lower triangle

```
                                    S
                                    a
                                    n
                              S
                              a   F           S
                              c   r       S   a
                        S  S  r   a       a   n
                     S  e  a  n   n  T  Y  n
                     o  a  o  m   c  a  a     D
                     n  t  k  e   i  c  k  J  i
                     o  t  a  n   s  o  i  o  e
                     m  l  n  t   c  m  m  s  g
                     a  e  e  o   o  a  a  e  o
```

Mean	Office	
2.6140	Sonoma	
2.7371	Seattle	
2.7988	Spokane	*
2.7989	Sacramento	*
2.8224	San Francisco	*
2.8467	Tacoma	*
2.8577	Yakima	*
2.8726	San Jose	*
2.9233	San Diego	*

Table I.4   ANOVA table for the hypotheses in Appendix G.   *(Continued)*

Null Hypothesis 2: No difference in physician quality across months

Source	df	Sum of squares	Mean squares	F ratio	F prob.
Between groups	8	2.8366	.3546	1.8586	.0627
Within groups	1326	252.9604	.1908		
Total	1334	255.7969			

No significant differences

Null Hypothesis 3: No difference in overall rating of exam scores across offices

Source	df	Sum of squares	Mean squares	F ratio	F prob.
Between groups	8	27.7563	3.4695	4.7607	.0000
Within groups	1274	928.4666	.7288		
Total	1282	956.2229			

Group	Count	Mean	Standard deviation	Standard error	95% confidence interval for mean
Yakima	170	4.0824	.8244	.0632	3.9575 to 4.2072
Seattle	166	3.8976	1.0481	.0813	3.7370 to 4.0582
San Fran	147	4.2041	.8019	.0661	4.0734 to 4.3348
Tacoma	168	4.0893	.7802	.0602	3.9704 to 4.2081
San Jose	172	4.2035	.7409	.0565	4.0920 to 4.3150
Sacramento	150	4.0400	.7408	.0605	3.9205 to 4.1595
Spokane	174	4.2069	.8553	.0648	4.0789 to 4.3349
San Diego	58	4.2931	.6756	.0887	4.1155 to 4.4707
Sonoma	78	3.6923	1.1877	.1345	3.4245 to 3.9601
Total	1283	4.0873	.8636	.0241	4.0400 to 4.1346

(*) Indicates significant differences, which are shown in the lower triangle

```
                        S
                        a
                        n
            S
            a  F           S
            c  r        S  a
         S  S  r  a        a  n
      S  e  p  a  n  T  Y  n
      o  a  o  m  c  a  a     D
      n  t  k  e  i  c  k  J  i
      o  t  a  n  s  o  i  o  e
      m  l  n  t  c  m  m  s  g
      a  e  e  o  o  a  a  e  o
```

Table I.4   ANOVA table for the hypotheses in Appendix G.   *(Continued)*

Mean	Office		
3.6923	Sonoma		
3.8976	Seattle		
4.0400	Sacramento		
4.0824	Yakima	*	
4.0893	Tacoma	*	
4.2035	San Jose	*	*
4.2041	San Fran	*	*
4.2069	Spokane	*	*
4.2931	San Diego	*	

Null Hypothesis 4: No difference in overall rating of exam scores across months

Source	df	Sum of squares	Mean squares	F ratio	F prob.
Between groups	8	16.9757	2.1220	2.8782	.0035
Within groups	1274	939.2472	.7372		
Total	1282	956.2229			

Group	Count	Mean	Standard deviation	Standard error	95% confidence interval for mean
January	144	4.2708	.7684	.0640	4.1443 to 4.3974
February	144	4.1736	.8050	.0671	4.0410 to 4.3062
March	157	4.1783	.7638	.0610	4.0579 to 4.2988
April	149	4.0940	.8648	.0708	3.9540 to 4.2340
May	158	4.0506	.9155	.0728	3.9068 to 4.1945
June	135	3.9407	.9601	.0826	3.7773 to 4.1042
July	128	4.0781	.8749	.0773	3.9251 to 4.2312
August	134	4.1045	.8341	.0721	3.9620 to 4.2470
September	134	3.8657	.9322	.0805	3.7064 to 4.0250
Total	1283	4.0873	.8636	.0241	4.0400 to 4.1346

(*) Indicates significant differences, which are shown in the lower triangle

```
                    S
                    e           F
                    p           e   J
                    t       A   b   a
                    e     A u   r M n
                    m J   J p g u a u
                    b u M u r u a r a
                    e n a l i s r c r
                    r e y y l t y h y
```

Table I.4 ANOVA table for the hypotheses in Appendix G.   *(Continued)*

Mean	Month		
3.8657	September		
3.9407	June		
4.0506	May		
4.0781	July		
4.0940	April		
4.1045	August		
4.1736	February		
4.1783	March		
4.2708	January	*	*

As can be seen in Table I.4, there are significant differences seen across the different offices on the measure of physician quality and overall rating of the exam. Patients in the Sonoma office rated their physician lower compared to all other offices (except Seattle patients). Additionally, Sonoma and Seattle patients tended to be less satisfied with the overall exam compared to the rest of the patients from the other offices. There was a significant difference across the months with respect to the overall rating of the exam. The months of June and September had significantly lower scores compared to the month of January of that same year, suggesting a downward trend.

Appendix J
Regression Analysis

To understand the application of regression analysis, let's first look at an example of the relationship between two variables: (1) a person's level of satisfaction with perceived quality of service received from a company in terms of availability; and (2) the person's level of overall satisfaction with service. Perceived quality of availability is defined as the extent to which the customer perceives the company as being available to provide service whenever he or she needs it. Overall satisfaction with the service is defined as the extent to which the customer is generally satisfied with the way he or she was treated by the company. Measures were developed to assess both variables on a five-point scale. A higher number on either scale represents better service.

We use these measures on a sample of 10 people and subsequently obtain two scores: X_i, which represents perceived quality of availability, and Y_i, which represents overall satisfaction. The data are presented in Table J.1. The first column in the table provides the names of 10 people who were given the questionnaire. The second and third columns present the scores on perceived availability and overall satisfaction, respectively, for each of the 10 people.

A graphic representation called a *scatterplot* indicates the relationship between these two variables. This is seen in Figure J.1. As one would expect, there is a positive relationship between these two variables. That is, customers who perceive the company as more available to provide services when needed have higher levels of satisfaction. The relationship can be summarized by a line, a regression line, which indicates the degree of relationship between X and Y. This relationship can also be described by an equation

$$Y = a + bX + e$$

where b and a are constants representing the slope and intercept of the regression line, respectively. The error associated with the prediction is labeled as e.

Table J.1 Hypothetical data for variables X and Y.

Customer	Xi	Yi	$(Xi)^2$	$(Yi)^2$	$XiYi$
Lance A.	3	5	9	25	15
Jackson B.	1	2	1	4	2
Brian F.	3	3	9	9	9
Joe F.	5	4	25	16	20
Kim P.	2	2	4	1	2
Lamona F.	2	2	4	4	4
Bob H.	4	4	16	16	16
Tom H.	3	4	9	16	12
Jenifer K.	1	1	1	1	1
Wade G.	4	3	16	9	12

$$\Sigma Xi = 28 \quad \Sigma Yi = 29 \quad \Sigma Xi^2 = 94 \quad \Sigma Yi^2 = 101 \quad \Sigma XiYi = 93$$

$$r = \frac{10(93) - (28 \times 29)}{\sqrt{([10(94) - (28)^2][10(101) - (29)^2])}} = .726$$

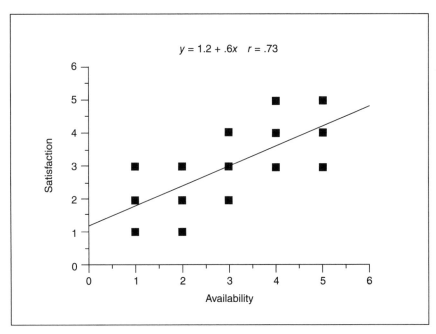

$$y = 1.2 + .6x \quad r = .73$$

Figure J.1 A scatterplot representing the relationship between perceived availability and overall satisfaction with service.

The intercept is the predicted score for Y when X is equal to zero, the point at which the line intersects the Y axis. The slope represents the change in Y given a unit change in X. The values of a and b describe the regression line. Different values of each will necessarily lead to different regression lines. For a given relationship between two variables, there is a regression line that best fits the scatterplot. The parameters, a and b, for the best fitting regression line are calculated by the following equations.

The formula for b is

$$b = \frac{n\Sigma X_i Y_i - (\Sigma X_i)(\Sigma Y_i)}{n\Sigma X_i^2 - (\Sigma X_i)^2}$$

We use b to calculate a.

$$a = \frac{\Sigma Y_i - b\Sigma X_i}{n}$$

These two equations are used to calculate the best fitting regression line. For the data in Table J.1, the regression slope is calculated to be

$$b = .756$$

and the intercept is calculated to be

$$a = .782$$

Therefore, the regression equation for predicting Y (overall satisfaction) from X (perceived availability) is

$$Y = .782 + .76X$$

This equation can be used to make predictions of Y for any given level of X. If a person had an X score of 4.5, their predicted score for Y would be 4.2. If a person had an X score of 1.25, their predicted score for Y would be 1.73.

DETERMINING THE DEGREE OF FIT

An important step in regression analysis is to determine how well the regression line represents the data or how well the regression line fits the data. We determine this fit with an index called *Pearson* r^2. This index varies from 0 to 1.0. This index approaches 1.0 as the data lie closely near the regression line. The index approaches 0 as the data are widely dispersed around the regression line. The formula for the *Pearson* r^2 is

$$r^2 = \frac{[n\Sigma X_i Y_i - \Sigma X_i \Sigma Y_i)]^2}{[n\Sigma X_i^2 - (\Sigma X_i)^2][n\Sigma Y_i^2 - (\Sigma Y_i)^2]}$$

This index can be interpreted as the percentage of variance in Y (the criterion) that is accounted for by X (the predictor). So, if r^2 is equal to .70, we say that 70 percent of the variance in Y is accounted for by differences in X. Conversely, we could also say that 30 percent of the variance in Y is not accounted for by differences in X (this is essentially the variance that is unexplained by the X variable). The r^2 for data presented in Table J.1 is calculated to be

$$r^2 = \frac{[10(93) - (28)(29)]^2}{[10(94) - (28)^2][10(101) - (29)^2]} = .528$$

The r^2 indicates that about 53 percent of the variance in Y is accounted for by differences in X.

PEARSON *r*

The r^2 is an index that describes how well the data fit a straight line. However, the r^2 does not tell us the direction of the relationship between the two variables. The linear relationship between two variables can be indexed by a single number, the *Pearson correlation coefficient,* denoted by the letter r. The Pearson r indicates the strength and direction of relationship between two variables. It can vary from –1 (a perfectly negative relationship between two variables) to 1 (a perfectly positive relationship between two variables). A negative relationship indicates that, as one variable increases, the other variable decreases. A positive relationship indicates that, as one variable increases, the other variable also increases.

The equation for the Pearson r is

$$r = \frac{n\Sigma X_i Y_i - \Sigma X_i \Sigma Y_i}{\sqrt{[n\Sigma X_i^2 - (\Sigma X_i)^2][n\Sigma Y_i^2 - (\Sigma Y_i)^2]}}$$

Table J.1 includes data on two variables, X and Y. Using the previous equation, we determine the extent to which variables X and Y are related to each other. The direction of their relationship is positive, and the strength of their relationship is $r = .73$. The amount of variance in Y accounted for by X (r^2) is calculated by squaring the correlation coefficient ($r^2 = .73^2 = .53$).

Figure J.2 illustrates various strengths and directions of relationships. A high correlation (either positive, Figure J.2(a), or negative, Figure J.2(b)) indicates that there is a substantial relationship between the two variables. Figures J.2(c) and (d) indicate that there is a moderate relationship between the two variables. In fact, we know, by the size of the correlation coefficient, that the relationship between X and Y is stronger in the two former figures. For example, the two variables in Figure J.2(a) have a positive correlation of .84, while the two variables in Figure J.2(c) have a moderate positive correlation of .45.

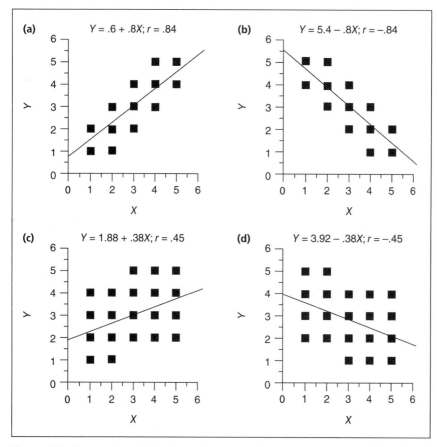

Figure J.2 Scatterplots indicating various strengths and directions of relationships between two variables.

TESTING SIGNIFICANCE OF FIT

We test the significance of the *r* by first transforming the *r* statistic to a *t* statistic. The formula for the transformation is

$$t(n - 2) = \frac{r\sqrt{n - 2}}{r\sqrt{1 - r^2}}$$

We can calculate the *t* from the *r* in our present example. In our example *n* = 10 and

$$t(8) = \frac{.73\sqrt{8}}{\sqrt{1 - .53}} = 3.01$$

We can determine if the *t* represents a significant effect (see Appendix H).

SUMMARY

The relationship between two variables can be described by a straight line, a regression line. The regression line allows us to predict values of Y (with a degree of error) from given values of X. The degree of fit of data around the regression line is indexed by the correlation coefficient, denoted by r. It is an index of the linear association between the two variables. The correlation coefficient can range from -1 (perfect negative relationship) to 1 (perfect positive relationship). A correlation of zero indicates no linear relationship between two variables.

MULTIPLE REGRESSION

In simple linear regression, we examine the relationship between two variables. We might want to examine the relationship of overall satisfaction with many other factors within the customer survey, such as reliability, availability, and professionalism. Instead of examining each factor separately (for example, calculating simple correlation coefficients), another approach would be to examine all factors simultaneously in their prediction of overall customer satisfaction. This method is referred to as *multiple regression analysis*. Multiple regression analysis allows us to determine which variable or variables best predict overall customer satisfaction. For example, it might be conceivable to think of overall satisfaction as a result of several factors, some factors more important than others. Although all the variables may be significantly correlated with overall customer satisfaction, multiple regression analysis determines which factors are *the best* predictors of overall customer satisfaction. *Best* is defined as factors that uniquely predict customer satisfaction.

Essentially, multiple regression analysis examines all the factors and selects the factors that account for most of the variance in customer satisfaction with the criterion that the factors account for a unique and significant amount of the variance in customer satisfaction. So, it is possible that, although five factors may be significantly correlated with overall customer satisfaction, a multiple regression analysis could result in a finding that only one factor accounts for a unique portion of the variance in customer satisfaction. The other factors, due to overlap with the first factor, may not add any explanation to the prediction of customer satisfaction. Graphically, we could look at this in a Venn diagram (see Figure J.3).

In this diagram, the circles represent the variance in each of the variables. The overlapping portions of the circles represent shared variance among the variables. We see that one factor, availability, explains most of the variance in customer satisfaction (larger overlap) compared to professionalism. Additionally, we see that professionalism does share a large amount of variance with customer satisfaction. However, we see that the unique

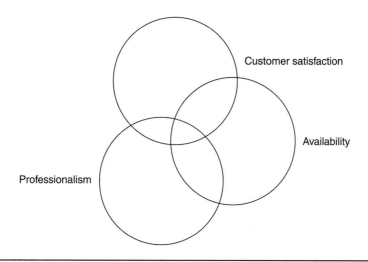

Figure J.3   A Venn diagram.

variance professionalism shares with customer satisfaction is almost cut in half after we take into account the variance professionalism and availability both share with customer satisfaction. Multiple regression analysis could be used to see whether the unique variance of professionalism significantly predicts customer satisfaction.

There are various methods of multiple regression analysis. The different multiple methods vary with respect to how the factors are included (or retained) in the final regression equation. These methods are forward selection, backward elimination, and stepwise selection. Using the *forward selection* method, the variable that has the highest correlation with customer satisfaction is entered into the equation first. Next, the factor that explains the greatest and unique amount of variance (after the first factor has been entered) is entered into the equation and tested for its significance. If the factor is significant, it remains in the equation and the next factor that explains the greatest and unique amount of variance (after the first two factors have been entered) is entered in the equation and tested for significance. This process is conducted until the remaining factors do not contribute any significant variance to the prediction of customer satisfaction.

Using *backward elimination*, all factors are included into the equation from the start. Each factor's unique contribution to the explanation of customer satisfaction (after controlling for the other factors) is tested. The factor whose unique variance does not account for a significant amount of variance and explains the least amount of variance in customer satisfaction is dropped from the equation. Each factor is again tested to see if its unique variance accounts for a significant amount of variance. The process of elimination is iterated until all factors in the equation account for a significant amount of variance in customer satisfaction.

In *stepwise selection*, both forward selection and backward elimination procedures are used. In the first step, the variable that has the highest correlation with customer satisfaction is entered into the equation. Next, the factor that explains the greatest and unique amount of variance (after the first factor has been entered) is entered into the equation and tested for its significance. In the next step, however, the first variable that was entered into the equation is tested to see if it explains a unique amount of variance in customer satisfaction after the second variable has been added to the equation. If the first variable does add unique explanation to customer satisfaction, it remains in the equation. If it does not, it is dropped. This process is conducted with the remaining variables. With this method, it is possible to determine which factors were initially good at predicting customer satisfaction at the early stages of the analysis but may have lost their usefulness at later stages after more variables have entered the equation.

These methods of multiple regression are presented here to show you the various methods you can use to determine the factors that best predict overall customer satisfaction. Readers are referred to the bibliography to learn more about multiple regression analysis.

Example

Using the patient satisfaction questionnaire, we are able to use simple linear regression to determine the relationship of office quality and physician quality. Specifically, we will regress office quality *(Y)* on physician quality *(X)*. First, the two variables are plotted to give us a general idea of the relationship between them. This scatterplot is presented in Figure J.4. As can be seen in this figure, the relationship between the two variables is positive.

In the next step, we conduct a simple regression analysis. The results of this regression analysis are presented in Table J.2. As we can see, the relationship between physician quality and office quality is slightly positive $(r = .27)$. Also, the percent of variance of physician quality that is accounted for by office quality is only 7 percent. Table J.2 also includes the final regression equation for the prediction of physician quality *(Y)* from office quality *(X)*.

Next, we could determine which variables are related to the overall rating of the exam. First, let's examine the simple correlations among the variables. These are located in Table J.3. As we can see from the correlation matrix, overall rating of the exam is positively correlated with physician quality and office quality. Overall rating of the exam is negatively correlated with wait time; patients who spend more time waiting for the doctor also report lower levels of satisfaction with the exam compared to patients who spend less time waiting for their doctor.

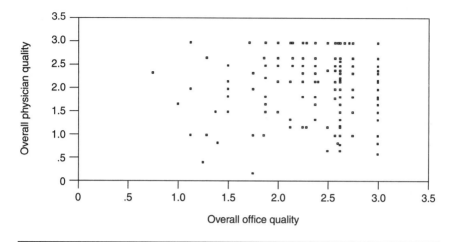

Figure J.4   Scatterplot of the relationship between physician quality and office quality.

Table J.2   Regression analysis predicting physician quality from office quality.

r	.27
r^2	.07
Regression equation:	$Y = a + bX$; $Y = 1.78 + .376X$
Significance test:	$t(1329) = 10.21$; $p < .0001$

Table J.3   Correlations among the patient satisfaction variables.

	Physician	Office	Wait time
Physician quality	—		
Office quality	.34	—	
Wait time (minutes)	−.07	−.14	—
Overall rating of the exam	.60	.30	−.11

Note: N for correlations ranges from 797 to 1336. All correlations significant at the .05 level.

Next, we conduct a multiple regression analysis (using a stepwise approach) using physician quality, office quality, and wait time as the predictor variables and overall rating of the exam as the outcome variable. The results of the analyses are presented in Table J.4. As we can see from the multiple regression approach, the best predictor of the overall rating of the exam is physician quality, followed by office quality, and wait time. The effects of the latter two variables are significant but not that substantial. Thus most of the variance in overall rating of the exam can be explained by the satisfaction level with the physician.

The next appendix covers another procedure that extends the concept of correlational analysis. This procedure, factor analysis, determines the relationship between observed variables and hypothetical variables.

Table J.4   Stepwise regression analysis of the patient satisfaction questionnaire.

	Scale	ΔR^2	*p*
Overall rating of the exam	Physician quality	.3554	.01
	Office quality	.0189	.01
	Insurance quality	.0031	.05
	Total for four variables in the equation	.3774	.01

Appendix K
Factor Analysis

Factor analysis is a general term that refers to a number of statistical techniques used in questionnaire development. There are several types of factor analysis, each with its own particular method for generating results. Because these methods often result in the same conclusions regarding interpretation of the data, this discussion will be very general and will not focus on one particular method of factor analysis; it will instead describe the general factor analytic technique.

Generally, factor analysis is used when you have a large number of variables in your data set and would like to reduce the number to a manageable size. For example, the 12 items presented in Figure K.1 might be used to assess service quality of a particular organization. You might think that they represent 12 dimensions of customers' attitudes, but upon inspection, we see that they might not really represent 12 different dimensions.

For example, items 1, 2, and 3 are similar to each other and might be represented by a broader dimension called *availability of the provider*. In addition, items 4, 5, and 6 might represent *responsiveness of the provider*, and items 7, 8, and 9 represent *professionalism*. Items 10, 11, and 12 represent *overall satisfaction with the service*.

Let's say that we had a large number of people complete the questionnaire. A factor analysis of the resulting data would tell us whether there is a smaller set of more general dimensions (like availability and responsiveness). We reduce the original number of variables to a smaller number of dimensions so we can more easily interpret the information contained in the data. If we want to see the interrelationship (correlation coefficients) between these 12 variables, we would have to calculate and interpret 60 correlations. This may be difficult, since we are not able to understand what all of the interrelationships would indicate. By reducing the number of dimensions—say, reducing the 12 variables to the four dimensions suggested earlier—we now have to calculate and interpret only six relationships.

---

1. I could get an appointment with the merchant at a time I desired.

2. The merchant was available to schedule me at a good time.

3. My appointment was at a convenient time for me.

4. The merchant was quick to respond when I arrived for my appointment.

5. The merchant immediately helped me when I entered the premises.

6. My appointment started promptly at the scheduled time.

7. The merchant listened to my opinion about what I wanted.

8. The merchant conducted herself/himself in a professional manner.

9. The merchant was courteous.

10. The quality of the way the merchant treated me was high.

11. The way the merchant treated me met my expectations.

12. I am satisfied with the way the merchant treated me.

Figure K.1 Customer opinion statements concerning service quality and overall satisfaction.

In general, factor analysis examines the relationships between a large set of variables and tries to explain these correlations using a smaller number of variables. Initially, factor analysis uses the overall correlation matrix of the variables and determines which items share an underlying dimension. Factor analysis mathematically identifies the number of factors or underlying dimensions that best represent the observed correlations between the initial set of items. Generally, in the set of existing items, those that are highly correlated with each other will be represented by a single factor or dimension.

After the number of factors or dimensions has been identified, the next step in factor analysis is to determine which items fall within their respective dimensions. This is done by a mathematical procedure called *rotation*. This rotation will clarify the dimensions' relationships with the items. As with the general method of factor analysis, various methods of rotation exist. Generally, these different rotation methods result in the same conclusions regarding which dimensions represent a given set of items.

EXPLORATORY AND CONFIRMATORY USES OF FACTOR ANALYSIS

Factor analysis explores the possibility that our variables can be reduced to a smaller, undetermined number of factors. That is, we do not know the number of factors that represent our variables nor which variables load on which factors. Factor analysis, in this situation, will identify which variables load on their respective factors. Factor analysis can also be used in a confirmatory manner in which we go into the analysis with some guess as to the outcome. In other words, we think we know the number of factors and which variables load on which factors. (The term *confirmatory factor analysis* is used here to illustrate how factor analysis can be used and is different from the more sophisticated approach of confirmatory factor analysis using significance testing.) This use of factor analysis is guided more by hypothesis testing. We expect the results from the factor analysis to confirm our hypothesis of the variables in our data set. For example, if we develop a questionnaire designed to assess certain dimensions of service quality, we expect that the items on our scale represent their respective factor or dimension.

HYPOTHETICAL FACTOR ANALYSIS

The results of the factor analysis (the number of factors and factor rotation) are presented in a tabular format called a *factor pattern matrix*. The elements in the factor pattern matrix represent the regression coefficient (like a correlation coefficient) between each of the items and the factors. These elements indicate the degree of relationship between the variables and the factors.

Table K.1 presents a hypothetical factor pattern matrix representing the results of a factor analysis that identified the existence of three factors that represented nine items. Items 1 through 3 have a high loading on factor I and small loadings on the other factors. Items 4 through 6 load highly on factor II, and items 7 through 9 load highly on factor III. A factor's definition is determined by the content of the items that load on it.

This hypothetical factor analysis indicates it would be reasonable to think of the data set as containing three variables rather than nine. Therefore, instead of looking at each variable as its own separate dimension, we would believe that there are three dimensions, each composed of three items. To obtain a score for each of the dimensions, we might combine the variables associated with a given factor to represent that dimension. That is, we would combine all the items that loaded highly on factor I to get a measure of that dimension. We would do the same for the items associated with factor II and factor III.

Table K.1 A factor pattern matrix with the factor loadings from the results of a hypothetical factor analysis of the responses to nine items.

	Factor		
Items	**I**	**II**	**III**
1	.80	.05	.07
2	.77	.04	.21
3	.45	.11	.13
4	.02	.55	.04
5	.10	.77	.21
6	.11	.88	.16
7	.09	.08	.72
8	.30	.21	.77
9	.21	.22	.67

Now we would have three dimensions with which to work. These dimensions are useful summary variables for drawing conclusions about the data. Furthermore, we could now more easily interpret the interrelations (correlation coefficients) among these dimensions.

ACTUAL FACTOR ANALYSIS

This next example is taken from actual data obtained from a beauty salon using a customer satisfaction questionnaire. Although the questionnaire contained the items listed in Figure K.1, only items 1 through 6 are included in this example. The first three items were written to reflect an availability dimension, while the last three items were written to reflect a responsiveness dimension. A method of factor analysis, called *principle factor analysis,* was performed. This initial factor analysis resulted in the factor pattern matrix presented in Table K.2.

As this factor pattern indicates, the factor analysis identified the existence of two factors or dimensions representing these six items. We expected this. However, it might be unclear as to which items represent factor 1 and which represent factor 2. All of the six items seem to load fairly high on factor 1. Factor 2 seems to reflect a bipolar scale; some items load positively on the factor, while others load negatively on the factor. The interpretation of the factor pattern matrix becomes even more difficult as the number of items and factors increases. To make the results of the factor analysis more meaningful, we use *rotation.*

On the initial factor pattern matrix, a method of rotation, called *varimax rotation,* was conducted. Other methods of rotation were used and, as

Table K.2 The factor pattern matrix resulting from the factor analysis of six items designed to measure perceived availability and perceived responsiveness.

Unrotated factor matrix

	Factor 1	Factor 2
Item 1	.727	.683
Item 2	.842	.425
Item 3	.321	.861
Item 4	.807	−.537
Item 5	.604	−.652
Item 6	.84	−.361

expected, resulted in the same pattern of results as varimax rotation. Therefore, this presentation will only include the results of varimax rotation. The rotated factor pattern matrix appears in Table K.3. In this factor pattern matrix, the interpretation of the factors is more clear. Factor 1 is clearly represented by the last three items, while factor 2 is clearly represented by the first three items.

As expected, we found the existence of two factors that underlie these six items. In a sense, we used factor analysis to confirm our expectations. By design, the first three items reflected an availability dimension of service while the last three items reflected a responsiveness dimension. The factor analysis confirmed our hypothesis as to the number of factors that these six items represent, thus making us more confident that the items measure what they were designed to measure.

Example

From the patient satisfaction questionnaire, we derived an overall measure of physician quality by averaging the responses to the six questions related to physician quality. We can use factor analysis to determine whether this method of averaging the items is reasonable. The factor analysis would tell us the number of underlying factors that describe the correlations among the six items of physician quality. The six items measuring physician quality are presented in Figure K.2.

The next step would be to determine the correlations among these six items. The correlation matrix for the six physician quality items is presented in Table K.4.

Table K.3 The result of the factor analysis after rotating the factors.

Orthogonal transformation solution—varimax

	Factor 1	Factor 2
Item 1	.14	.987
Item 2	.391	.858
Item 3	−.288	.873
Item 4	.966	.086
Item 5	.879	−.131
Item 6	.881	.244

Physician quality			
	Yes	**No**	**Not sure**
1. Introduced himself/herself to me.	Y	N	?
2. Asked me how I was injured/became ill.	Y	N	?
3. Listened to me.	Y	N	?
4. Treated me with respect.	Y	N	?
5. Was professional in doing the examination.	Y	N	?
6. Spent enough time with me (not rushed).	Y	N	?

Figure K.2 Physician quality items.

As we can see from the correlation matrix, all items are positively correlated with each other. The pattern of correlations, however, is not clear. Some items show high correlations with other items ($r = .58$) while other items show low correlations with other items (.14). A factor analysis examines the entire correlation matrix and helps us make sense of these correlations. Perhaps one underlying factor can explain the pattern of correlations we see in Table K.4.

The results of the factor analysis (factor pattern matrix) is presented in Table K.5.

Table K.4 Correlation matrix for the six physician quality items.

	1	2	3	4	5	6
Question 1	1.00					
Question 2	.22	1.00				
Question 3	.15	.22	1.00			
Question 4	.31	.20	.56	1.00		
Question 5	.26	.14	.48	.58	1.00	
Question 6	.17	.22	.47	.42	.41	1.00

Table K.5 Factor pattern matrix for the six physician quality items.

	Factor 1
Question 1	.35531
Question 2	.26187
Question 3	.69985
Question 4	.78311
Question 5	.69716
Question 6	.59329

The results of the factor analysis suggest that the six items could be described by one underlying factor. As is indicated in the factor pattern matrix, one factor can explain the correlations among the variables, suggesting that all six items are measuring one underlying factor that is responsible for the variance in the items. Therefore, the creation of a new variable called overall *physician quality* by averaging the six items does make sense, both logically and statistically.

Summary

Factor analysis identifies the number of underlying dimensions that account for the relationship between many items. Since factor analysis allows you to determine which items measure similar things, it is often used as a means of data reduction.

Appendix L
Table of Random Numbers

These random numbers were generated with a computer program and range from 1 to 99,999. Each number had an equal chance of being generated.

92513	21156	20618	78167	87337	80703	00468	84107	58120	15456
17743	07198	90623	93143	58624	99172	90774	32892	43015	03868
64861	63732	82018	99240	11925	87715	08917	64625	51627	20766
79728	09753	43999	23550	20290	45512	06476	50545	49641	68162
20515	97350	04927	87226	11553	40866	70782	20944	65761	08406
55469	10628	09666	09906	94742	11203	99330	38092	26386	38890
95834	67434	10367	25356	03517	11773	12159	61605	79374	73538
38344	94791	86959	90375	39792	31626	16217	75227	59118	48758
58805	62440	80292	69705	80900	53725	19260	63853	52996	41111
13310	73409	14683	72271	83141	31214	06020	36270	89706	59971
63713	76433	82594	13916	49596	51822	19609	27454	85470	89592
74104	73061	81653	70740	30044	11351	97125	92733	73051	84786
78861	42464	71587	29797	69687	98987	73885	91051	56021	55387
36915	77574	29370	77071	38475	39808	26999	61025	74503	48624
04771	12920	35438	84635	57077	71178	05781	95589	19444	50655
38792	98613	08548	65459	46643	31589	26608	93722	71904	98448
22358	87444	47701	58366	28319	66264	90515	16041	62258	35767
85925	79736	54218	88132	33224	19743	29210	26962	79052	44391
52972	54548	85857	60644	12414	63024	30719	47093	57483	98950
01504	34410	87397	45152	13270	70784	40097	74700	36362	27201
47310	81172	43366	95102	12440	66368	71484	84735	78198	65864
52773	71303	43874	52350	50081	87145	08226	45971	87660	77714
10822	41517	94528	27204	34618	21898	92037	77282	00834	91593
45122	47428	78536	16203	47494	40969	75182	44961	04057	75998
57860	98766	70665	22204	50186	92901	43092	01484	94901	38907
97394	86975	63503	83789	66147	18745	98056	56883	09887	68377
04824	69980	08281	08365	81162	14938	15126	14297	97930	87086
72933	93269	88155	37800	46676	45646	93489	83874	82111	62150
16305	67104	66060	28206	53165	79230	01372	53440	27867	09628
02674	21739	07376	51503	39818	77886	66043	53012	66435	65773
72311	39822	42810	19800	96401	27412	36409	69962	93899	11187
20706	35672	86437	61921	65572	92677	95636	57183	58219	63017
42718	18888	63674	90418	40960	08617	24701	31349	72595	34379
24010	42118	44494	68694	33997	26586	86540	52297	74910	56444
32067	87027	19144	18467	40376	35642	05817	27684	19042	03323
44569	68369	59771	39055	17045	64723	65400	66571	75542	65935
08487	63190	89557	44757	52447	62902	87699	50010	63877	96156
85834	44712	33304	54909	75046	49907	64365	42403	61689	72287
05150	00751	15552	87821	72474	73283	88592	61628	12753	78396
17670	88611	90535	04493	23554	07028	19741	00796	12694	65857
05221	65192	51547	52682	81566	94180	78802	47901	76064	54259
20977	74751	03998	78282	64292	48037	09946	02345	61880	45268
57906	12627	93767	06761	55512	53175	26354	73948	55615	53165
28352	33164	93269	93833	58574	62083	13382	00109	46278	49877
94165	27864	64602	68693	53619	64668	07040	33622	33066	40964
56693	42385	00601	65723	54104	63014	05768	07673	88769	42281
09131	74506	63078	30882	59738	70331	63669	16305	60160	72148
17652	95540	87088	89126	16730	79871	48653	37999	25753	89591
63576	61256	93052	49509	39740	39844	73818	30614	29605	62099
40912	46784	97819	67113	23390	79137	50734	33970	71863	79725

Bibliography

Allen, M. J., and W. M. Yen. 2002. *Introduction to Measurement Theory*. Long Grove, IL: Waveland Press.

American Educational Research Association, American Psychological Association, and National Council on Measurement in Education. 1985. *Standards for Educational and Psychological Testing*. Washington, DC: American Psychological Association.

Anderson, E. W., C. Fornell, and S. K. Mazvancheryl. 2004. "Customer Satisfaction and Shareholder Value." *Journal of Marketing* 68 (October): 172–185.

Ang, L., and F. Buttle. 2006. "CRM Software Applications and Business Performance." *Journal of Database Marketing & Customer Strategy Management* 14:4–16.

Camp, R. C. 1989. *Benchmarking: The Search for Industry Best Practices That Lead to Superior Performance*. Milwaukee, WI: ASQ Quality Press.

Campbell, D. T., and D. W. Fiske. 1959. "Convergent and Discriminant Validation by the Multitrait-Multimethod Matrix." *Psychological Bulletin* 56:8–105.

Cronbach, L. J. 1951. "Coefficient Alpha and the Internal Structure of Tests." *Psychometrika* 16 (3): 297–334.

Cronbach, L. J., and P. E. Meehl. 1955. "Construct Validity in Psychological Tests." *Psychological Bulletin* 52:281–302.

Dawes, R. M. 1972. *Fundamentals of Attitude Measurement*. New York: John Wiley & Sons.

Dillman, D. A. 2006. *Mail and Internet Surveys: The Tailored Design Method*. New York: John Wiley & Sons.

Dillman, D. A., R. D. Tortora, and D. Bowker. 1998. "Principles for Constructing Web Surveys." http://survey.sesrc.wsu.edu/dillman/papers/websurveyppr.pdf (accessed February 14, 2008).

Edwards, A. L., and K. C. Kenny. 1946. "A Comparison of the Thurstone and Likert Techniques to Attitude Scale Construction." *Journal of Applied Psychology* 30:72–83.

Fishbein, M. 1967. *Readings in Attitude Theory and Measurement.* New York: John Wiley & Sons.

Fornell, C., S. Mithas, F. V. Morgensen, and M. S. Krishan. 2006. "Customer Satisfaction and Stock Prices: High Returns, Low Risk. *Journal of Marketing* 70 (January): 1–14.

Gruca, T. S., and L. L. Rego. 2005. "Customer Satisfaction, Cash Flow, and Shareholder Value." *Journal of Marketing* 69 (July): 115–130.

Gupta, S., D. Hanssens, B. Hardie, W. Khan, V. Kumar, N. Lin, N. Ravishanker, and S. Sriram. 2006. "Modeling Customer Lifetime Value." *Journal of Service Research* 9 (2): 139–155.

Hayes, B. E. 2008a. "Customer Loyalty 2.0: The Net Promoter Score Debate and the Meaning of Customer Loyalty." *Quirk's Marketing Research Review,* October, 54–62.

———. 2008b. *Measuring Customer Satisfaction and Loyalty: Survey Design, Use and Statistical Analysis Methods.* 3rd ed. Milwaukee, WI: ASQ Quality Press.

———. 2008c. "The True Test of Loyalty." ASQ *Quality Progress,* June, 20–26.

Heskett, J. L., W. E. Sasser, and L. A. Schlesinger. 1997. *The Service Profit Chain.* New York: The Free Press.

Keiningham, T. L., B. Cooil, T. W. Andreassen, and L. Aksoy. 2007. "A Longitudinal Examination of Net Promoter and Firm Revenue Growth." *Journal of Marketing* 71 (July): 39–51.

Kerlinger, F. N. 1973. *Foundations of Behavioral Research.* 2nd ed. New York: Holt, Rinehart, and Winston.

Likert, R. A. 1932. "A Technique for the Measurement of Attitudes." *Archives of Psychology* 140:1–55.

Lissitz, R. W., and S. B. Green. 1975. "Effect of the Number of Scale Points on Reliability: A Monte Carlo Approach." *Journal of Applied Psychology* 60:10–13.

Morgan, N. A., and L. L. Rego. 2006. "The Value of Different Customer Satisfaction and Loyalty Metrics in Predicting Business Performance." *Marketing Science* 25 (5): 426–439.

Net Promoter. 2007. http://www.netpromoter.com.

Nunnally, J. M. 1978. *Psychometric Theory*. 2nd ed. New York: McGraw-Hill.

Reckase, M. D. 1990. *Scaling Techniques. Handbook of Psychological Assessment*. New York: Pergamon Press.

Reichheld, F. F. 2003. "The One Number You Need to Grow." *Harvard Business Review* 81 (December): 46–54.

———. 2006. *The Ultimate Question: Driving Good Profits and True Growth*. Boston: Harvard Business School Press.

Reichheld, F. F., and W. E. Sasser. 1990. "Zero Defections: Quality Comes to Service." *Harvard Business Review*, 68 (September–October): 105–111.

Reinartz, W., M. Krafft, and W. Hoyer. 2004. "The Customer Relationship Management Process: Its Measurement and Impact on Performance." *Journal of Marketing Research* 41:293–305.

Thurstone, L. L. 1929. "Theory of Attitude Measurement." *Psychological Bulletin* 36:224–241.

Index

Belong to the Quality Community!

Established in 1946, ASQ is a global community of quality experts in all fields and industries. ASQ is dedicated to the promotion and advancement of quality tools, principles, and practices in the workplace and in the community.

The Society also serves as an advocate for quality. Its members have informed and advised the U.S. Congress, government agencies, state legislatures, and other groups and individuals worldwide on quality-related topics.

Vision

By making quality a global priority, an organizational imperative, and a personal ethic, ASQ becomes the community of choice for everyone who seeks quality technology, concepts, or tools to improve themselves and their world.

ASQ is...

- More than 90,000 individuals and 700 companies in more than 100 countries

- The world's largest organization dedicated to promoting quality

- A community of professionals striving to bring quality to their work and their lives

- The administrator of the Malcolm Baldrige National Quality Award

- A supporter of quality in all sectors including manufacturing, service, healthcare, government, and education

- YOU

Visit www.asq.org for more information.

ASQ Membership

Research shows that people who join associations experience increased job satisfaction, earn more, and are generally happier*. ASQ membership can help you achieve this while providing the tools you need to be successful in your industry and to distinguish yourself from your competition. So why wouldn't you want to be a part of ASQ?

Networking

Have the opportunity to meet, communicate, and collaborate with your peers within the quality community through conferences and local ASQ section meetings, ASQ forums or divisions, ASQ Communities of Quality discussion boards, and more.

Professional Development

Access a wide variety of professional development tools such as books, training, and certifications at a discounted price. Also, ASQ certifications and the ASQ Career Center help enhance your quality knowledge and take your career to the next level.

Solutions

Find answers to all your quality problems, big and small, with ASQ's Knowledge Center, mentoring program, various e-newsletters, *Quality Progress* magazine, and industry-specific products.

Access to Information

Learn classic and current quality principles and theories in ASQ's Quality Information Center (QIC), *ASQ Weekly* e-newsletter, and product offerings.

Advocacy Programs

ASQ helps create a better community, government, and world through initiatives that include social responsibility, Washington advocacy, and Community Good Works.

Visit www.asq.org/membership for more information on ASQ membership.

*2008, The William E. Smith Institute for Association Research